Ridiculous Grace
and
Scandalous Mercy

Reflections on the
Gift and Duty of Mercy

To Mike

May you always feel the warmth of God's ridiculous grace and the comfort of His scandalous mercy.

God bless you

Jeff

ENDORSEMENTS

Jeff Armbruster's third book, *Ridiculous Grace and Scandalous Mercy*, reads as a fireside chat with a good friend. The reader is challenged to examine how their life has been lived, how they have treated those around them and how they have lived their faith. Have we shared our many Graces and have we shown to others the Mercy we have been given? The Reflections are touching, witty and thought-provoking. A thoroughly wonderful read.

Rebecca Sullivan

We've all had the experience of listening to a lecture, hearing a sermon, reading an article or book which, though it made an impression on us in the moment, left nary a trace of itself in our long-term memory or in the overall trajectory of our lives. The only lessons that make a lasting impact on the way we think and how we live are the ones we reflect seriously upon. Through such reflection, alone or with others, they are able to carve out a place in our memories and begin to shape the choices we make. In his latest book, *Ridiculous Grace and Scandalous Mercy, Reflections on the Gift and Duty of Mercy*, Jeff Armbruster has done the hard work we all need to do – invest quality time in serious reflection on the astounding gift of God's mercy. While each of us must do this important work for ourselves, Jeff's book will serve as a wise companion for anyone who wishes to interiorize the way in which our lives have been transformed by the mercy of God, and how we are duty bound to extend that mercy to others.

Rev. Daniel P. Ketter, JCL
Archdiocese of Atlanta

Ridiculous Grace and Scandalous Mercy is a very honest, authentic, and insightful work. It provides the answer to what is next, following *Live Humbly, Serve Graciously's* call to live as we are mandated through baptism serving God's people. Relevant scriptures on mercy and the like are inserted throughout the book and invite you to conduct a personal reflection and examination. References to great saints, bible stories, and the Catechism of the Catholic Church support the writing and educate the reader. It reminds us of the gifts of prayer and the sacrament of reconciliation that we have as Catholics. It shares hope of the promise of God's mercy and His love for all of us. It even provides practical ways to begin to extend mercy to others. I was enlightened by each page. The book fed my spirit, was a vehicle for self-discovery, renewed my appreciation for all God's gifts, and inspired me to intentionally love and serve others every day.

LaRhonda Julien

Pope Francis, reminds us in, *The Name of God is Mercy*, that, "The first and only step required to experience mercy is to acknowledge that we are in need of mercy." In *Ridiculous Grace and Scandalous Mercy*, author Jeff Armbruster offers an insightful collection of real-world and heartfelt reflections that beautifully illustrate the Pope's assertion that God's mercy is "The Lord's strongest message." Jeff describes with finesse and emotion the opportunities we all have in our daily lives, not only to experience, but also to help others experience God's mercy and compassion.

In the words of St. John Vianney, "Our sins are nothing but a grain of sand alongside the great mountain of the mercy of God." Jeff's reflections on the gift and duty of mercy shows how we are all called to participate in the mercy of our Lord, particularly in the way we show others mercy.

Deacon Bill Boyd
Mary Our Queen Catholic Church, Peachtree Corners, GA

In his book, *Ridiculous Grace and Scandalous Mercy - Reflections on the Gift and Duty of Mercy,* Jeff Armbruster gives us a grace-filled account of our spiritual journey towards God's endless mercy. The reader is empowered to want more and to experience more of God's mercy. It is as if Jeff is speaking to us in person through the pages.

Deacon Robb Ciezki
Saints Peter and Paul Catholic Church, Hamburg, NY
Campus Minister/Religion Teacher
St. Mary's High School, Lancaster, NY

The author states, "I am neither a theologian nor philosopher," and perhaps that is precisely why this book is so impactful. Jeff has clearly accumulated a wealth of knowledge from which the reader can draw. After quoting one obscure work, no doubt new to 99% of readers, he asks, "Could the power of God's love, mercy and compassion at the hour of death be described more beautifully?" My answer is, no. It was unlike anything I have ever read and gives me great hope. Such discoveries are one of the great joys of this book.

Another joy is the depth to which we are exposed to the many facets of God's mercy. To quote one section, "The outcomes were diametrically different because of one thing and one thing only. Peter trusted in God's mercy – Judas did not." Anyone that lives with regrets and tends to focus on their worst moments, will benefit greatly by reading this book because it takes them on a joyful walk into God's glorious garden of mercy.

But today's world often pressures us to be silent when mercy demands we speak. When it says stay seated and do nothing, mercy demands we stand up and act. In short, having received God's boundless mercy; we must share it. Easy to say, hard to do. Consider this book a how-to manual.

Eric Anderson
COO, Clearwave Corporation

Lord have mercy – scandalous or otherwise – Jeff Armbruster teaches and inspires once again! Call it fate, serendipity, or the Holy Spirit (I choose the latter), but I always seem to read Jeff's writings when life is a bit, or more than a bit perhaps, off-center. Jeff's history lessons, stories, and practical teachings always seem to bring me back to center. His latest book, especially in his discussions around St. John Henry Newman's prayer, *The Mission of My Life*, reminds us all that we are each put on this earth for some unique purpose – and I won't deign (too much anyway) to know what God has determined to be Jeff's unique purpose, but I suspect it has something to do with inspiring people through his written words to serve one another. As Jeff puts it, to learn how to be "third" (read on and you'll understand). Thank you, Jeff - through God's grace and scandalous mercy and a hearty helping of your wisdom I hope that I can stand alongside you one day . . . in third.

Chris Dillon
Partner, Holland & Knight

Ridiculous Grace and Scandalous Mercy is another powerful book by Jeff Armbruster. I found myself with a pencil or highlighter in my hand the entire time while reading as there were so many points, quotes and messages that I would circle or underline so that I could re-visit to let those words sink into my mind and my heart even further. This book will certainly be a primary tool for Adoration reflection, Catechesis and continued self-examination for me.

Bob Chapin
Senior Vice President, CharterBank

Jeff Armbruster carefully takes the reader on a comprehensive journey into the marvelously ridiculous and scandalous mercy of God. He skillfully weaves his own experiences and Catholic faith with Scripture as well as writers from a breadth of perspectives. And in the end, I learned new and real ways to share the grace of God with the people in my life. A blessing!

Dr. Allen Hunt, Senior Advisor, *Dynamic Catholic*
Best-Selling Author of *Everybody Needs to Forgive Somebody*

The mercy of God stands alone at the root of any tree of theological musing and lies beyond our logical comprehension. As Christians, we might wonder about the many ways God has gifted us with His grace, because on our path of sanctification, these gifts strengthen us. *Ridiculous Grace and Scandalous Mercy*, provides us a remarkable collection of focused reflections on our Lord's mercy. These reflections, more than any other single work that I have read, impart a deep and meaningful appreciation of this infinite mercy of God that is, in the clever and bold words of the author, both ridiculous and scandalous.

David Hancharik
Technical Director, ViaSat, Inc.

Insightful, practical, real and relevant. Words that not only describe Jeff Armbruster's new book, *Ridiculous Grace and Scandalous Mercy*, but words that also describe the author himself. In his latest work Jeff combines the personal, the biblical, and the spiritual to offer a look at grace and mercy that most have never experienced. Who else could combine scripture with geology and engineering to tell a warm, engaging story about the importance of grace and the unrelenting mercy of Christ our Lord? Only Jeff. I was blessed by this book and I feel certain you will be as well.

David McCullough

With his latest work, Jeff shares a series of meditations that are practical and useful for addressing many of the day-to-day spiritual challenges faced by all of us. Each reflection is based on sound Catholic doctrine and expresses Jeff's deep faith. In much the same way it did in his first two works, Jeff's writing style, particularly the way he relates his personal experiences, helps the reader absorb and cling to often complex spiritual concepts. I highly recommend this book to any Christian searching for a resource to deal with life and its challenges!

JR Allred
President, Dalton Carpet One

As someone who's benefited from Jeff Armbruster's experience and wisdom over the years, I'm grateful to have so many of his reflections on the important subject of God's mercy written down to study and practice. Jeff's deeply thoughtful and forthright approach presents some very complex subjects in an easily accessible way. *Reflection XIV – Mercy Is About Being "Others-Focused"* – alone is worth reading three, four, five, as many times as it takes for this essential message to sink in.

With poignant stories, prayer-filled meditations, and most importantly, a blueprint on how practicing humility, generosity, and employing our God-given gifts to help others are the necessary requirements needed to receive and share God's mercy, this book is a timely reminder that we are forgiven when we forgive those who wrong us, we are loved when we love the unlovable, and we are offered mercy when we show mercy to others. Jeff's *Ridiculous Grace and Scandalous Mercy* is an excellent explanation about the unfailing grace and mercy God offers us all. Read it, reflect upon it, and pass it on.

Brandon Doty
President, Reasoned Marketing

Many years ago, I came to the realization that God loves me in spite of my sin and desires to pour out His mercy on me. Jesus was waiting for me right then and there. That awareness changed the course of my life. God is all holy and He desires me (and you) to be in communion with Him. For that, you do not, in this life, need to be perfect; you need to be forgiven, to be healed and to be contrite and desire holiness. So, it was with great anticipation that I awaited this latest book from Jeff Armbruster. Jeff did not disappoint with *Ridiculous Grace and Scandalous Mercy*.

Motivated by the *Extraordinary Jubilee Year of Mercy* and his self-reflection on how his observance of that year affected his spiritual life, Armbruster has put together a series of personal reflections on God's mercy that will strengthen your awareness of God's merciful love for you and His desire to forgive you, heal you, and lead you home through this place of pilgrimage to our true home. His reflections on God's Love and

Grace that focus on the Lord's compassionate Mercy and Forgiveness are both encouraging and empowering. Saint John Paul II has written that this Mercy, *"raises man above his weakness to the infinite heights to the holiness of God."* So, I encourage you to prayerfully read *Ridiculous Grace and Scandalous Mercy*, meditating on these reflections, as you seek an ever-deepening union with God.

Deacon Mike Bickerstaff

Director of Adult Education & Evangelization

St. Peter Chanel Catholic Church, Roswell, Georgia

Editor-in-Chief, Integrated Catholic Life, Inc.

First printing August 2021

ISBN# 9798508475321

NOTE: Unless otherwise noted, throughout this book, all passages from Sacred Scripture were taken from the *New American Bible, Revised Edition (NABRE),* and downloaded from the U.S. Conference of Catholic Bishops website, usccb.org.

Cover design by Lillian Moore and the author.

Printed by Kindle Direct Publishing

Ridiculous Grace
and
Scandalous Mercy

*Reflections on the
Gift and Duty of Mercy*

Jeffrey T. Armbruster

Foreword by
Rev. Lawrence J. McNeil

DEDICATION

This book is dedicated to my dear friend, Deacon Jim Stone.

Jim had significant impacts on me in ways I am still discovering. He gifted me with his friendship, sincerity, spirituality, prayerfulness and marvelous sense of humor. Over the twenty or so years I knew Jim, he prayed for me and with me, challenged me, pushed me and loved me unconditionally. He is already greatly missed.

This book is also dedicated to my wife, Laurel;
to our children and their spouses,
Amy and Dan, Dave and Patti;
to our grandchildren Zach, Ellie, Nick, Ryan
and any others we may be blessed with;
and to each of you who choose to read even a
small portion of this work.

My fondest hope is that in some way you will each feel the grace and mercy showered onto you unconditionally by God and know the peace that comes from those gifts.

You are each truly special gifts from God

CONTENTS

ACKNOWLEDGEMENTS

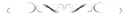

S HOULD YOU CHOOSE to take your valuable time to read the pages that follow, please understand that most of what you encounter is the result of what I have learned from many others and represents the gifts they have generously shared or given me.

At the top of the list of those from whom I have learned much and to whom I am eternally grateful and owe much is, Laurel, my wife of 52 years. She has endured much during that time, including addresses in six different states during our first 12 years of marriage as I pursued my career. Laurel has loved me unconditionally, taught me much, and challenged me often. Her insights are remarkable. She lifts me up when I am down, and brings me back to earth when I fly off on a tangent. She continues to give me gifts beyond what I deserve by simultaneously being my strongest supporter, most severe critic and best friend. She makes me be a better person. Most important, though, she has been my spiritual partner and soul mate throughout our lives together. We have grown together spiritually in ways I could never have foreseen, in our prayer life, in raising our family, in how we live our lives. Her love of God, trust in Jesus Christ for all things, and openness to the Holy Spirit's guidance constantly force me to up my game. My love for the Lord has been profoundly influenced by her. She truly lives her life devoted to getting me, our children and their families, and our extended families and friends to heaven and devotes much spiritual, emotional, mental and physical energy to that commitment. Her generosity and graciousness to me, our family and all those she encounters reflects a genuine understanding of what it means to strive, always, to be third. I am indeed blessed to have this woman walking hand-in-hand with me through life.

Our children, Amy and David, and their spouses Dan and Patti provide incredible support and encouragement as do our grandchildren, Zach, Ellie, Nicholas and Ryan. Life is so much fuller because of each them, their joy and spirit. We are eternally blessed because of them.

My parents, Jane and Frank, provided not only a firm foundation for life, particularly by the admirable way they lived their lives, they also provided lifelong encouragement to me and my siblings to grow and give. My faith foundation was firmly established under their guidance. How could they ever be adequately thanked for setting that firm base? The manner in which my sister Becky practices her faith, too, is an inspiration.

There are so many others who have given me so much through their (and our) life experiences that trying to name them all would surely result in forgetting some. However, I would like to offer special thanks to my niece, Theresa Ford, and to our dear friend, Loretta Boyd, who each spent many hours working on my original manuscript, editing, shaping and recommending ways to express my ideas clearer. I owe both of them a huge thank you.

I am also very grateful to my grandniece, Lillian Moore, for applying her artistic talents to the design and creation of the cover of this book. Starting with an idea I had, and working collaboratively with her, Lil produced the beautiful cover for this work. The photographic base was taken during morning prayers while sitting on the beach looking east. The sky displayed what seemed a wonderful metaphor for our lives. No matter the storminess and darkness we might feel, the light of God's love, grace and mercy is always juxtaposed to it. All we need to do is be open. Thank you, Lillian, for putting your special gifts to work. You are special.

And to our dear Ellen Storeim, how could I ever thank you for the love, energy and talent you poured into the internal layout of these words? You are much appreciated.

In addition, there are many, many friends who have loved and taught me much though their generosity and experiences. One of those dear friends, Father Larry McNeil, has had a huge impact on my life in so many ways. His unconditional love and support for more than 40 years have been such a blessing. Thanks to the Holy Spirit for nudging me to sit and talk with him those many years ago, when my courage to do so was lacking. The spiritual and emotional support he has provided me and our family has been a true gift. To him I will always be grateful. The words of the Foreword to this book are lovingly and gratefully acknowledged – what a blessing to work with him on this project.

Thanks, too, to the many trusted friends that agreed to take their valuable time to read and assess the final version of my manuscript, then write endorsements that are included here. Their encouragement has lifted my spirit immensely.

I would also like to thank the remarkable group of guys I have met with at Mary Our Queen parish, nearly every Friday morning at 6:30 AM for more than 15 years. Early versions of about half of the material contained in this volume were compiled, massaged, and shared with them as part of our round-robin sharing of "speaker" duties within the group. They have been extremely supportive and tolerant as I shared my thoughts and feelings on a wide range of spiritual topics. They have been an important part of my spiritual journey for many years.

And finally, I am grateful to the many with whom I share my faith. I have prayed with them and for them and they have prayed for me and my family. Many of the insights shared here come from them. They are each a blessing!

FOREWORD

THE PURPOSE OF a foreword in a book is to introduce the writer to the reader. I have known Jeff Armbruster and his family for well over 40 years. Our friendship began one night when he had come to the priests' residence in the parish to speak to one of the other priests, who happened to be away. As a result, he got stuck with me. And looking back on that night, and the many years since, I am immeasurably enriched as a result of that chance encounter.

Jeff spent his career working for the U.S. Geological Survey in water resources. His love of science and engineering, and his search for knowledge and truth, combined with his faith, have been the strong motivators for his journey in life. He has also spent many years doing consultation work as well as helping others to become authentic leaders in life and not simply in a profession.

Apart from God and his faith, the first and foremost gift in his life is his wife, Laurel, as well as his children and grandchildren. The book you are reading here is the fruit of his journey, the journey of a committed scientist and Catholic to live out the love of faith, marriage and parenthood in this world in which we live.

I suspect that one of the things that led you to pick up this book is its strange title: *Ridiculous Grace and Scandalous Mercy – Reflections on the Gift and Duty of Mercy*. It is meant to stop us in our tracks and reread it – sure that our eyes have misled us.

The title reminds me of a Mass I celebrated several years ago at which the lector introduced the Psalm response to the congregation, inviting them to reply to the verses of the Psalm with the response, "The Lord is kind <u>of</u> merciful." Of course, the correct response was, "The Lord is kind <u>and</u> merciful." We all got a chuckle. But like the title of this book, the lector's "error" revealed a deeper truth – we are afraid of absolutes – we are much more comfortable with relative statements and relationships, because they comfort us with the feeling that God does not demand everything from us – that He is kind of merciful and therefore we can be relative in the mercy we reflect to others.

It is like saying the Our Father (Lord's Prayer): "Forgive us our trespasses as we forgive those who trespass against us." I have often thought that we hope God does not hear the second half. We want Him to be absolute in forgiving and loving us, but us forgiving others absolutely – not so much.

But as Jeff challenges us – that is exactly what God offers us and what He expects from us. As we read the Scriptures we are confronted with the absolutes of love and grace. Abraham is expected to sacrifice his only son, no questions asked. God sacrifices His only Son, no holding back. As we look at the Sacraments, we discover this – absolute, alive and fruitful. We will never understand love until we are willing to empty ourself into the other. We will never understand what it means to be forgiven until we can radically forgive. St. Faustina quotes Christ as reflecting that "the greater the sinner, the greater the right he has to my mercy," which endures forever.

That's why I can invite you to read this book. Discover the ridiculousness of grace and the scandalous quality of God's mercy. And discover that mercy isn't simply God's gift to us, but rather also our duty to God and our brothers and sisters. Read it and you will find a treasure!

Rev. Lawrence J. McNeil
Retired Pastor, Basilica of the Sacred Heart of Jesus, Hanover, PA
Retired Adjunct Professor, Mount Saint Mary's
Seminary, Emmitsburg, MD

PROLOGUE

O N THE SECOND anniversary of his election as successor of St. Peter, March 13, 2015, Pope Francis I declared the first ever *Extraordinary Jubilee Year of Mercy*. The celebration would extend from December 8, 2015, to November 20, 2016. While there had never been a Jubilee Year dedicated to mercy alone, many of our popes have spoken, written and taught about God's mercy in beautiful and heartening ways.

As I read the Pope's Bull of Indiction (2015), *Misericordiae Vultus (The Face of Mercy)*, I was genuinely enthusiastic about the Church's public declaration of the importance of God's mercy, and about how a year of focused attention by the universal Church on God's mercy would allow us to internalize illuminating new insights about this extraordinary gift He freely gives each of us. I was equally excited about the possible spiritual growth I might personally gain during the year. As my interest grew, I realized that I would need to dive headlong into reading, studying, writing and reflecting not just on mercy, but also on the related components of God's love, and grace and how these three gifts relate to compassion, forgiveness and service to others. A side benefit of this deep dive for me was being invited to share my thoughts with a variety of audiences on the realities of mercy as a gift (that we receive) and mercy as an obligation (that we must share with others).

So, near the end of the *Jubilee Year*, I decided to take a step back and try to assess what effect(s), if any, the celebration had on my personal spiritual growth. I wondered what the year-long attention to God's radiant mercy meant for me; what I learned; and what I came to understand more clearly than before. Did I come away more enlightened than before? Did any of this focused emphasis on God's bounteous mercy change my attitudes, words, and actions toward others? Would I be able to lead my life in a more civil, tolerant, loving and service-oriented direction than before this celebration? Because of all the craziness in our world today, the timing of the *Jubilee* for me, was critical. If there was ever a time when the world needs God's mercy, it is now. If there was ever a time when each of us needs to reach out to others in merciful and compassionate ways, it is now. Only by better understanding this beautiful virtue can we seek God's mercy more sincerely, and only by understanding more deeply our obligation to be merciful to others will others experience our mercy poured out on them.

If, by chance, you are surprised by, or are more than just a little curious about the origin of the title of this book, I would like to offer a few words of explanation. As I began to write, then compile my reflections, it occurred to me that the whole notion of God's grace being given without condition is ridiculous. Why, in heaven's name, would Almighty God shower us (me) with His grace, knowing each of us is a sinner? Such a notion is absurd, silly, unreasonable and preposterous. But, in spite of the fact that each of these terms seems to carry a negative connotation, they accurately define ridiculous. Interestingly, however, in recent decades ridiculous has taken on other, quite different meanings – awesome, extravagant and excessive. This more contemporary set of definitions also provides appropriate and precise descriptions of God's grace, and, in my opinion, does so even more accurately than the first!

While thinking about God's gift of mercy, I had a similar train of thought – the immensity of God's mercy extends beyond and violates any set of standards or norms I have ever considered. *Beyond boundaries* is a very simple definition of what scandalous means. To be sure, though, scandalous is one of those terms that often elicits strong emotions because it usually means disgusting, distasteful, offensive and shocking. I think it is safe to say most of us would consider each of these words to have negative implications. The one exception is *shocking*, mostly because it carries within its own definition opposite meanings. Some of the synonyms for shocking include startling, astonishing, amazing, unexpected, extraordinary, and remarkable. I would submit that each of these definitions is actually an extremely appropriate and accurate descriptor of God's gift of mercy. It is *startling* and *astonishing* how we are shown mercy. *Amazing*, too, that even though we are responsible for Christ's suffering and death, He showers us with His unconditional love. One might expect that the Son of the Living God would die for those who are righteous, but how very *unexpected* He would die for us sinners.

Romans 5:7-8 clearly says,

> *Indeed, only with difficulty does one die for a just person, though perhaps for a good person one might even find courage to die. But God proves his love for us in that while we were still sinners Christ died for us.*

Such *remarkable* gifts showered onto unworthy recipients could not be judged any other way except *extraordinary*. Conclusion? God's mercy is truly scandalous!

The reflections on God's love, mercy and compassion that make up this work were significantly influenced by the writings of our current pope and four of his five predecessors on the Chair of Peter – Pope Emeritus Benedict XVI, St. John Paul II, St. John XXIII, and St. Paul VI. The specific works of Pope Francis that I found most enlightening were his, *Bull of Indiction – Misericordiae Vultus;* and his more recent, *The Name of God is Mercy.* In addition, I have drawn heavily from Father (now Cardinal) Raniero Cantalamessa's, *The Gaze of Mercy;* Father Benedict Groeschel's, *Heaven In Our Hands – Living the Beatitudes;* C. S. Lewis', *Mere Christianity;* the writings of Bishop Robert Barron (mostly from posts on his online global media ministry, *Word on Fire*); St. Augustine; St. Teresa of Calcutta; St. Faustina and others. The central themes of most reflections were stimulated by daily Mass readings; meditations from the *Word Among Us* (a Catholic periodical that focuses specifically on the daily Mass readings); the *Book of Christian Prayer (Liturgy of the Hours)*; homilies heard or books I was blessed to discover.

A special note about the writings of St. John Henry Newman is in order here because I reference him frequently throughout this work. The words and message of his prayer, *The Mission of My Life*, inscribed a profound and indelible mark on my heart the very first time I heard it more than a half-dozen years ago and frankly they have nagged me ever since. In fact, this prayer was the underlying inspiration for my most recent book, *Live Humbly, Serve Graciously – Reflections on Baptism, Mission and Service*. But beyond his inspirational prayer, I discovered that a remarkable amount of his writing, on a variety of topics, particularly about the Blessed Mother and purgatory influenced me as well. Because I refer to him so much, most of the time I will simply refer to St. John Henry Cardinal Newman as, "Newman."

Sacred Scripture provides a rich treasury of references to love, grace, mercy, compassion and forgiveness, and I have drawn inspiration from many of them. Some narratives are accounts of events that took place in Jesus' three-year public life. Many are parables He personally used to teach the crowds that gathered around or followed Him. Others are lessons He fashioned specifically for His beloved disciples. Still others He carefully created to educate and inform His critics. The lessons all revealed important concepts to help them (and us) begin to understand not only the love that He and His Father had for them, but also how each of them had the responsibility to share the love bestowed on them with others. I have used several of these narratives and parables in more than one reflection because of their spiritual richness and insight – specifically the *Samaritan Women at the Well,* the *Woman Caught in Adultery,* and the *Pharisee and Tax Collector* simultaneously praying in the temple. A narrative from the Old Testament I used more than once is the story of King David, particularly his Psalm 51, the *Miserere.* Hopefully, the reuse of these passages will not be a distraction.

When I began writing this book, I did not intend it to be a sequel to *Live Humbly, Serve Graciously,* but as it began to take shape, I realized that my earlier work actually serves as the foundation for this one. Because God's unconditional gifts of love, mercy and compassion are so intimately interwoven with humility, baptism, mission and service, I found myself drawing from my earlier book far more than I anticipated. My point in telling you this is that if you read *Live Humbly,* you will likely see some ideas presented here that you may think you have read elsewhere – well, you have. Congratulations for having such a good memory! But, if you have not read the earlier work, hopefully, I have provided sufficient linkages here that each point will stand alone and make sense.

The original versions of about half of these reflections were talks I prepared for the Men's Spiritual Fellowship at my church over the past 15 or so years. The remainder are based on talks prepared for a variety of audiences, specifically to celebrate and shed light on the *Jubilee Year of Mercy;* and newly developed material based on situations experienced, books read and conversations with a wide range of people far brighter and more deeply spiritual than I. While my reflections on love, mercy, grace, compassion and forgiveness are less than exhaustive, and while I am neither a theologian nor philosopher, my fondest hope is that you will find something in this book that is useful in your personal spiritual journey. You might want to consider reading these reflections no more than one or two at a time.

Ridiculous Grace and Scandalous Mercy

Reflection

I

Ridiculous Grace and Scandalous Mercy
(A Love Story About Mercy and Compassion)

Have mercy on me, God, in accord with your merciful love;
in your abundant compassion blot out my transgressions.

(Psalm 51:3)

T HE CATECHISM OF the Catholic Church (CCC) defines *grace* as: "the free and undeserved help that God gives us to respond to His call to become children of God, adoptive sons, partakers of the divine nature and of eternal life". To put an exclamation point on the importance of God's grace, consider this – our very *justification* comes from the grace of God. The source of the *favor* spoken about is a love so grand, so deep, so undeserved, so intimate that it is, in truth, beyond our meager human ability to understand or appreciate. Even mystics down through the ages, such as St. Bernard of Clairvaux, St. Teresa of Avila, St. John of the Cross, St. Francis Assisi, and St. Faustina failed to fully comprehend (operative term here is *fully*) this mystery. Suffice it to say, even without fully understanding the meaning of "God is Love," this simple declaration is the very essence of our Christian heritage.

If there were a single season of the liturgical year best suited to focus our personal prayer and reflection on our Loving Father's love, grace and mercy, it would be Lent. During no other time of the year does the Church so keenly emphasize Jesus' sacrificial giving of Himself for our individual good through her daily mass readings, liturgies and the gift of sacramental forgiveness, than she does during Lent. In the lead up to Easter, our attention should rightly be centered on Jesus' humiliation

1

and suffering because He was betrayed, scourged, crucified and died because of our sinfulness. Reflecting on those sacrifices should drive us to our knees in humility, gratitude and sorrowfulness, leading to a firm commitment to amend our lives. Only then will our afflicted souls be healed and able to gloriously celebrate His Resurrection. Having said that, not to be reflective year-round would be tantamount to diminishing the immensity of God's unconditional gifts to us because, frankly, we are collectively a sinful, perverted, *stiff-necked* people.

The reality that God has flooded each of us with His grace from the very moment of our conception, is, quite simply, *ridiculous*. Despite our sinful natures, He continuously showers us with divine favor. In spite of all we have done, particularly rebelling against God's law – given to us for our own good and well-being – Jesus allowed Himself to be the target of unbelievable humiliation, torture and suffering. So, the *Good* – no, so the *Perfect* one took on the burden of my sins and, in doing so, suffered agony beyond description. Though we might try to mentally imagine what the events of Holy Thursday and Good Friday would have been like, we cannot really do so. Even many who have tried to watch Mel Gibson's extraordinary 2004 cinematic production, *The Passion of the Christ*, have found it impossible to view the most graphic scenes because of the sheer brutality of the events surrounding Christ's persecution and death. Yet as gruesome as they were, historians who have studied accounts of Jesus' death claim the violence portrayed in the movie was not even close to the violence Jesus actually endured. So, focusing on the season of Lent and events of Holy Week are appropriate because they vividly remind us of God's love poured out on each of us individually. God's Son, Jesus, came into the world, then suffered and died for us. Think about those realities. At what level does any of this make rational sense? None I know of. None I can imagine. Only through the prism of faith does God's unconditional love and generosity make sense. We are His people and He is our God. What a remarkable love story.

Sacred Scripture contains numerous stories and narratives that shed light on and help us to understand the remarkable relationship between God and us, His creations. One story that immediately comes to mind is that of King David. The details of his story are recorded primarily in First and Second Samuel. Numerous commentaries have been written about David's journey. You know the story, the drama, the highs and lows, so I will not burden you with all that here. But by way of brief summary, David arrogantly committed adultery with Bathsheba, wife of Uriah the Hittite, then, even more arrogantly, colluded to cover up his affair, ultimately becoming an accomplice in Uriah's murder. Let us be clear, David knew he had sinned – in fact, he knew he had sinned in epic proportions! He also knew the traditional burnt offerings customarily offered for sins would be woefully inadequate reparation for his actions. So, for quite a while, he took no action at all. Not until God sent His prophet Nathan to hold David accountable did he act. Nathan did not condemn David; rather he told him a story about a rich man who stole a lamb from a poor man and then asked what he would do in the same situation. David did not recognize that *he* was the rich man. Then, Nathan told him, "That man is you." He was horrified. Once confronted, David, the chosen one of God, finally took action and used his God-given poetic genius to pour out his heart, begging his creator for mercy and compassion. He wrote:

Have mercy on me, God, in accord with your merciful love; in your abundant compassion blot out my transgressions. Thoroughly wash away my guilt and from my sin cleanse me. For I know my transgressions; my sin is always before me. Against you, you alone have I sinned; I have done what is evil in your eyes. So that you are just in your word, and without reproach in your judgment. Behold, I was born in guilt, in sin my mother conceived me. Behold, you desire true sincerity; and secretly you teach me wisdom. Cleanse me with hyssop, that I may be pure; wash me, and I will be whiter than snow. You will let me hear gladness and joy; the bones you have crushed will rejoice.

Turn away your face from my sins; blot out all my iniquities. A clean heart create for me, God; renew within me a steadfast spirit. Do not drive me from before your face, nor take from me your holy spirit. Restore to me the gladness of your salvation; uphold me with a willing spirit. I will teach the wicked your ways, that sinners may return to you. Rescue me from violent bloodshed, God, my saving God, and my tongue will sing joyfully of your justice. Lord, you will open my lips and my mouth will proclaim your praise. For you do not desire sacrifice or I would give it; a burnt offering you would not accept. My sacrifice, O God, is a contrite spirit; a contrite, humbled heart, O God, you will not scorn. Treat Zion kindly according to your good will; build up the walls of Jerusalem.

Then you will desire the sacrifices of the just, burnt offering and whole offerings; then they will offer up young bulls on your altar."

David's gut-wrenching plea is immortalized as Psalm 51, often referred to as the *Miserere*, a prayer treasured for millennia because of its beautiful, sincere and passionate plea for compassion, forgiveness and mercy. Far too often, in our fast-paced, secular world, the spirituality of this beloved prayer and the gift it highlights are mostly forgotten. For those who may not be familiar with the Liturgy of the Hours (Breviary) that clergy and religious (and many lay Catholics) use as the framework for their prayer lives, Psalm 51 is prayed every Friday morning as a clear reminder of our need to beg God for His mercy and compassion. The Liturgy of the Hours is organized around the repetition of a specific collection of psalms and other Scripture passages and prayers over a four-week cycle. The prayers and psalms are different for each day in the cycle – except one. Psalm 51 is part of Morning Prayers every Friday, without exception. That it is the only psalm repeated every week is, in my opinion, significant because it serves as a constant reminder of our own sinfulness and the need to regularly beg for God's mercy and forgiveness. I would suggest rereading the Psalm, carefully studying the words – if you do, you will clearly understand why it is repeated every Friday, the customary day of remembrance of Jesus' crucifixion and death. In one of my final conversations with my dear friend, Jim Stone, before he died, after having prayed the Liturgy of the Hours Morning Prayers (on Friday) with him, I confided in him that every time I prayed Psalm 51, it impacted me deeply. In a quiet voice, but with a glimmer in his eye, he smiled and said, "It's supposed to!" And, so it is!

While some of the imagery in Psalm 51 may be unfamiliar to us, I believe the sentiment is pretty clear. The "Chosen One of God," the "man after God's own heart," knew he had sinned and in response, fell to his knees, poured out his heart and shamelessly begged for forgiveness. *"Have mercy on me, God, in accord with your merciful love; in your abundant compassion blot out my transgressions."* Each time I repeat the first verse of this psalm, I must conclude that God's love is endless, that His willingness to forgive me is unconditional, that His compassion is without bounds and His mercy endures forever. God's mercy is simply *scandalous* – an all-perfect God extends His tender mercy to me, His sinful creation. Remarkable.

How interesting that God chose to send one of His personal messengers to get David's attention. How interesting that God chooses, even today, to insert His personal representative into the middle of encounters between us, the sinner, and Him. Sound familiar? For those of us who practice our faith in the Catholic Christian tradition, we experience the wisdom of such interventions each time we receive the Sacrament of Reconciliation, confessing our sins to a priest, who acts in *persona Christi*.

From the establishment of the priesthood until today, the Catholic Church has continued to grant both the visible and spiritual reality of God's mercy to us sinners through the Sacrament of Reconciliation. The Church teaches the conditions required for our forgiveness include acknowledging our sinfulness, admitting our guilt, repenting for our offenses against God, confessing our transgressions to Christ's representative (the priest), promising to amend our lives, begging for forgiveness – then be willing to be forgiven. God's mercy is not just His love directed toward us; it is also His invitation for us to let go of our burden of guilt. If God Himself forgives and forgets, why can't we? It is important that we remember, once forgiven, we are forgiven, once and for all.

One of the earliest references to God's mercy in Scripture is Deuteronomy 7:9:

> *Know, then, that the LORD, your God, is God: the faithful God who keeps covenant mercy to the thousandth generation toward those who love him and keep his commandments.*

Just imagine, God promised to keep His covenant with His faithful to the thousandth generation. Curiously, if we consider a generation to span twenty-five years, we must conclude the whole of human existence up to now has only made a small time down-payment on the length of God's promise of mercy. So even if we interpret the *thousand generations* literally, God promises to continue showering us with mercy for many thousands of years hence. Almost surely, though, the author of Deuteronomy simply meant, God will keep His promise forever. One of my favorite passages in all of scripture, Psalm 118:1, supports this claim:

"Give thanks to the Lord for He is good, His mercy endures forever."

To me, the message could not be any clearer or any more reassuring.

Compassion is another gift our loving Father bestows on us in abundance. Not surprising, the notion of compassion is beautifully extolled in the Psalms, at least a dozen times, mostly in the context of forgiveness. While reflecting on this gift should always be on our minds, during Lent we ought to more thoroughly examine our hearts to see whom we should reach out to and forgive. We should apologize for injuries inflicted, for words spoken that hurt another, for attitudes that were arrogant, for feelings discounted, or for thoughtlessness perpetrated . . . shall I go on? In short, because we have chosen to go our own sinful way, we are encouraged to reach out to those we have hurt in any way by our thoughts, words, actions, or inactions and not only beg God for His mercy and forgiveness for our offenses but also make reparations to those we have harmed. Maybe I should have said, "Particularly during Lent, I should beg for God's forgiveness for the pain I personally inflicted on Jesus as His flesh was violated during His scourging and crucifixion."

Our understanding of God's mercy and compassion can be deeply enriched by reflecting on the events that occurred in the days leading up to Good Friday. During this holiest of weeks, we hear three different Gospel accounts of Jesus' Passion. In Luke's account, however, there are two events which seem to be quite different, even though they are really intriguing parallels – one is the narrative of Peter's three denials of Christ, the second is Judas' betrayal. At the Last Supper, Peter was warned he would deny Christ, and even though he declared he would not, he did.

Those denials were sins of enormous gravity. Yet Jesus' infinite mercy was shown Peter almost immediately as He walked past Peter while being led from the room where He had been questioned by Caiaphas. In Luke 22:61-62, we are told:

> *And the Lord turned and looked at Peter. And Peter remembered the word of the Lord . . . And he went out and wept bitterly.*

Father Raniero Cantalamessa (2015), "Preacher to the Papal Household" for more than 35 years, observed "Jesus' gaze uncovers Peter's sin and wakes him up from his lack of self-consciousness better than the cock's crowing does. Jesus' gaze is a gaze of kindness that offers forgiveness. There is no anger, no irritation in it; the only reproach, gentle and silent, is that of a wounded affection. Jesus' gaze of mercy obtains the result that a reproachful gaze would not have had." Clearly, no sin is too great for God's mercy.

So, what about Judas? Why does his story end so differently than Peter's? Interestingly, scholars agree Judas had genuine remorse for what he had done, as did Peter, because in Matthew 27:4 we are told Judas was so distraught at what he had done he cried out, *"I have sinned in betraying innocent blood!"* He immediately went and returned the thirty pieces of silver, and then . . . The outcomes were diametrically different because of one thing and one thing only. Peter trusted in God's mercy – Judas did not.

John 8:1-11 is another familiar story from which we can learn much about God's mercy – the story of the woman caught in adultery:

> *Jesus went to the Mount of Olives. But early in the morning he arrived again in the temple area, and all the people started coming to him, and he sat down and taught them. Then the scribes and the Pharisees brought a woman who had been caught in adultery and made her stand in the middle. They said to him, "Teacher, this woman was caught in the very act of committing adultery. Now in the law, Moses commanded us to stone such women. So what do you say?" They said this to test him, so that they could have some charge to bring against him. Jesus bent down and began to write on the ground with his finger. But when they continued asking him, he*

straightened up and said to them, "Let the one among you who is without sin be the first to throw a stone at her." Again he bent down and wrote on the ground. And in response, they went away one by one, beginning with the elders. So, he was left alone with the woman before him. Then Jesus straightened up and said to her, "Woman, where are they? Has no one condemned you?" She replied, "No one, sir." Then Jesus said, "Neither do I condemn you. Go, and from now on do not sin anymore."

Over the centuries, much speculation has been raised about what Jesus might have been writing in the dirt during this encounter. At the beginning of the fifth century, St. Jerome, one of the Church's most esteemed theologians and a Doctor of the Church, speculated Jesus might simply have been writing the names of the Scribes and the Pharisees in the sand. Interesting thought, though no one really knows. But Jesus' purposeful distraction achieved its intended result. With His challenge, *"Let the one among you who is without sin be the first to throw a stone at her,"* the gathering got very quiet, very quickly as, one-by-one the Pharisees disappeared, leaving Jesus and the woman alone. Did Jesus reprimand her? Did He even raise His voice? He did neither. Instead, He told her to go and sin no more. His kindness to her was beautiful. I, personally would do well to remember Jesus' merciful response and be far less judgmental in all my dealings with others than I am. *"Let the person without sin cast the first stone."*

Like so many stories in Holy Scripture we are not told what happens next, even though the people involved probably lived many years after their encounter with Jesus. So, what do you suppose happened next for this woman as she left Him that unforgettable day? Surely, His refusal to condemn her affected her to the core, after all, His loving act of mercy saved her life, not just physically, but spiritually as well. Maybe she was so grateful to Jesus she became one of His followers. Maybe she went back to her husband to reconcile. We will never know. But one thing she likely did not do was go back to living the way she had in the past. She surely was changed by her encounter with God's mercy. Similarly, when we open ourselves to His grace, our gratitude for what Jesus has done for us should lead us to follow Him more closely by softening our hearts, inspiring us in response to be more loving and merciful toward others. His love, grace and mercy also strengthen us against further temptation to sin.

While the encounter with this woman is only one example, I find it fascinating how many times Jesus found Himself in socially awkward situations, ignored the social norms set by the Scribes and Pharisees (who used by them as *cattle prods* on others) and did not back away. How often did the religious leaders of His time accuse Him and others of wrongdoing, yet seem not to understand their personal need to look into a mirror? Many similar questions could be asked. But my point here is rather than being controlled by man-made rules or by accusing others, Jesus consistently and very simply offers us compassion and mercy, scandalous levels of mercy.

Day after day during Lent, the daily mass readings focus on the healing power of God's love, almost begging the question, "Do you want to be (spiritually) well?" in much the same way Jesus asked the paralyzed man who waited at the well at Bethesda if he wanted to be (physically) well. All we need to do to be healed is simply ask God for His grace – regardless of whether we are seeking mental, physical, emotional, or spiritual healing. To be sure, all of us have some degree of suffering in our lives and we all need healing. But truthfully, the only things separating us in our wounded state from being spiritually healthy are a refusal to admit our brokenness and a reluctance to ask for His grace and mercy. God desperately wants us to be well – and He patiently awaits our plea for healing.

Even without our conscious knowledge, God constantly showers us with ridiculous amounts of grace that we neither deserve nor can we earn. His love for us is beyond all understanding. When God's love is directed toward us who are sinners, we experience scandalous levels of His mercy that we likewise neither deserve, nor can we earn. And even though His gifts to us are unconditional, we are encouraged to put our faith into action, not to earn grace and mercy, but quite the opposite – to thank Him for the mercy and grace He has already granted us. Putting our faith into action quite naturally leads to living the Corporal and Spiritual Works of

Mercy. Our personal response to God's grace and mercy is simply being open to and living out the good works St. Paul wrote about in his letter to the Ephesians 2:8-10:

> *For by grace you have been saved through faith, and this is not from you; it is the gift of God; it is not from works, so no one may boast. For we are his handiwork, created in Christ Jesus for the good works that God has prepared in advance, that we should live in them.*

Would like to offer a final summary thought or two. God's love, particularly in the context of Jesus' passion and death as an expiation for our sinfulness, is an extraordinary gift. In spite of our sinfulness, blindness, indifference, irreverence and callousness toward Him, He loves us anyway, unconditionally. One of the most dramatic truths about the relationship we have with our Father God is His insistence on showering us with boundless, ridiculous amounts of grace, no matter what we do. When that ridiculous grace is focused toward us sinners, we experience scandalous levels of His mercy. When we open ourselves to God's unearnable gifts of love, mercy and compassion, we will be flooded with them! Nothing else in our human experience even comes close as a parallel. St. Faustina taught, "For the sake of your sorrowful passion, have mercy on us and on the whole world. "

Reflection

II

Lord, Show Us the Radiance of Your Mercy

But the tax collector stood off at a distance and would
not even raise his eyes to heaven but beat his breast
and prayed, 'O God, be merciful to me a sinner.'

(Luke 18:13)

THE RADIANCE OF God's mercy is revealed to us in a variety of ways –
in sacred scripture, through the lives of the saints, by the actions of
others, and by our own actions, to name only a few. Even though the
Church focused heavily on mercy during the Jubilee Year, she did not
waiver from following the normal three-year cycle of daily mass readings
during that time. Coincidentally, however, virtually all of the Gospel
readings at Mass for the final two months (or so) were taken from St.
Luke's Gospel. I find this important for several reasons. First, St. Luke
was a remarkably well-educated, dedicated evangelist and physician who
traveled hundreds of miles to preach the Gospel to the Gentiles and was
the companion of St. Paul to the end of Paul's life. St. Luke witnessed
and was privy to Paul's accounts of God's mercy to him. Second, between
his Gospel and the Acts of the Apostles, St. Luke contributed more to
the New Testament than any other writer and much of his narrative
focuses heavily on stories and parables illustrating Jesus' mercy to all
He encountered. Third, many of the most widely recognized, endearing
and instructional stories demonstrating God's mercy are found in Luke's
Gospel and nowhere else. So, had St. Luke not allowed himself to be
used as God's instrument in his writing, we would have been deprived of
some of the finest illustrations of God's love, mercy and compassion ever

written. And finally, while much could be said about Luke, possibly his most engaging, and likely least mentioned characteristic, was his love for and belief in God's complete and unconditional mercy. We get very vivid pictures of that love by the way he paints beautiful, clear portraits of God's patience with sinners – and by extension with each of us. Many scholars have observed that St. Luke's stories are startling because they show God reaching out to marginalized people and welcoming them into his kingdom. While the stories below are familiar, I found each of them quite worthy of review simply because they speak loudly about God's endless mercy. Revisiting St. Luke's Gospel was particularly helpful in guiding my reflections on the *Year of Mercy*.

In Chapter 7:40-47, St. Luke relates the beautiful and powerful story of a sinful woman who anointed Jesus' feet while a Pharisee named Simon looked on in judgment and disbelief. Do you remember the exchange?

> *Jesus said to him in reply, "Simon, I have something to say to you."*
> *"Tell me, teacher," he said. "Two people were in debt to a certain*
> *creditor; one owed five hundred days' wages and the other owed*
> *fifty. Since they were unable to repay the debt, he forgave it for both.*
> *Which of them will love him more?" Simon said in reply, "The one, I*
> *suppose, whose larger debt was forgiven." He said to him, "You have*
> *judged rightly." Then he turned to the woman and said to Simon,*
> *"Do you see this woman? When I entered your house, you did not*
> *give me water for my feet, but she has bathed them with her tears*
> *and wiped them with her hair. You did not give me a kiss, but she*
> *has not ceased kissing my feet since the time I entered. You did not*
> *anoint my head with oil, but she anointed my feet with ointment.*
> *So, I tell you, her many sins have been forgiven; hence, she has*
> *shown great love.*

The Pharisee was only concerned about following rules and social appearances. By contrast, Jesus chose to pour out God's mercy and compassion on the sinful woman because her actions toward Him were a clear indication of her love of Him and her desire for repentance. Two very different responses to the same series of events – one was judgmental, the other loving.

The beloved parable of the Good Samaritan (Luke 10:29-37), tells the story of a [hated] Samaritan who encountered a [Jewish] man who had been beaten by thugs and left to die.

"Who is my neighbor?" Jesus replied, "A man fell victim to robbers as he went down from Jerusalem to Jericho. They stripped and beat him and went off leaving him half-dead. A priest happened to be going down that road, but when he saw him, he passed by on the opposite side. Likewise a Levite came to the place, and when he saw him, he passed by on the opposite side. But a Samaritan traveler who came upon him was moved with compassion at the sight. He approached the victim, poured oil and wine over his wounds and bandaged them. Then he lifted him up on his own animal, took him to an inn and cared for him. The next day he took out two silver coins and gave them to the innkeeper with the instruction, 'Take care of him. If you spend more than what I have given you, I shall repay you on my way back.' Which of these three, in your opinion, was neighbor to the robbers' victim?" He answered, "The one who treated him with mercy." Jesus said to him, "Go and do likewise."

The Samaritan modeled the very essence of God's mercy as he cared for the injured man, even as other passers-by (including a priest) ignored him. Jesus' message should be quite clear. But just how often are we willing to cheerfully show love, mercy and compassion to a perfect stranger, maybe one who is dirty or smells bad, or has a different skin color, is from a different religious tradition, or has a different country of origin than our own? An essential element of mercy and compassion is *agape*, an unconditional love that does not have eyes, ears or nose.

One of the most beloved stories in the New Testament, also from St. Luke's Gospel and read during Lent, is the story of the Prodigal Son. In that narrative, the Pharisees criticized Jesus for daring to eat with sinners – in their eyes, doing so was scandalous. "Sinner" was an identity, so to them Jesus was keeping company with the lowest of the low. Jesus' loving response was the parable of the Prodigal Son. Though normally known by this name, the story might actually have a somewhat misleading title. Rather than being called the parable of the Prodigal Son (focusing on the son who woke up, decided to go home and beg forgiveness from his dad), some scripture scholars suggest this might equally meaningfully be called the "Parable of the Forgiving Father". But upon further reflection, the story is not just about one son or just a father – it is a story about two sons and their father, and all three are needed to make the parable complete. This story clearly assures us of our heavenly Father's infinite love for us. Regardless which title you prefer, the parable has two distinct goals: first, God wants everyone to know His love, and second, He wants those who know His love to experience it more deeply.

In a sense, the prodigal son was "dead" because of the sins he committed when he was away from home. But the moment he returned, it was if he had come back to life. The Father was only concerned with bringing his son home. We are meant to see that for Jesus the present moment of conversion and turning away from our sinfulness is the most important moment. Jesus used this rebellious fellow to describe people who have not yet accepted the love God has for them. They need to turn and come home to Him. They need what might be called an "initial conversion." These are people God asks us to mercifully lift up in prayer in a special way – particularly if they are loved ones who might be far from the Lord. May they all experience an initial conversion!

The prodigal son's older brother, by contrast, was already "alive." He was faithful to his dad and hardworking on his behalf. But he needed a conversion, too. While he may have been obedient to his father, lots of sinful thoughts occupied his mind, particularly when his younger brother returned. He needed an "ongoing conversion," a deeper turning away from his habits of resentment, anger, and self-righteousness.

The Pharisees, like the elder brother in the story, could not see their own sinfulness because they were so focused on seeing the sins of others; they were stuck in the past with no look at the present. What about us? Even if we believe in Jesus, pray every day and go to Mass regularly, we still need ongoing conversion. Even when trying to do our best to live good lives and care for our families, we can fall into judgmental, self-righteous, self-centered, arrogant ways of thinking and behaving, so we still need ongoing conversion. God asks us to keep turning to Him for help and healing. No matter how big or small our sins, God is always waiting with open arms to welcome us home. Through this parable, we are meant to see that for Jesus, the present moment is the most important moment of conversion. We cannot change the past, but in accepting this reality, we can learn an important lesson about God: He lives in the present. As thirteenth century mystic, Meister Eckhart said, "God is a God of the present. He takes and receives you as He finds you – not what you have been, but what you are now." Therefore, it is necessary to truly accept our identity, not in sinfulness, but in Christ as "*a new creation*," (2 Cor 5:17). Turning to Christ in repentance allows reconciliation with Him and acceptance of His mercy, which is always greater than our worst sin. Each moment can be a moment of conversion, and our God waits patiently to run out and meet us on the road just as the father did in the parable.

Referring to the Prodigal Son, Luke 15:20 says:

> *While he was still a long way off, his father caught sight of him, and was filled with compassion. He ran to his son, embraced him and kissed him.*

The word vitally important in this passage is *compassion*. As often happens, some words simply do not translate well from one language to another – like *compassion* in this passage. There are at least six Hebrew words for our English word *compassion*. In the Hebrew text of this story, the word *compassion* is *rachamim* (emphasis on the *ha*), a word loosely translated as "mother love," the kind of deep love a mother has for the unborn child in her womb, the kind of profound love that can at the same time hurt deeply and be joyful and wondrous. In spite of the term "mother love," feeling such compassion does not require being a woman. While the prodigal son probably did not deserve *rachamim*, his father was so overjoyed to see his son that he showered him with both love and compassion, sent for clean clothes, ordered a ring be put on his finger, and charged his servant with preparing a celebration. Would not any of us as parents welcome a prodigal daughter or son back in the way this father did or as our loving Father-God welcomes us whenever we stray? Hopefully we would. Almost surely, we would. Or would we? One thing we can be assured of – God does because His mercy is unconditional.

How about ours?

Rachamim is not a word familiar to most of us, certainly was not to me. I heard the word for the first time in a sermon several years ago as the homilist made it come alive while preaching on this parable. He said as wonderful as the dad's gift to his son was, and as hard as it may be to believe, most of us reject our Loving Father's *rachamim*. At an alarming rate, we do so by refusing to accept our God's compassionate forgiveness for our sins. Another, more blunt way of saying the same thing is that most of us reject God's mercy. While our rejections take many forms, most are founded in arrogance, self-righteousness, and pride. One example I remember the priest mentioning in his homily that morning is our reluctance to fully confess our sins in confession, either because we are too proud to admit our wrongdoings, or because we rationalize and convince ourselves that what we have done is not really sinful, when in fact it is. Another is that we convince ourselves that the sin we committed is so great God could not possibly forgive us, but nothing could be further from the truth. To receive the gift of *rachamim* and benefit from it, all we need to do is humble ourselves before God, tell the truth, and then humbly accept the wonderful mercy and forgiveness He showers on us. Mercy is His love turned toward us, the sinners!

While many more stories and parables about God's mercy are recorded in Luke's Gospel, I would like to include just one more here. In Luke 17:11-19, we read about Jesus healing 10 lepers:

> *As He continued His journey to Jerusalem, He traveled through Samaria and Galilee. As He was entering a village, ten lepers met [Him]. They stood at a distance from Him and raised their voice, saying, "Jesus, Master! Have pity on us!" And when He saw them, He said, "Go show yourselves to the priests." As they were going they were cleansed. And one of them, realizing He had been healed, returned, glorifying God in a loud voice; and he fell at the feet of Jesus and thanked Him. He was a Samaritan. Jesus said in reply, "Ten were cleansed, were they not? Where are the other nine? Has none but this foreigner returned to give thanks to God?" Then He said to him, "Stand up and go; your faith has saved you."*

Why is this story important? Because of the 10 healed, only the Samaritan (remember they were enemies of the Jews) returned to thank Jesus. God is not concerned with labels; He simply loves an open heart and is willing to shower such hearts with His mercy. Am I willing to humbly accept God's mercy and forgiveness and thank Him for it? Or am I content with keeping God at arms-length?

Simply praying Psalm 118:1, *Give thanks to the Lord for He is good, His mercy endures forever*, is a beautiful way to acknowledge and thank God for his compassionate goodness. And if I truly want to grow closer to Him, there are many prayers, particularly in our Catholic tradition that are humble petitions for God's mercy – not just for ourselves, but for our families and friends, and for perfect strangers as well. One such prayer is said as part of praying the rosary, the *Fatima Prayer:*

Oh, my Jesus, forgive us our sins, save us from the fires of hell, and lead all souls to Heaven, especially those in most need of Your Mercy.

The beauty of this prayer is our sincere plea for mercy, not just for our own sinful selves, but also for those "most in need of Your Mercy." If we take the words of this prayer to heart, we are actually begging God to have mercy on those at the very margins, even on those who have consciously separated themselves from the state of grace by their own choices. In short, we pray for God to have mercy on everyone, including the most hardened criminals and terrorists and our next-door neighbor who may be a pain in the neck! Why would we consider doing such a thing? Because we have no knowledge of what goes on in another person's heart. So, praying for God's mercy on them is entirely proper – and, each time we do, we fulfill one of our most sacred obligations as members of the Body of Christ.

Praying for someone begs the questions: Are we really serious about helping those who seem not to care what they do, who they hurt, or what mischief they may cause? Are we genuinely praying for those some might consider unsavable? Hopefully, we are. Actually, we must! In all candor, though, each time I waiver or question my intentions, I must force myself, either in the moment or post facto, to rightfully remember the proper order of things – I do not receive mercy because I have shown mercy to others, I must show mercy to others because God has already shown me His love, mercy and forgiveness. God is always the originator; we are always the responders. Also worth remembering, we cannot out-give God! Dr. Scott Hahn, Director of the St. Paul Center for Biblical Theology, has a wonderful explanation of why Christ suffered and died for us and, in so doing, showered us with His mercy (and by extension why we should pray for and be merciful to others). "He paid a debt He didn't owe, because we owed a debt we couldn't pay."

A beautiful prayer that focuses exclusively on God's mercy is the *Divine Mercy Chaplet*, inspired by Divine revelations made to Sister Faustina, recorded in her extensive diary (1981). Each time the chaplet is prayed, we recite three prayers specifically focused on mercy:

> Eternal Father, I offer you the body and blood, soul and divinity of your dearly beloved Son, Our Lord Jesus Christ, in atonement for my sins and the sins of the whole world.

And,

> For the sake of His Sorrowful Passion, have mercy on us and on the whole world.

Then at the conclusion,

> Holy God, Holy Mighty One, Holy Immortal One, have mercy on us and on the whole world.

The words of these three short prayers cause me to ask an *either – or* question: "Am I really pleading for mercy for myself and all others, not collectively, but individually?" or am I simply saying the words? Hopefully, I am sincere, not just going through the motions in spite of the number of times I may pray the chaplet!

The relationship between love and mercy is profound. I think it useful to consider the following bit of wisdom from Peter Kreeft's book (2016), *How to be Holy – First Steps in Becoming a Saint*: "Most of our worst sufferings come from relationships with other people. Most of our greatest joys do, too. Because people have faults and weaknesses – everyone does especially any idiot who thinks he doesn't – we must (1) accept this as a fact of life – the machine called the human psyche doesn't work perfectly. And (2) the most important thing to do about this is to remember that we are almost always causing others sufferings just as much as they are causing us to suffer. (3) So, stop judging and just LOVE." Love leads to and is the foundation for compassion and mercy.

Using Kreeft's observation as context, I believe one very important lesson I learned during the *Year of Mercy* was the definition of mercy offered by Bishop Robert Barron (2016): "Mercy is what *love* looks like when it turns toward the sinner." Because I am a sinner, I pray I will continue to remind myself of this reality, particularly when I am *most* in need of His mercy; and, because mercy has been showered on me as a gift without condition, I can do nothing less toward others. My duty as a baptized member of the Body of Christ, is willingness to show unconditional mercy, compassion and forgiveness to everyone around me – not just to those I love and to those who love me, but to those who may challenge my very belief in the radiance of God's mercy.

Reflection

III

God's Mercy Endures Forever

Give thanks to the Lord for He is good, His mercy endures forever.
(Psalm 118:1)

WHEN ASKED TO define mercy, Pope Francis replied, "Mercy is the divine attitude which embraces, it is God's giving Himself to us, accepting us, and bowing to forgive. Jesus said He came not for those who were good but for the sinners. He did not come for the healthy, who do not need the doctor, but for the sick. For this reason, we can say that mercy is God's identity card. God of mercy, merciful God." (Francis I, 2016)

In the parable of the Pharisee and the Tax Collector from Luke 18:9-14, we read:

> *He then addressed this parable to those who were convinced of their own righteousness and despised everyone else. "Two people went up to the temple area to pray; one was a Pharisee and the other was a tax collector. The Pharisee took up his position and spoke this prayer to himself, 'O God, I thank you that I am not like the rest of humanity – greedy, dishonest, adulterous – or even like this tax collector. I fast twice a week, and I pay tithes on my whole income.' But the tax collector stood off at a distance and would not even raise his eyes to heaven but beat his breast and prayed, 'O God, be merciful to me a sinner.' I tell you, the latter went home justified, not the former; for everyone who exalts himself will be humbled, and the one who humbles himself will be exalted."*

What is surprising about this story is that the tax collector, who would likely have been a despised member of society at that time, was *justified*. Reread the passage. Jesus said so! Such a reality should give each of us hope that mercy will be poured out on us, too! We are reminded again in this narrative that God looks into our hearts not at labels others might use to describe us. Are we courageous enough in our lives to do the same, or are we more concerned about what people might think or say or do in response to our humility?

In candor, though, I find it pretty easy to see myself in the role of the Pharisee, looking into the mirror and seeing a righteous reflection, after all, I work hard, pray hard, do charitable work and donate generously – nearly throwing my shoulder out of its socket patting myself on the back for doing so. But Jesus invites us to follow the example of the tax collector, who says,

"O God, be merciful to me a sinner."

The tax collector's simple, enormously humble plea, is all any of us need utter to be engulfed by our loving Father's mercy. How simple – but how difficult it is for most of us to bow humbly to receive this amazing gift. Ironically God, Himself, bows to forgive us, and He bows to shower us with His mercy!

My initial exposure to the concepts of God's grace and mercy was as a young child in Catholic school. The beloved Franciscan, Dominican and Ursuline nuns who were my teachers did a wonderful job helping me grasp the fundamentals of those realities. In my innocent mind, all of what I learned about mercy made sense, including memorizing prayers that mentioned mercy. But as a freshman in high school, I ran head long into a portrayal of mercy that made absolutely no sense to me – in English class, not religion. It was my first encounter with William Shakespeare. Unfortunately, his genius was lost on me at the time. Hold that thought for just a moment!

During the last half dozen years or so, likely inspired by the literature written in support of activities of the *Jubilee Year of Mercy*, I began to read and reflect a great deal on mercy. A nagging recollection of those painful moments with Shakespeare emerged so I went back and reread what most literary scholars agree is one of Shakespeare's most famous soliloquys, taken from Act IV, Scene I of, *The Merchant of Venice*. Shakespeare's words landed on a far more receptive mind and heart:

> The quality of mercy is not strained.
> It droppeth as the gentle rain from heaven
> Upon the place beneath. It is twice blest:
> It blesseth him that gives and him that takes.
> 'Tis mightiest in the mightiest; it becomes
> The throned monarch better than his crown.
> His scepter shows the force of temporal power,
> The attribute to awe and majesty,
> Wherein doth sit the dread and fear of kings.
> But mercy is above this sceptered sway;
> It is enthroned in the hearts of kings;
> It is an attribute of God himself;
> And earthly power doth then show like God's
> When mercy seasons justice.

What beauty. What eloquence. And while scholars continue to debate whether Shakespeare was a religious author, his brilliant insight about the greatest gift anyone could receive from or give to another is, in my mind, deeply spiritual and captures the very essence of mercy. We receive mercy from God – we convey it to others. Others receive from God – they convey to us. Those who receive mercy and understand what they have received are recognizable, because they in turn are those who show mercy to others no matter whether they are king, nobleman or peasant.

Jackie Francois-Angel, in *Beautiful Mercy* (a chapter in Kelly (2015)), says, "Mercy is one of those theological concepts that seems pretty abstract. I know I have experienced mercy from God and from others. I also know there are times when I've been merciful. But I always thought of mercy as just having to do with forgiveness." My own simple, early understanding of mercy parallels Frances-Angel's; but mercy is far more complex.

Around the turn of the fifth century, St. Augustine taught that mercy and misery are two sides of the same coin. One concept makes little sense in the absence of the other. "When we ask for God's mercy, we are essentially asking Him to heal our heart that is in misery. And our hearts can be in misery not just from sin, but from the deep hurt caused by a broken relationship with a family member, from the suffering of infertility, from the pain of a physical or mental illness, from losing a job, from being betrayed or abandoned, from spiritual or physical poverty, and so on . . . I realize that I've experienced God's mercy much more than I could ever count. And I've also realized that I, in turn, have given mercy to others in more ways than just by forgiving someone who has wronged me." (Jackie Francois-Angel, in Kelly (2015)).

In my own sinful misery, I longingly desire God's mercy, so does it not make sense that I, too, must show mercy to others in their misery? And because God is merciful to me, who am I to presume who else God grants mercy? *For the sake of His sorrowful passion, have mercy on us and on the whole world.* (A prayer from, *The Divine Mercy Chaplet*)

A simple search of the Old and New Testaments reveals several hundred references to mercy, more than a hundred in the Psalms alone! What is the significance? Why is this gift mentioned so frequently? The answer to these two questions can be summed simply by way of Psalm 57:2:

> *Have mercy on me, God, have mercy on me. In you I seek refuge. In the shadow of your wings I seek refuge till harm pass by.*

This verse is beautifully highlighted by a psalm-prayer taken from the Liturgy of the Hours – Morning Prayers:

> Lord, send your mercy and your truth to rescue us from the snares of the devil, and we will praise you among the peoples and proclaim you to the nations, happy to be known as companions of your Son.

Our lives would be truly enriched, if only we would internalize this ancient message.

Many New Testament stories highlight how Jesus modeled God's mercy during His public ministry. One example is Jesus' meeting Zacchaeus, the little short guy in the sycamore tree, described in Luke 19:1-10. Jesus saw him in the tree – out on a limb – and very likely had a smile on His face as He looked up and saw such a prominent person doing something so silly. He no doubt saw the almost childlike look on Zacchaeus' face. To be sure, Jesus knew he was one of the despised tax collectors, but called him down anyway and said, *"I am coming to your house for dinner tonight"* – no doubt quite the scandal. While in this man's house, with no prompting from Jesus except for a merciful gaze, Zacchaeus basically admitted he was a crook – then told Jesus he would give half of his possessions to the poor and repay four-fold anything he had extorted from anyone. The enthusiasm of his initial childlike encounter with Jesus was transformed into a deeply mature conversion. Remarkable.

Jesus' encounter with the Samaritan woman at the well (John 4:1-42), is another well-known account that sheds even more light on how God treats us mercifully. You may recall Jesus approached the woman who had come to a community well to draw water, and ask her for a drink. For a Jewish man to ask a Samaritan woman for a drink of water was evidently an absolute social no-no! Yet Jesus made the request and then courteously engaged her in somewhat casual conversation, still another no-no. He asked about her family only to be told of an irregular marital relationship. While Jesus was clear with her about her relationships with the men she had lived with, He did not scold her, humiliate her or talk down to her in any way. Instead, after an open and loving conversation about her living arrangements, Jesus chose this sinful woman to be the very first person to whom He would reveal He was the Messiah!! That His Father loved her was enough for Him. Simply beautiful. How mercifully He treated the woman. (Additional insights from this same story appear elsewhere in this work.)

Pope Francis provided clear focus on mercy when he declared the first-ever *Jubilee Year* dedicated exclusively to mercy, even though many of his predecessors directed much attention to mercy as well. While I looked back only fifty years or so, much to my surprise, except for Pope John Paul I (whose papacy lasted only 33 days), every pope during that time spoke and wrote eloquently, not just about the importance of the gift of mercy, but also the duty of mercy.

Pope Francis' teachings are remarkably parallel to and complementary of the teachings of his recent predecessors. In his opening remarks to the Second Vatican Council in the early '60's, St. John XXIII said, "Now the Bride of Christ wishes to use the medicine of mercy rather than taking up arms of severity . . . The Catholic Church, as she holds high the torch of Catholic truth at this Ecumenical Council, wants to show herself a loving mother to all: patient, kind, moved by compassion and goodness toward her separated children."

Using an idea first proposed by St. Augustine, Saint Paul VI summarized the essence of his own spiritual life, thus: "My poverty, the mercy of God. That I may at least honor who you are. God of infinite bounty invoking, accepting, and celebrating your sweet mercy." (Francis I, 2016).

St. John Paul II (1980) enhanced the ideas of his predecessors with his encyclical, *Dives in Misericordia* (*Rich in Mercy*), in which he affirmed the Church lives an authentic life only when it professes and proclaims mercy, the most amazing attribute of the Creator and Redemptor, and when it leads humanity to the font of mercy. The Pope's message was deeply influenced by and linked to revelations received directly from the Lord through a Polish nun and mystic, Sister Maria Faustina Kowalska (Kowalska, 1981). John Paul II was so significantly moved by his deepened understanding of God's mercy through her, he established Divine Mercy Sunday, celebrated the first Sunday after Easter. Pope John Paul II canonized Sister Faustina during the celebration of the first Divine Mercy Sunday services. *For the sake of His sorrowful passion, have mercy on us and on the whole world.*

Pope Emeritus Benedict XVI added to our understanding of mercy when he taught, "Mercy is in reality the core of the Gospel message; it is the name of God Himself, the face with which He revealed Himself in the Old Testament and fully in Jesus Christ, incarnation of Creative and Redemptive Love. This love of mercy also illuminates the face of the Church, and is manifested through the Sacraments, in particular that of the Reconciliation, as well as in the works of charity, both of community and individuals. Everything that the Church says and does shows that God has mercy for man." (Francis I, 2016)

Pope Francis poetically described mercy as, "The bridge that connects God and man, opening our hearts to a hope of being loved forever despite our sinfulness." What a beautiful image of God's never-ending love for us, who are truly unworthy of His love and grace. He continued, "[the Church] is authentic and credible only when she becomes a convincing herald of mercy," a mercy that "knows no bounds and extends to everyone without exception… How much I desire that the year to come (speaking about the *Jubilee Year of Mercy*) will be steeped in mercy, so that we can go out to every man and woman, bringing the goodness and tenderness of God…May the balm of mercy reach everyone, both believers and those far away, as a sign that the kingdom of God is already present in our midst." (Francis I, 2015).

Throughout his adult life, Pope Francis has passionately focused on mercy as the central theme of his own personal spirituality. That he declared the *Jubilee Year of Mercy* should not have surprised anyone. His papal motto, displayed on his coat of arms, is the same one he used as a bishop; *miserando atque eligendo*, ("by having mercy, by choosing Him"). His motto was taken directly from a homily preached by St. Bede the Venerable on the calling of Matthew to be an apostle: "Jesus saw the tax collector and by having mercy chose him as an Apostle saying to him: 'Follow me.'" This particular homily, preached by Saint Bede, has taken on special significance in the Pope's life and his spiritual journey, for it was on the feast of St. Matthew that a young, seventeen-year-old Jorge Bergoglio was touched by the mercy of God and felt the call to religious life in the footsteps of Saint Ignatius of Loyola. The homily, which focuses on divine mercy, is also included in the Liturgy of the Hours – Office of Readings, on the Feast of Saint Matthew, offering special mercy when prayed.

Oddly, many pundits have criticized Pope Francis for his teachings on mercy, essentially suggesting he is being too soft on sinners, letting them off the hook without consequences. In commentaries written during the *Jubilee Year of Mercy*, Bishop Robert Barron (2016) observed, "A good deal of confusion stems from a misinterpretation of Francis' stress on mercy . . . It is not correct to say that God's essential attribute is mercy.

Rather, God's essential attribute is love, since love is what obtains among the three divine persons from all eternity." Barron continued, "Mercy is what love looks like when it turns toward the sinner. To say that mercy belongs to the very nature of God, therefore, would be to imply that sin exists within God himself, which is absurd…. Many receive the 'message of divine mercy' as tantamount to a denial of the reality of sin, as though sin no longer matters. But just the contrary is the case. To speak of mercy is to be intensely aware of sin and its peculiar form of destructiveness."

While many argue that mercy, even God's mercy, is limited by the demands of justice, Pope Francis, with similar logic as that used by St. Augustine, reminds us that mercy and justice are "two dimensions of a single reality that unfolds progressively until it culminates in the fullness of love." The Pope continued, "Preaching mercy…is not the same as ignoring sin or withholding correction. Instead, mercy invites repentance and conversion and ensures the sinner that once God forgives a sin, He forgets it…Many of those who insist first on God's justice are like the Pharisees who thought they could save themselves by following the letter of the law but ended up simply placing 'burdens on the shoulders of others and undermined the Father's mercy'…God's justice is His mercy. Mercy is not opposed to justice, but rather expresses God's way of reaching out to the sinner offering him a new chance to look at himself, convert and believe." (Francis I, 2016).

I believe inspiration for the Pope's comment here is fully founded in Wisdom 12:13, 16-19. There we are told:

> *For neither is there any god besides you who have the care of all, that you need show you have not unjustly condemned. For your might is the source of righteousness; your mastery over all things makes you lenient to all. For you show your might when the perfection of your power is disbelieved; and in those who know you, you rebuke insolence. But though you are master of might, you judge with clemency and with much lenience you govern us; for power, whenever you will, attends you. You taught your people, by these*

deeds, that those who are righteous must be kind; and you gave your children reason to hope that you would allow them to repent for their sins.

Father Raniero Cantalamessa (2015) further clarifies: "The mercy of God, whether in the Sacrament of Reconciliation or apart from it, does not have conditions, but it does require a sinner's repentance. Without repentance, mercy is not possible. To pretend otherwise would mean 'getting away scot-free' with God: but it is written, *Do not be deceived; God is not mocked, for whatever a man sows, that he will also reap*' (Galatians 6:7). In His omnipotence God can do all but one thing: He cannot, on His own, make a heart become 'broken and contrite' as described in Psalm 51:17. To do that He needs the consent of our free will. This is not actually a condition but a limitation God placed on Himself when He created us as free beings. God 'can invite someone by His grace and knock at the door, but He will not break it down if the person has barricaded himself or herself inside by rejecting Him.'"

Evil cannot simply be ignored or covered up – in fact, it must be destroyed. But that happens only when we sinners, individually, assume responsibility for what we have done and claim it as our own. And only we can do that, not God. He is the innocent one; we are the guilty. But the moment we admit our sinfulness, a miracle happens – God's infinite mercy floods us.

All of what I have shared this far is about God's gift of mercy to us. But there is another, very real dimension of mercy, specifically, that we each have a duty to extend mercy to others. While reflections on the *duty of mercy* will be provided later, providing a foundation for those reflections is fitting here.

In Matthew 5:7, we are told,

"Blessed are the merciful, for they will be shown mercy"

and in Matthew 6:12,

"Forgive us our debts, as we forgive our debtors."

On the surface, both passages might lead us to believe that the mercy we receive from God is the result of the mercy we show toward others and in proportion to it. If this were the case, though, according to Cantalamessa (2015), "the relationship between grace and good works would be completely turned upside down and it would cancel out the purely gratuitous character of the divine mercy that God solemnly proclaimed to Moses" in Exodus 33:19:

> *I will make all my goodness pass before you, and I will proclaim my name, "Lord," before you; I who show favor to whom I will, I who grant mercy to whom I will.*

So, what does all of this mean? Very simply, it means we should show mercy because we have received mercy, not in order to earn it. Said another way, I should be merciful to others because God has already been merciful to me! In full agreement with this reciprocation, as anointed priests, prophets and kings each of us is obliged to be merciful to others, loving them unconditionally and with compassion – only by doing so are we truly living out our baptismal responsibility of the stewardship of Jesus' kingship.

Lord, I beg you to give me sufficient humility that I can plead as the tax collector did, *'O God, be merciful to me a sinner.'*

What a truly magnificent love story!

Reflection

IV

Thank You, Jesus, for Your Gifts of Grace and Mercy

Rejoice in the Lord always. I shall say it again, rejoice!
(Philippians 4:4)

Gᴏᴅ'ꜱ ɢʀᴀᴄᴇ ᴀɴᴅ mercy flow to us in many ways. Sometimes we are comforted in our disappointment. Sometimes we find relief in our misery. Sometimes we experience respite in our suffering. Still other times, God shows His mercy by providing us with a roadmap for how He intends for us to live our lives, sharing our gifts with others, and being thankful to Him in all things. St. Paul provides useful context in 2 Corinthians 1:3-7:

> *Blessed be the God and Father of our Lord Jesus Christ, the Father of compassion and God of all encouragement, who encourages us in our every affliction, so that we may be able to encourage those who are in any affliction with the encouragement with which we ourselves are encouraged by God. For as Christ's sufferings overflow to us, so through Christ does our encouragement also overflow.*

One thing we can be sure of, each of us was created for a specific purpose, one unique to us. That being said, just how does all of this diversity within the human family fit together and why is that important? The beginning of St. Matthew's Gospel (1:1-17) provides some interesting insight. This lengthy passage chronicles the genealogy of Jesus – tracking no less than forty-two generations from Abraham to Jesus. Each person mentioned in this detailed list of often tongue-twisting names, whether good or bad, smart or challenged, holy or not so holy, an exile or not, each and every one had his mission – a remarkably important mission – being part of the long line of imperfect humans that led finally to the birth of Mary's perfect child, our Savior, Jesus – both God and Man. If each member of those forty-two generations had his own unique, God-given role to play, it surely is not too much of a stretch "to believe that each of us, too, plays an important role in what God is doing in this outpost of His eternal kingdom." (*The Word Among Us*).

St. John Henry Newman's prayer, *The Mission of My Life*, goes to the very heart of what it means to trust that God has a plan for our good, and in spite of what we might do to upset those plans, He will always offer us His grace, mercy and forgiveness to carry on.

The Mission of My Life

God has created me to do Him some definite service.
He has committed some work to me which He has not
committed to another.
I have my mission.
I may never know it in this life,
but I shall be told it in the next.
I am a link in a chain,
a bond of connection between persons.
He has not created me for naught.
I shall do good; I shall do His work.
I shall be an angel of peace,
a preacher of truth in my own place,
while not intending it if I do but keep His commandments.
Therefore, I will trust Him,
Whatever I am, I can never be thrown away.
If I am in sickness, my sickness may serve Him.
In perplexity, my perplexity may serve Him.
If I am in sorrow, my sorrow may serve Him.
He does nothing in vain.
He knows what He is about.
He may take away my friends.
He may throw me among strangers.

He may make me feel desolate,
Make my spirits sink,
Hide my future from me.
Still, He knows what He is about.

The words and message of this prayer inscribed a profound and indelible mark on my heart the very first time I heard it a half-dozen years ago and frankly they have nagged me ever since. "God has created me to do Him some definite service. He has committed some service to me that He has not committed to another. I have my mission." What a remarkable description of the "why" I was (we were) created. In simple terms, I was created to serve and shower love and mercy on others just as God has showered those gifts on me. Another way to interpret this message is that I must lead my life by living the Spiritual and Corporal Works of Mercy, to make them an integral part of who I am and what I do. While the details of His plan for me are still often sketchy in my mind and heart, one thing I know for sure – God intends for me to emulate His love and mercy and to extend those gifts to those around me including family, friends and perfect strangers.

God has created us uniquely, each with the talents needed to do His work. In a homily preached several years ago, my dear friend Deacon Jim Stone asserted quite clearly, "God has created each of us with talents, the fruits of which many have already used selflessly in this wonderful community of love called the Church." He went on to say that "some have not yet been motivated to use their gifts in helping build the Kingdom." Some of us have talents we have chosen not to share, for whatever reason. Still others may want to share themselves but simply may not yet know how. By the grace of God, many freely share their gifts by helping others, and in doing so, show them both love and mercy. Our world is much richer because of them, just as God intended.

But listening for guidance from the Holy Spirt can be hard work. In fact, over the past five or six years, I have spent a great deal of time trying to discern the details of just what the first three sentences of Newman's prayer means in my life. While my journey has yielded some fruitful results, under no circumstances have I been provided the complete answer, but that's okay. Newman cautioned, "I may never know [my mission] in this life, but I shall be told it in the next." I am continuing the discernment process in all I do.

Spiritual leaders throughout human history, guided by the Holy Spirit, have provided human witness to help us understand who we are and why we are here. For example, John the Baptist spent his entire life using his unique God-given talents serving as the prophet of the Most High, dedicated to leading others to Christ. One day he was grilled by priests and Levites sent by the Jews in Jerusalem. They asked him (John 1:19-21):

> "Who are you?" he admitted and did not deny it, but admitted, "I am not the Messiah." So they asked him, "What are you then? Are you Elijah?" And he said, "I am not." "Are you the Prophet?"

John humbly replied that he was not the Prophet. When they pressed him further, he responded:

> "I am the voice of one crying out in the desert." (John 1:23)

How remarkable! Jesus' front-man, humbly shunned any recognition of importance, even though he, himself, had quite a following. Instead, John the Baptizer was totally focused on the work he was sent to do – to prepare the way of the Lord. Clearly, John knew he was not Jesus, yet he chose to spend his entire life being the voice that announced Jesus' coming. From his infancy, John knew, through the words spoken to him by his father (Luke 1:76-79, New Latin Vulgate):

> You, my child, shall be called the prophet of the Most High; for you will go before the Lord to prepare his way; to give his people knowledge of salvation by the forgiveness of their sins. In the tender compassion of our God the dawn from on high shall break upon us, to shine on those who dwell in darkness and the shadow of death, and to guide our feet in the way of peace.

John's example is one we should follow – remember who we are and to whom we belong, be willing to serve – then stand firm and resist when other voices tempt us to do something else. Also, be ready to courageously remind others who they are and support them when they need help. If we carefully and faithfully listen to that *nagging voice* in our hearts (the Holy Spirit), we will be guided in the ways of love and mercy to those in need around us. We, too, must be prophets of the Most-High God because our mission is to do His work. And, whether we know it or not at any given moment, He continues to guide us in a myriad of ways to do just that.

We all know Jesus began His public life at the Wedding Feast of Cana, as described in John 2; but it is easy to miss some of the subtle lessons imbedded in that narrative (and from other events in Jesus' ministry, as well.) "Few of us have ever seen water transformed into wine, the blind receive sight, or the dead raised to life…[but] let's be careful not to minimize the more hidden works God does within the human heart. It is every bit as miraculous when a person learns to hear God in prayer, when the bonds of shame and guilt are broken through repentance, or when a wounded heart is healed through forgiveness." (*Word Among Us*). As unaware as we might be in the moment, we really are spiritually transformed whenever we read Scripture, pray or meditate or show love and mercy to someone in need. Even though our transformation may not be immediately evident to us, know this: we are becoming *good wine*. All that the Lord accomplishes is good, so when positive changes happen it is spiritually healthy to recognize and affirm them. Newman (2018) provides loving insight: "God has created all things for good; all things for their greatest good; everything for its own good…He knows what I can do, what I can best be, what is my greatest happiness, and He means to give it to me." Because He has a plan for each of us, we need to follow that plan as closely as we can and courageously refuse to entertain any conversations (most of which go on between our ears) that would tempt us to do otherwise.

Jesus made exceptional wine for the wedding guests, and through His grace and mercy, He makes extraordinary changes in us, too. Every day, Jesus is changing us – not all at once, but in the right way, at the right time, and in the right order – all because He loves each one of us, personally! God never tires of showering us with His grace and mercy. In response, if we feel we should help someone in need, act on that feeling, listen to our inner voice. Why? Because God is almost surely using us to answer that other person's prayer! Each time we reach out in love, we will be changed. We should remind ourselves of His love and power frequently throughout the day, asking Him to change the water of our lives into fine wine. He will do it – in abundance.

The *aha message* for me in this is that every day, Jesus, in His mercy, is changing me – not necessarily all at once, but in *the right way*, at *the right time*, and in *the right order*. The notion of God changing me in this way only makes sense in a [time] context I can understand, even though there is no time or space for God. God IS (He lives) only in the present, so He meets me where I am, in the present.

I heard a presentation a couple of years ago by Dr. Bill Thierfelder, President of Belmont Abbey College, about the importance of living in the present moment. Thierfelder contended that the best place to meet God is not in the past, not in the future, but in the present, simply because, for God the only time *is* the present. In his book, *Less Than a Minute to Go*, Thierfelder (2013) says that compared to God, "Your life is faster than a billionth of a second. Knowing what is most important in life, your strongest purpose, will enable you to accept and make the sacrifices necessary to double your talents. By living, working, and playing in the present moment you will experience peak performances and remain in perfect union with God. Your love in thought, word and deed for God and neighbor is the answer to the most important question that you will ever be asked: 'Do you love me?'" There is no better way to show our love and thankfulness to Him than by letting His love for us overflow to them.

About a dozen years ago, a dear friend helped me remodel the kitchen in our old house. Early in the project, I clearly recall an occasion when we were making a particularly complicated cut in some hardwood flooring, and the piece fit perfectly the first try, my friend jubilantly declared, "Thank you, Jesus!" Frankly his comment surprised me. Not sure why, but it did. Many additional times over the next three weeks we worked together, I heard my friend say the same thing, to the point I found myself imitating his comment. As the result of this experience, I have continued to thank Jesus, out loud, when outcomes are positive. But we are asked to do so much more!

Scripture tells us that we should be thankful to God in all things. 1 Thessalonians 5:18 says:

"In all circumstances give thanks, for this is the will of God for you in Christ Jesus."

Is St. Paul teaching us to be thankful for all of our personal bumps in the road and all of our tragedies big and small, in addition to positive outcomes? That is exactly what he is doing! Steel is annealed and made stronger by hammering it and gold and silver are refined by fire. Bushes, flowers and fruit-bearing plants are more beautiful and fruitful when pruned. Our bodies are made stronger when we stress them through exercise. Why mention such? Because we need to remind ourselves regularly that God never sends us a burden heavier than we are capable of carrying. So, when hard times come our way, is God training us for heavier burdens? Fact is, we will never really know. But one thing we do know is that we are made stronger spiritually, physically, mentally and emotionally by faithfully facing and accepting all that God puts in our path and being thankful to Him for the challenges.

In his letter to the Philippians 4:4-7, St. Paul says:

Rejoice in the Lord always. I shall say it again: rejoice! Your kindness should be known to all. The Lord is near. Have no anxiety at all, but in everything, by prayer and petition, with thanksgiving, make your requests known to God. Then the peace of God that surpasses all understanding will guard your hearts and minds in Christ Jesus.

So, in addition to being thankful for the *gifts* we are given and for the challenges we face, we should also make our *petitions* in thanksgiving as well. While, "Thank you, Jesus," is entirely appropriate for me to pray in all things, I must admit, "Thank You, Jesus," is hard to say when I hit my thumb with a hammer, cut my hand with a razor knife, or bump my head on an open cabinet door. But, slowly, very slowly I am learning to do that.

Thierfelder also maintains that if we truly want to live in the moment saying, "Thank You, Jesus," for all things, we must by logical extension be confident God is using all things for our good – successes and failures, delights and sorrows. In simple terms, we must have sufficient faith and hope in all things that God really is leading and guiding us to the place where we can eventually complete the mission for which He uniquely created us, which always includes, in some way, shape or form, showering love, mercy and compassion on those in need. So, in the breath immediately following, "Thank you, Jesus," we would do well to add, "Jesus, I trust in you." Our declaration of trust allows us then to grow into and live the essence of another important part of Cardinal Newman's prayer:

> "I have my mission. I may never know it in this life, but I shall be
> told it in the next. I am a link in a chain, a bond of connection
> between persons. He has not created me for naught. I shall do
> good; I shall do His work. I shall be an angel of peace, a preacher
> of truth in my own place, while not intending it if I do but keep
> His commandments. Therefore, I will trust Him, Whatever I am,
> I can never be thrown away."

In a conversation with my dear friend, Jim Stone, I shared this idea of combining my thanks to Jesus in all things and declaring trust that He will use all events for my good. In reply, Jim suggested I needed to add the probing question, "Jesus, what would you have me do?" As important as the first two declarations are, his question presented a remarkably difficult challenge for me. The more I have thought about the, "Jesus, what would you have me do?" the more it has become a constant daily (or should I say multiple-times-a-day) personal challenge. How should I extend grace and mercy to others in response to each event put before me – just what does Jesus want me to do? Again, Newman provides brilliant counsel:

> "I am a link in a chain, a bond of connection between persons.
> He has not created me for naught. I shall do good; I shall do His
> work. I shall be an angel of peace, a preacher of truth in my own
> place, while not intending it if I do but keep His commandments."

What is Jesus asking of me? Of you? While mulling over that thought, I was reminded of the opening lines of the homily preached several years ago at a dear friend's funeral. "Chris walked each step of his life with Jesus." What a remarkable tribute to Chris. What a remarkable challenge to me, and to you, too. Walking each step with Christ means he walked with others gracefully and mercifully! Can I do the same?

Recently, words spoken at a funeral by one of the six daughters of another friend caused a similar feeling to wash over me. She lovingly read recollections she and each of her siblings had about the most memorable thing they learned from their dad. Each recalled something different. But something struck me as being the common denominator among the various lessons they recalled – all were lessons taught or modelled by their dad consistently over their entire lifetimes. Not a single event, not for a week or two – but for a lifetime by him. In listening to the daughter-spokesperson, I was reminded, too, of a statement I included in a eulogy I gave at my mother-in-law's funeral, specifically, "the legacy you leave is the life you lead." Legacy is not what we talk about, instead – legacy is about what we do, how we lead our lives, how we love others. People who leave a genuine, positive legacy generally are not even aware of doing so – they lead their lives, do good, help others in every way they can, and the legacy finds them, particularly in those they love and serve.

Needless to say, all of these ideas and events caused me to start thinking about whether the way I lead my life is heading me in the right direction. Stephen Covey (1989), in his, *Seven Habits of Highly Effective People*, asked a compelling and related question. If you were given the opportunity to attend your own funeral and listen to what others were saying about you, would you be able to honestly say, in all of your actions, you are doing now what is necessary so others could truthfully say those things about you?

One of St. Teresa of Calcutta's most widely referenced teachings is, "God does not ask us to be successful, He asks us to be faithful." To be faithful, we must be willing to frequently ask, "Jesus, what would you have me do?" In addition, we must also be willing to frequently and honestly answer the question Jesus asks us, "Who do you say that I am?" Both the asking and the answering are difficult, yet both yield clear guidance for us. Do my words and actions toward others reflect the mercy God has showered on me? Does my behavior model a true understanding that Jesus is my Lord and Savior? If loving others and showing them mercy were a crime, would my actions be sufficient to convict me?

Archbishop Charles Chaput (2012), in his book, *Render Unto Caesar*, asks and answers another important question, "What needs to be done by Catholics today for their country? The answer is: *Don't lie*. If we say we're Catholic, we need to prove it. America's public life needs people willing to stand alone, without apologies for the truth of the Catholic faith and the common human values it defends. One person can make a difference – if that individual has a faith he or she is willing to suffer for." That *one person* must be the *one* each of us sees in the mirror when we are brushing our teeth. Loving unconditionally and extending mercy to the vulnerable are visible elements of being that *one person* Archbishop Chaput spoke about!

The immensity of God's love became manifest when He mercifully sent His Son to save me, so I am now challenged to thank Him by unconditionally loving, serving and showering mercy on others. What does it take to make that a reality each day? I believe following the guidance contained in Newman's, *Mediation on Christian Doctrine* (1848), offers a wonderful benchmark:

> O Ruler of Israel . . . I give myself to Thee. I trust Thee wholly. Thou are wiser than I – more loving to me than I myself. Deign to fulfill Thy high purposes in me whatever they be – work in and through me. I am born to serve Thee, to be Thine, to be Thy instrument. Let me be Thy blind instrument. I ask not to see – ask not to know – I ask simply to be used.

Thank you, Jesus, for your gifts of love, grace and mercy. Help me show my gratitude by being your loving servant.

Reflection

V

Drink from the Well That Never Runs Dry

"To the thirsty I will give a gift from the spring of life-giving water.
(Rev. 21:6)

FROM TIME TO time, during what seems to be a relatively short period, I seem to be exposed to multiple, highly-related events, ideas, conversations, etc. Such a nexus produced the overwhelming inspiration for this reflection. But the title, as I will explain later, has been looking for development for some time.

A while back I watched a beautiful video on the Catholic website, FORMED, on the topic of God's *boundless love*. While I make no claim to be able to add to the scholarship and wisdom of Father David, the priest who gave the presentation, I would like to share some of the thoughts that have been percolating in my heart and head since that viewing.

By way of background, I was educated as a civil engineer, and spent nearly four decades with the Water Resources Division of the U.S. Geological Survey. The first 15 years or so with USGS, I was actively involved doing water-resources data collection and research, so much of the water-detail included here simply reflects my natural way of processing information. My hope is the details will not be a distraction.

Nearly all of Father David's talk about God's unwavering love for us was delivered while he stood beside the Niagara River, on the Canadian side of Niagara Falls. The background of the massive river and the conversation about God's unconditional love was beautifully symbolized for me by what appears to be an endless supply of water surging over the falls. (By way of full disclosure, the flow of the Niagara River can be shut off completely by upstream reservoirs – although it is rarely done.) Regardless, Jesus' boundless love and the water analogy had more than just a fanciful attraction for me.

On the heels of watching that video, the Gospel reading the very next Sunday was from John 4, the familiar story of Jesus and the "Woman at the Well." The encounter between Jesus and the Samaritan woman is generally thought by biblical scholars to have occurred at the site of *Jacob's well*.

As wells go, Jacob's well was not really very deep, but likely deeper than other wells or cisterns that might have been dug during that time. Let's be clear, though, dug wells are just that, dug – with a shovel or similar implement. If you think about it, you should not be surprised that such wells have the obvious hazard of sloughing or collapsing walls, so they are not usually too deep.

Jacob's well was different because it was not *dug* as customarily done in that place and time. Instead, it was mostly chipped out of solid rock, 135 feet of solid rock, likely limestone, that tends to be relatively soft compared to other types of rock. So, while the sides of the well would have been competent (that is, they would not have easily caved in), Jacob's well would have been solid and structurally sound – an important feature in maintaining its stability over time. But as with wells completed in most all types of rocks, the water level would have been relatively deep below the land surface as compared to dug wells. Remarkably, Jacob's well dependably supplied water to Jacob's family and ancestors in their short-term history, but while not precisely true, it has consistently yielded water for the nearly four millennia since then. Data show the well has been dry only for short periods during the driest of summers! And in case you forgot about the geographic setting, Jacob's well is in the desert.

How could such a well be a dependable source of water (nearly all the time)? A brief primer on groundwater flow might be useful. Wells completed into rock yield water either by seepage directly from the pores in the formation itself, from a variety of fractures in the rock that can extend for many miles away or from both sources. Because Jacob's well has been a very reliable source of water to people of the region for thousands of years, no doubt the water is from both sources.

The Samaritan woman, as a routine part of her normal daily chores, would have come to the well with either a wooden bucket or terracotta one and a piece of rope long enough to reach the water – with a little extra, just in case. Let's do the math. A pint of water weighs one pound. So, to gather even a single gallon of water, she would have had to lower the bucket more than a hundred feet, scoop up the water, then lift it to the surface. The bucket would likely have weighed a pound or two, the rope another couple of pounds, plus eight pounds per gallon of water. Clearly, people of the time used far less water than we do today, but just imagine the amount of work to provide water for just two people for a day! And what about providing for any livestock they might have been raising? No wonder people in the desert seldom bathed! Even with the mechanical advantage of using a pully to assist with the water gathering, the work was still notable. Recall, too, the gospel account adds the detail that the Samaritan woman came to the well at midday. Because she came during the heat of the noon-day sun, the difficulty of the work she had to do to get the day's water would have been amplified simply because of the heat and unrelenting sun.

So, when Jesus asked the Samaritan woman for a drink, to accommodate Him she would have to do some serious lifting over a reasonable period of time. St. John pointed out that any conversation between the two would have violated several social no-noes. But a conversation happened anyway.

In a recent article, *Jesus Offers You Living Water*, published in the online Catholic magazine, *Integrated Catholic Life*, my friend Deacon Mike Bickerstaff (2019) pointed out, "[The conversation] is all the more startling when we place it in the context of the Person of God asking one of His creations to aid Him."

How did that conversation go? We hear Jesus say, in John 4:10-11:

"If you knew the gift of God and who is saying to you, 'Give me a drink,' you would have asked him and he would have given you

*living water." (The woman) said to him, "Sir, you do not even
have a bucket and the cistern is deep; where then can you get this
living water?"*

Bickerstaff observed,

"Gently and ever so carefully, Jesus begins to reveal to this
woman who He truly is and what He has to offer to her. He
understands all about her and what is in her heart. He recognizes
an opening and begins to prompt her to respond to His call.
Can we not see this in our own lives and encounters with Him?
Maybe like the woman of Samaria, there have been times when
we are emotionally, spiritually, and physically down; times when
maybe we feel alone and estranged from those around us. And
Jesus, passing by, encounters us where we are and calls out to
us. Do we listen for His loving voice? When we hear Him, do
we mistake and doubt His meaning? Like Nicodemus, introduced
to us earlier in John's Gospel, this woman at first responds only
at the surface, misunderstanding "living water" to mean only
water from a moving source, such as a stream. Her physical needs
were inhibiting her from, instead of leading her to the deeper
understanding of Christ's words, but as we will see, she was open
to the truth."

*Jesus answered and said to her, "Everyone who drinks this water
will be thirsty again; but whoever drinks the water I shall give will
never thirst; the water I shall give will become in him a spring of
water welling up to eternal life." The woman said to him, "Sir, give
me this water, so that I may not be thirsty or have to keep coming
here to draw water." (John 4:13-15)*

"Although the door to the woman's heart opened wider, she
still did not fully understand His meaning. Nonetheless, she
expressed the desire for what she understood Him to offer, and
Jesus was ready to lead her even deeper. "Do we allow the troubles
of our day, our daily sufferings and trials, our responsibilities, our
secular distractions, and particularly our sins to keep us from the

only One who can satisfy all our needs? We need not and must not let them do that; Jesus is prepared to take us deeper and meet our every need when we simply let him."

Jesus said to her, "Go call your husband and come back." The woman answered and said to him, "I do not have a husband." Jesus answered her, "You are right in saying, 'I do not have a husband.' For you have had five husbands, and the one you have now is not your husband. What you have said is true."

The woman said to him, "Sir, I can see that you are a prophet. Our ancestors worshiped on this mountain; but you people say that the place to worship is in Jerusalem." Jesus said to her, "Believe me, woman, the hour is coming when you will worship the Father neither on this mountain nor in Jerusalem. You people worship what you do not understand; we worship what we understand, because salvation is from the Jews. But the hour is coming, and is now here, when true worshipers will worship the Father in Spirit and truth; and indeed the Father seeks such people to worship him. God is Spirit, and those who worship him must worship in Spirit and truth."

The woman said to him, "I know that the Messiah is coming, the one called the Anointed; when he comes, he will tell us everything." Jesus said to her, "I am he, the one who is speaking with you." (John 4:16-26)

"As the encounter continues, Jesus lets the woman know that He knows . . . knows all about her, about her past and her present. And it is not that He does not care about all of that – He does care – but He cares in an unexpected way; He offers her healing and forgiveness through the grace of living water so that she may be sanctified and never thirst unproductively again. Eventually He reveals that He is the Living Water that will be for us a "spring of water welling up to eternal life". She comes to know that He is indeed greater than Jacob at whose well they talk. He is the answer to every prayer. And on realizing this, she cannot wait to go and spread the good news, leaving behind her cares and even the vessels she brought with her to collect water. That's what we do when we receive great news. We share our joy with others. She even went to share hers with the very people she was trying to avoid by coming to the well at noon."

Bickerstaff continued:

"As a Samaritan and as a woman with many husbands and an outcast, she had every reason the world gives to ignore Jesus and remain as she was. But she didn't. And neither should we. Jesus knows where we are and what we feel. He knows all our triumphs and failures. He knows our sins. He made each of us for Himself and He wants to purify us and give us every good thing, drawing us ever closer to Himself. But He will never force the matter, only invite us; gently and lovingly. Do you want to know such joy? Do you want to receive from Jesus the living water that never runs dry?"

In case the full importance of the story might be missed, we need to understand that Jesus picked this woman, a woman to whom social custom forbade Him to speak, to be the very first person He chose to reveal Himself as the Messiah. He chose her – a stranger, an outcast, likely an adulterer – to reveal His divinity. To understand such a story of seeming conflict requires what Richard Rohr (2009) calls *dualistic thinking*, the ability to hold and process what might seem like opposites at the same time and make sense of it.

Jesus's unconditional love for the woman is the same unconditional love He has for each of us. Isaiah 45:15 provided a simple but beautiful description of His endless love:

"Can a mother forget her infant, be without tenderness for the child of her womb? Even should she forget, I will never forget you."

Psalm 100 (using the translation from the Liturgy of the Hours) adds still further assurance of God's eternal love and mercy:

Cry out with joy to the Lord, all the earth.
Serve the Lord with gladness.
Come before Him, singing for joy.

Know that He, the Lord, is God.
He made us we belong to Him,
We are His people, the sheep of His flock.

Go within His gates, giving thanks.
Enter His courts with songs of praise.
Give thanks to Him and bless His name.

Indeed, how good is the Lord,
Eternal His merciful love.
He is faithful from age to age.

Clearly, "*He is faithful from age to age,*" is about drinking from the well that never runs dry. I have come to truly treasure the beautiful, comforting and assuring message the words of this psalm provides.

The opening (and closing) verse of Psalm 118 (which are identical), is one of my favorites: "*Give thanks to the Lord for He is good, His mercy endures forever.*" In the most recent translation of the Bible currently used by the Church for all daily Mass readings, the New American Bible Revised Edition (NABRE), these words are slightly different, but equally beautiful and comforting: "*Give thanks to the Lord for He is good; His love endures forever.*" Regardless, whether mercy or love or forgiveness or the saving power of God, we are lovingly assured we will never be abandoned.

Reflecting back on how water gets to a well, we should remember that it must flow there. The reference to *living water* traditionally came from flowing streams, as it did from the gate of the temple referred to in Ezekiel 47:1:

Then he brought me back to the entrance of the temple, and there! I saw water flowing out from under the threshold of the temple toward the east, for the front of the temple faced east. The water flowed out toward the right side of the temple to the south of the altar.

So even if *living water* is defined as flowing water – as was understood by the people of Jesus' time – water can be flowing (albeit, slowly) in a rock formation.

God's boundless love and mercy are often difficult for us to understand. Some would even argue the *why* of these gifts is impossible to understand. But just look, as an example, at the season of Lent and the events of Holy Week and Easter for insight into understanding the unconditional nature of God's interrelated gifts of love, grace and mercy. In, *Live Humbly, Serve Graciously*, I offered the following:

> How much does God love you? How much does He love me? How much does He love each and every one of us, individually? Let me answer by way of a visual image. Picture yourself on Calvary, observing Jesus being tortured. You are close enough for Jesus to hear you, so you ask – *"Jesus, how much do you love me?"* With one hand already nailed to the cross, He boldly stretches the other arm as far as he can so it too can be nailed, and replies – *"How much do I love you? I love you this much."*

God is first. He originates, invents and creates time itself. In Scripture, God is never passive. He speaks. He questions. He challenges. He plans. He initiates. He acts. He is always the one who loves me before I even know of Him or love Him. His mercy is His love directed toward me, the sinner. I am essentially the perpetual responder. *Agape*, unlike the other three natural loves, is like God in that way. *Agape* is not a receptive, responding process but an initiating, creating source. Our loving actions must be driven by our loving thoughts which in turn must originate from a loving heart. A loving heart must be a humble heart. We have the capability, but do we have the will?

In Matthew 22:36-39, the Pharisees asked Jesus:

> *Teacher, which commandment in the law is the greatest? He said to him, "You shall love the Lord, your God, with all your heart, with all your soul, and with all your mind. This is the greatest and the first commandment. The second is like it: You shall love your neighbor as yourself."*

Love God. Love your neighbor. Jesus declares these commandments are the greatest, thus solidifying the reality that God is love and His love is the basis for all loving. One of the most remarkable epiphanies I have experienced in decades happened as I read Peter Kreeft's assertion (2004) that, "God cannot fall in love, not because He is less loving than we are but because He is more loving. He cannot fall in love for the same reason that water cannot get wet: it *is* wet. God *is* love."

Because God is love, and because love itself cannot receive love as a *passivity*, it spreads only as an *activity*. Remember, *agape* is not a feeling – *agape* is action. So, when we say God is Love, we are saying He is Love-In-Eternal-Activity.

The conversation between Jesus and the Samaritan woman from John's gospel, was the inspiration for the lyrics from one of my favorite contemporary Catholic hymns, "Lord, I Come," composed by Billy Funk. The song is frequently sung during Communion time at the weekly student mass at our grandchildren's school. The words are quite simple yet contain a profound message:

Lord, I come. Take my life.
I offer it to you a living sacrifice.
By your grace. By your blood.
I come into the Holy of Holies.

All I want to do is dwell in your presence.
And drink from the well that never runs dry.
All I want to see is the light of your beauty.
Just one glimpse, just one drink.
And my soul is satisfied.

The phrase, "Drink from the well that never runs dry," hit me squarely between the eyes the very first time I heard it and it continues to nag and impact me deeply. Maybe the connection is profound because of my hydrology background, but the spiritual and emotional impact of that simple thought forces me to concede the complex, pure and perfect reliance on an eternal reality of life, love, grace and mercy that comes only from our all-loving Triune God.

One final thought. Our joy, our example to others, our spiritual reality moving forward is to joyfully, "drink from the well that never runs dry."

Could the ultimate joy that comes from Christ's death and resurrection for the expiation of my (our) sins be a finer example of what the living water delivers? Even though I (we) am truly unworthy because of my (our) sinfulness, to receive God's mercy and compassion, He chooses to shower me (us) anyway with those gifts, every moment, of every day, simply because He loves me (us).

- Will I humbly choose to love others and have my entire existence reflect the loving God in whose image I am created?
- Will my merciful actions toward others reflect the mercy I have already received from Him?
- Will I be compassionate in my treatment of others in a way that reflects the compassion I have been shown?

I pray my answers will be, "Yes, Yes and Yes," today and beyond.

Reflection

VI

No Greater Mercy Than This

No one has greater love than this, to lay down one's life for one's friends.
(John 15:13)

Today, on virtually every public square and even in many churches, the sanctity of life and the sacredness and purity of marriage are being directly assaulted. Quite remarkable is the fundamental shift of societal values over the past half-dozen decades or so: elective abortion used to be unthinkable and assisted suicide considered equally absurd and not right-minded. Yet in our country today, we know that both of these assaults on our sensibilities are not only legal, but staunchly defended by many as legitimate and moral. Supporters frequently use euphemisms such as a woman's right to choose, a woman's right to make decisions about her own body, and what is wrong with a person deciding to end his/her own life when he/she is riddled with disease or have a terminal condition with little to no hope for recovery.

Quite puzzling, however, are the many who claim to cherish life, but paradoxically support capital punishment and do not see the inconsistency of those two positions. We genuinely live in a world of contradictions – many of which, I believe, have been deeply influenced by an insidious moral relativism that, over time, has eroded God's truth. At no other time in modern history has the notion of mercy toward both the unborn and dying been so blatantly ignored, dismissed, or challenged than it is today.

Groschel (1994) points out the irony that so many in our world today look back on Pharaoh's slaughter of thousands of Hebrew male babies in the time of Moses and the massacre of millions of Jewish children by Hitler, and do not see the similarity of what goes on in our country today. "Today in our society it is the unborn children who are considered dispensable. No matter that these are tiny human creatures with beating hearts and measurable brain waves by the end of the third week of life. Who will be next? Children who suffer from physical defects? Mental patients and the aged? Who will speak out for true mercy in these critical days?"

Many of us arrogantly think we have created a higher, more civilized society as compared to some third-world countries – however, it does not take a great deal of reflection to show that rather quite the opposite is true. Peter Kreeft (2002), a professor of Philosophy and Theology at Boston College, in his book, *How to Win the Culture War*, tells of a doctor he knows, who spent two years working in the Congo to win the trust and confidence of the native people so he could eventually help them understand how their diet was killing them. Once that trust was established, those people, whom some would call primitive, asked him about America. He told them there were people who did not believe in God (to their astonishment), and that there were over a million mothers per year who paid doctors to kill their babies before they were born (to their total disbelief). They simply had no way of comprehending those realities of our society. Isaiah 49:15 is worth pondering:

"Can a mother forget her infant, be without tenderness for the child of her womb? Even should she forget, I will never forget you."

There can be no greater gift of mercy than protecting those who are defenseless – the unborn and those near death from disease. Kreeft (2002) stated: "If the God of life does not respond to this culture of death with judgment, then God is not God. If God does not honor the blood of the hundreds of millions of innocent victims of this culture of death, then the God of the Bible, the God of Abraham, the God of Israel, the God of the prophets, the God of orphans and widows, the Defender of the defenseless, is a man-made myth, a fairy tale, an ideal as insubstantial as a dream. But (you may object) is not the God of the Bible merciful and forgiving? He is indeed. But the unrepentant refuse forgiveness. And forgiveness, being a gift, must be freely given and freely received."

To be clear, I firmly believe the Church's teachings about God's love and mercy and His willingness to forgive any wrong, so long as the person is repentant and accepting of His forgiveness.

Newman's, *The Mission of My Life*, (the entire prayer can be found in Reflection 4), beautifully puts our value as individuals into perspective. Each of us, no matter our station in life, has been created in the image and likeness of God, to do Him some service not committed to anyone else. How remarkable. We have each been created to do Him some, unique service. We each not only have a distinct role; we also have an undeniable obligation to play our part in God's beautiful, marvelous and intricately complex grand plan for all of humanity. God's mercy and grace, both freely given to us, are major factors enabling us to live out our part in His plan. Our required response is extending mercy to our neighbors.

Respect for life in all stages is requisite. Choices, while not always easy, are simple – will they support life . . .or . . . death? We need look no further than to the final months of St. John Paul II's life to understand that even a life racked with physical suffering, is a life that continues to give, positively influence, and inspire others. The impact he had on hundreds of millions of Catholics and non-Catholics alike by the humble dignity he showed in his final days continues to reverberate around the world. What a beautiful expression of love to all, particularly our loving Father.

About 50 years ago, the Supreme Court came down on the side of a mother's right to decide whether the baby she carried would live or die, with the lives of tens of millions of babies being legally terminated as a result. Obviously, to the Justices who decided this case, a mother's right to not have a baby was far more important than the inalienable right to life of the defenseless baby in her womb. About Roe v. Wade, Mother Teresa (now St. Teresa of Calcutta) said simply, but profoundly, "When a mother can kill her baby, what is left of civilization to save?" Civilizations endure when all life is defended, and that fundamental defense is founded on unconditional love and mercy.

As Christians, we must courageously stand up for and be vocal about our beliefs on a wide range of issues, especially about the sanctity of life, because if we fail there, countless lives will continue to be snuffed out before they have a chance. Archbishop Wilton Gregory, in his pre-election message to the Archdiocese of Atlanta, in 2008, counseled the faithful about our voting responsibilities as Catholics using the words from our Nation's Declaration of Independence, "Life, liberty and the pursuit of happiness." He pointed out that even our nation's founding fathers used "Life" as the first and most prominent reason to pursue our independence. Archbishop Gregory concluded, "Without life, the rest is simply details."

I had the opportunity to hear Dr. Alveda King (Dr. Martin Luther King's niece and a non-Catholic) deliver a remarkable speech at the first Fortnight for Freedom celebration in Atlanta, in July, 2012. Her closing remarks that evening focused specifically on the mandates of the Affordable Care Act, but her message was much broader. With her tongue deeply imbedded into her cheek, she said the mandates *were* about women's rights – the right to higher incidences of heart disease and several forms of cancer, the right to take the life of an unborn baby, and the right to be promiscuous without repercussions. By the grace of God, recent rulings by the Supreme Court have provided some relief for many employers who have religious objections to the mandates related to birth control and abortions (Armbruster, 2016). But to be clear, not until all such offensive mandates in current federal law are removed will such attacks on our beliefs be eliminated. On the bright side, a 2020 ruling by the U.S. Supreme Court upheld the Little Sisters of the Poor's appeal against providing birth control coverage as part of employee health insurance.

So, what should we do? Sit around and accept what we know is wrong? Look the other way or refuse to engage in responsible dialogue with family, friends and colleagues when we hear conversations promoting politically correct "worm-speak" regarding the sanctity of life and marriage? As baptized Catholics, as people of good will, we have a moral obligation to courageously speak God's truth, to be a source of reason, and to do our very best to defend what we know to be morally correct. When we hear those who profess to be Catholic promoting the *freedom to choose* we need to courageously speak out and support the innate value of every human being, from the moment of conception. When we hear politicians promoting laws that would allow for the termination of a baby's life, at any point, including several days after a live birth, we must be the voice of those who do not yet have a voice that can be heard. When we hear of efforts to enact laws that permit assisted suicide, we must staunchly support the loving, merciful care of the sick and dying, insuring they are treated with dignity and respect until their natural death. Our practice of mercy toward others could not take on any more fundamental dimensions than these.

In His wisdom and mercy, God chose to include two separate but complementary components of humanity to continue His love story. The Catechism of the Catholic Church (#1605) clearly states: "Holy Scripture affirms that man and woman were created for one another: "It is not good that the man should be alone." The woman, "flesh of his flesh," his equal, his nearest in all things, is given to him by God as a "helpmate"; she thus represents God from whom comes our help. *Therefore, a man leaves his father and his mother and cleaves to his wife, and they become one flesh.*"

"God who created man out of love also calls him to love the fundamental and innate vocation of every human being. For man is created in the image and likeness of God who is Himself love. Since God created him man and woman, their mutual love becomes an image of the absolute and unfailing love with which God loves man. It is good, very good, in the Creator's eyes. And this love which God blesses is intended to be fruitful and to be realized in the common work of watching over creation: "And God blessed them, and God said to them: *'Be fruitful and multiply, and fill the earth and subdue it.'*"" (CCC, #1604). As clear as this message is, many in our society today argue validity of the opposite. The matrimonial covenant is itself a gift of mercy granted by God to both husband and wife, that, if accepted by them, will guide their lives together.

Ironically, a growing number of the "enlightened" choose to ignore human biology, and instead promote the notion that the love between any two persons should be sufficient reason for marriage. As Catholics, we steadfastly believe that "God Himself is the author of marriage." The vocation of marriage is written in the very nature of man and woman as they came from the hand of the Creator. With such richness of understanding, how have we managed to reach the point where the very foundation of God's plan for His continuation of creation, through holy matrimony, is challenged almost everywhere we turn – in the media, in our schools, in our society, and, most disturbingly, in many of our Churches, and, frankly, even in Catholic universities around the country. When we hear rhetoric that attempts to redefine marriage as a contract between any two people who love each other, we must insist that marriage is not a man-made societal instrument, rather it is a covenant between a man and a woman lovingly living out the reality of God's creation. It is simply remarkable how we have lost our focus.

The First Amendment to the U. S. Constitution reads: *Congress shall make no law respecting an establishment of religion or prohibiting the free exercise thereof; or abridging the freedom of speech or of the press; or the right of the people peaceably to assemble and to petition the Government for a redress of grievances.* What an extraordinary statement of freedoms. Freedom of religion, freedom of speech, freedom of the press, freedom to assemble and freedom to petition grievances. What a remarkable foundation for society. Yet in spite of these freedoms, our country is on the threshold of a serious moral crisis, one that seems to directly contradict John 10:10:

"I came so that they might have life and have it more abundantly."

Having said that, if we have faith in Jesus, we have to accept the reality that all good things come to those who believe. As hard as it may be to accept, God may, in fact, be using these attacks on life, marriage and religious freedom to draw us closer to Him – after all, our human limit is the place where God works most effectively in our lives. So…we must steadfastly keep our eyes fixed on Jesus and graciously accept his unconditional love, grace and mercy. While our circumstances may not change, our hearts surely will. Presidents come and go, governments come and go, crises come and go. But God is always there, is always on our side, and He always has our welfare as His priority. Thankfully, our heavenly Father is very patient.

But we, too, must be patient and remain ever vigilant to what goes on in our political processes because of the near continuous assault on issues of morality. We must be willing to express our views loudly and often to our legislative delegations, regardless of party affiliation and to White House comment lines. Who else will stand up if we do not?

There are many absolute truths given to us by our Creator. No frequency of denial will change them. Black is black. White is white. No matter how many times I might say black is white – it is not, and never will be. Similarly, our religious freedom is an inalienable right not conferred on us by our government, rather by our loving God. His grace and mercy poured out on us is a full-measure indicator of our dignity and worth. We must courageously defend that absolute right because it is the very foundation of our success as a republic, to the foundation of who we are as a society and as a Church. In a 2009 address at the University of Toronto, Archbishop Charles Chaput warned, "Evil preaches tolerance until it is dominant, then it tries to silence good."

Fortunately, we Catholics are not alone in our fight for the protection of life, marriage and religious freedom. In November 2009, a group of Orthodox, Catholic and Evangelical Christians, crafted what is called the *Manhattan Declaration*. They affirmed, "We are Christians who have joined together across historic lines of ecclesial differences to affirm our right – and, more important to embrace our obligation – to speak and act in defense of these truths." Hundreds of church leaders including dozens of Catholic bishops, have attached their signatures to this document. The signatories declared, "Because the sanctity of human life, the dignity of marriage as a union of husband and wife and the freedom of conscience and religion are foundational principles of justice and the common good, we are compelled by our Christian faith to speak and act in their defense." Is the declaration perfect? No! However, let us not allow the pursuit of *perfect* be the enemy of *extremely well done*. While our society is currently far from being aligned with God's truths, the principles supported by the *Fortnight for Freedom* movement, and, those outlined in the *Manhattan Declaration,* go a long way toward publicly framing the positions we must defend as a Christian society.

2 Chronicles 7:14 clearly advises:

> *If then my people, upon whom my name has been pro-*
> *nounced, humble themselves and pray, and seek my face, and*
> *turn from their evil ways, I will hear them from heaven and*
> *pardon their sin and heal their land.*

If there ever was a time in our country's history to humble ourselves, fall to our knees, and turn to God in prayer, it is now. If there ever was a time for us to beg for God's mercy for our wrongdoing, it is now. If there was ever a time for us to beg for God's mercy on our communities, country and society, it is now. If there ever was a time for us to pass laws defending life at all stages of development, the time is now. If there ever was a time to mercifully protect the lives of the unborn and the sick and elderly, the time is now. And, if there ever was a time to be merciful to our neighbors in all we do, the time is now. There is no greater love than this!

Reflection

VII

Understanding Mercy – Where Is God When Things Get Tough?

Have no anxiety at all, but in everything, by prayer and petition, with thanksgiving, make your requests known to God. Then the peace of God that surpasses all understanding will guard your hearts and minds in Christ Jesus.

(Philippians 4:6-7)

EVERY NOW AND then, life seems to throw a myriad of difficult situations at us all at once – or at least in a short period of time. For example, during the summer of 2018, my wife and I were simply deluged with difficult, troubling, and in a couple of cases tragic bits of news. A young friend had gone through a very difficult divorce and since had a hard time with steady full-time employment. He would get what seemed to be a good job, then the company would lose a contract or in one case the company went under. What a struggle. A dear friend was admitted into a special memory care facility because of advancing Alzheimer's. How difficult for her, her family and those who love her. A few months before, our 42-year-old nephew, one of my godsons, was diagnosed with and then began very difficult chemotherapy treatment for a rare form of *soft-tissue* cancer that for some unknown reason decided to attach to his liver. Because of the size and location of the tumor surgery was not an option. How unfair. My brother-in-law, dad of the nephew I just mentioned, had recently had his fourth stroke in just a week shy of a year, with motor skill damage to his left-side (and he is terminally left-handed). And he now has impairment to motor skills in his right hand, too. How difficult it was watching him suffer. And to add to my sister's family's burden, my sister tends to the needs of her 96-year-old mother-in-law who had recently fallen and was rehabbing. How physically and emotionally draining. A dear friend of more than 35 years was diagnosed with cancer, and one of my sisters-in-law had just her knee replaced. And another of my sisters-in-law was in the hospital for nearly two weeks with a pesky and debilitating condition that was finally diagnosed and treatment started. All of these situations, along with the prostate cancer that a close friend was and still is being treated for could easily be cause for reflection – *Just how could God permit such suffering, particularly for those who are faithful to Him*

In addition, within a relatively small community of friends within our church, another dear friend struggles with dementia and two others with a variety of heart and orthopedic problems. Wow, quite the litany of hard issues with which to grapple. Could not help being reminded of Rabbi Harold Kushner's (1981) very popular book, *When Bad Things Happen to Good People,* or an even more remarkable book by Peter Kreeft (1986), *Making Sense Out of Suffering.*

And if all these issues were not enough, one more family health-related situation occupied a great deal of our time and spiritual energy during that same short period. I had called my brother to wish him happy birthday, but he did not answer – so I left a voicemail. Called him the next day as I had promised and again wished him happy birthday, this time in person. Then I lightly added, "So, how is 78 treating you so far?" to which he answered, "not so well." When I asked if his AFIB was acting up, he said, "No," then told me he had been diagnosed with small cell lung cancer. Although I was not terribly surprised to hear of his illness, because he smoked for his entire adult life, hearing about it hit me particularly hard for a variety of reasons. With deep sadness, the relationship between my brother and me had been strained for some time, so there was that. To have a brother I shared a bedroom with until college being so far away emotionally was difficult. But hearing of his diagnosis was a gut-punch. Even more troubling than the worry over his physical condition was my concern about his spiritual well-being, although, in truth, I had no idea where he was in his spiritual journey. The unknown was likely what weighed so heavily.

While trying to wrap our spiritual and emotional selves around all of those issues, my wife and I read Jeremiah 14:17-22, and a reflection on it, from *The Word Among Us*. The passage is a narrative filled with tragedy and despair:

Let my eyes stream with tears night and day, without rest, over the great destruction which overwhelms the virgin daughter of my people, over her incurable wound. If I walk out into the field, look! those slain by the sword; If I enter the city, look! victims of famine. Both prophet and priest ply their trade in a land they do not know. Have you really cast Judah off? Is Zion loathsome to you? Why have you struck us a blow that cannot be healed? We wait for peace, to no avail; for a time of healing, but terror comes instead.

We recognize our wickedness, Lord, the guilt of our ancestors: we have sinned against you. Do not reject us, for your name's sake, do not disgrace your glorious throne. Remember! Do not break your covenant with us. Among the idols of the nations are there any that give rain? Or can the mere heavens send showers?

Is it not you, Lord, our God, to whom we look?
You alone do all these things.

Let's face it, our human nature usually predisposes us to more readily hear messages of hope, rather than listening to those of woe. Almost surely, that is why the people of Jerusalem found it so hard to accept Jeremiah's prophecies. He warned them that unless they turned back to God, they would suffer grievous consequences. Unfortunately, the Hebrews ignored Jeremiah. Unfortunately, too, everything he said came to pass – drought, famine, an invasion, and finally, exile. *Let my eyes stream with tears day and night.* That particular chapter of Hebrew history was truly bleak. What part of this tragic tale could possibly inspire us?

When we look around, we see at least as many problems in our own place and time as existed in Jeremiah's time. In fact, if we think about our current social condition only shortly, we too might be moved to tears, possibly despair.

- What of all the pain caused by abortion, drug addiction, and domestic violence?
- What of all the heartache of memory loss, mental health issues and the pain and suffering of frightening diseases like (but clearly not restricted to) cancer.
- What of the anguish of addictions of all sorts?
- What of the sadness and heartache that comes from marriages that fall apart?
- What about the pain of those who suffer from apathy, indifference and other forms of emotion challenges?
- What of the poor who live in unimaginable squalor?
- What of the difficulty so many face as they escape war in their own countries?

As people of faith, it is natural for us to empathize with others over the sadness, loss, and suffering that surrounds them, but our response cannot simply end with feelings of compassion – to do so would be unchristian. God does not want or intend us to resign ourselves to the tragedy, suffering and pain we see then just sit back and watch things get worse; rather, He anoints us through our Baptism to share in Jesus' three offices of priest, prophet, and king and showers us with His grace to carry out those offices. Our baptism is very much a call-to-action, very much an obligation to extend mercy to those around us who are suffering in any way. Sometimes we are called to be priests and minister His healing love in countless ways by serving those who are sick and hurting. At other times, we are called to act as prophets as we speak the word of God to people who have lost their faith, have lost hope, or don't think God loves them. And in still other situations, we are asked to share our kingly gifts by providing food, shelter and justice for the marginalized, the poor and the neglected. In all these ways we are actively challenged to use the very best talents we have been given by God to help those in need, regardless their circumstances, or our own.

Sadly, many critics of religion point to suffering as a reason not to believe in God. As Catholics, (as Christians) we can defend exactly the opposite position. God's will is not to cause suffering but to end it; that is why He sent His Son! Jesus came to free us from sin and to give us the "ministry of reconciliation." He came to bring heaven down to earth, and He now calls all of us to help build His kingdom here and now.

As we look about and both see and experience the pain and suffering around us, just as it says in the first verse of the passage from Jeremiah, our eyes should stream with tears. At the same time, our hands and feet should get busy bringing hope and healing to all God's people. Not surprising, psychologists have long recognized that one of the easiest ways to climb out of our own negative mental and spiritual spirals, is to reach out and *do* for others – as hard as that *doing* might seem.

> "Lord, give me compassion for the wounded people you have placed in my path. Give me the courage to reach out to them and the wisdom to help them as best I can." (Word Among Us)

So, what might our physical and metaphorical "hands and feet" be busy doing for others? How can we personally be involved assisting those in marriage crises, in employment crises, and in health crises that could easily be leading to death. Clearly, we can and should pray for others regardless of how we might feel, or how busy we might be. We can, even with small amounts of our time, be an open, receptive ear to those who need to be heard. We can help garner physical, mental and spiritual support for those in need by enlisting others who would gladly help, if only they knew of the need. We can run errands for or drive others to places they need to go – church, grocery, doctor, whatever. We can offer to clean their house when they do not have the time or emotional energy to do so themselves. We can reach out and do our very best to reconcile with those who are relationally distant. We can encourage others when they feel they have lost hope. We can invite others for dinner when the absence of a loved one aches more than they are willing or able to admit.

While one-on-one outreach is nearly always effective, sometimes more organized efforts are needed. Three ministries that quickly come to mind, that exist solely for these sorts of outreach, are the Saint Vincent DePaul Society, Catholic Charities, and Stephens Ministry. Local affiliates of each of these are easy to find and all welcome willing volunteers.

One of my favorite passages from the New Testament is James 2:14-17:

What good is it, my brothers, if someone says he has faith but does not have works? Can that faith save him? If a brother or sister has nothing to wear and has no food for the day, and one of you says to them, "Go in peace, keep warm, and eat well," but you do not give them the necessities of the body, what good is it? So also faith of itself, if it does not have works, is dead.

The essence of these four short verses is a real-world description of Jesus' commandment to love our neighbors as ourselves and is foundational to understanding Catholic social teaching. The passage instructs us how to live our daily lives and how to interact with family, with friends, with neighbors. And we are also instructed to reach out to those in need, whether they be close to us or not. As a cradle Catholic, growing up in a family where both of my parents were service-oriented, I think I have (or have almost) always been able to internalize what this means, even when I might have been short on executing. Both of my siblings have lived their lives taking seriously the essence of this passage as they have devoted countless hours helping others, each in their own way, without counting the cost or expecting anything in return. My wife gives generously of herself in helping those in need and who might be hurting in some way; and we tried, as best we could, to teach our children this same way of living and giving.

A couple of years ago, while preparing for a presentation at another parish, I clumsily stumbled on what was, to me, an epiphany. I found in Ephesians 2:8-10 what I should have known years ago and offer it here with the hope you will find it useful:

For by grace you have been saved through faith, and this is not from you; it is the gift of God; it is not from works, so no one may boast.

For we are his handiwork, created in Christ Jesus for the good works
that God has prepared in advance, that we should live in them.

Paraphrasing: "We are God's handiwork, created to assist Him in His good work."

The opening sentences of Newman's prayer, *The Mission of My Life,"* directly applies here: *"God has created me to do Him some definite service. He has committed some work for me that He has not committed to another. I have my mission."* Newman never said in this prayer or anywhere else living our mission would be fun or easy. In fact, he did not even claim that the *what* of our life's journey would be clearly known or obvious to us in this lifetime. What the prayer does says is that we must simply be open to our surroundings and to the urgings of the Holy Spirit, then to act on those urgings.

I am reminded of a beautiful passage from Sirach 2:4-6:

Accept whatever happens to you; in periods of humiliation be
patient. For in fire gold is tested, and the chosen, in the crucible of
humiliation. Trust in God, and He will help you; make your ways
straight and hope in Him.

But what of the pain, the suffering, the sickness, the despair and all of the other of life's worries, like those mentioned earlier? Hard as it might be at times to accept the will of God, the reality is, "[our] all-knowing, all-powerful, all-good God allows us to suffer, just as He allows us all sorts of things, because we have the freedom to behave as we will. But He has also provided a place with the greatest contentment we can imagine if only we listen to Him, listen to His Son, and listen to His Church" (Coren, 2012). Coren continues, "As to the specific issue of pain and suffering, C.S. Lewis, who watched his beloved wife die of cancer, put it this way: 'But pain insists upon being attended to. God whispers to us in our pleasures, speaks in our conscience, but shouts in our pains: it is His megaphone to rouse a deaf world.'"

Nowhere in sacred Scripture are we promised that faith in Jesus Christ guarantees we will enjoy a good life free of pain and/or darkness. In fact, quite the opposite – there are far more predictions of struggles on earth for the believer than there are of gain and success. What we are promised by our loving Father is if we live our faith, enduring all the pain, tragedy and hardship life throws at us, we are guaranteed a *perfect eternity*.

God's grand plan is for us to lead the best possible life here on earth, then return to Him for eternity; however, sometimes we need to be reminded of our goal when things are tough. Pain is a sharp, clear tool to achieve that purpose. A needle may be necessary to prevent disease or treat an infection; but nobody welcomes or enjoys the injection. While the injection can be painful, its intent is to prevent far greater suffering later; just as what may seem like even intolerable pain now leads to far greater happiness later.

An excerpt from the second Mass reading for the Feast of the Transfiguration, 2 Peter 1:16-18 says:

> *"We had been eyewitnesses of his majesty . . . while we were with him on the holy mountain."*

We might logically expect Peter to sing of the glory of the transfigured Christ. But he also described this glimpse into heaven as a light in the midst of darkness. Peter understood that Jesus had given him this vision as a way to encourage and prepare him for the darkness that would engulf him when Jesus faced His passion. In our own lives, sometimes it seems as if no matter where we look, we see darkness in the form of sickness, despair, war, poverty, crime, abortion, broken families. Because all these realities can discourage and tempt us to give up on our personal call to holiness, I think it critical that we, too, hold on to this vision. Remember it when tempted to give up hope. Remember it when overwhelmed. Remember it when we are angry. Remember it when the burden is really heavy. Remember it when we share the suffering of a loved-one.

St. Peter reminds us vividly that the transfiguration of Christ reveals the true, unchanging foundation to all of reality. Jesus is glorified. He is the Father's beloved Son. He reigns over everything. Even if evil seems triumphant, Jesus' light is still stronger than the darkness. Even when devastating sickness seems unfair, Jesus' courage to live in the moment will provide strength. Even when we don't know how to help another in need, Jesus' example will show us the way to shower others with love.

St. Paul loving taught the Thessalonians (2 Thess. 1:11-12):

To this end, we always pray for you, that our God may make you worthy of his calling and powerfully bring to fulfillment every good purpose and every effort of faith, that the name of our Lord Jesus may be glorified in you, and you in him, in accord with the grace of our God and Lord Jesus Christ.

Do we have courage to live our lives looking forward, rather than dwelling on the past? Do we have the courage to use the grace bestowed on us each day to do the work of our baptism, that is, be priest, prophet and king to all those we encounter? Do we have the courage to use the talents we were gifted with to fully participate in God's intricate plan for all mankind? Are we willing to go where we might be uncomfortable and challenge ourselves to do at least one charitable thing for someone else each day?

Yes, we are exposed to and are sometimes even surrounded by what seems like overwhelming levels of suffering, sickness, and sadness – and, yes, all of that can weigh us down. But God always, mercifully, gives us sufficient grace to lighten our loads and overcome the challenges. Always. God gives us the strength to deal with our own personal struggles, and to reach out to help others with theirs. Always. Our God is an awesome God who wants only good for us, even when we might be confused by His path for us and for those around us. St. Teresa of Avila often said, "God writes straight with crooked lines."

A year has passed since the events described earlier. Our family and friends find ourselves in equally or possibly even more difficult circumstances than a year ago. My brother-in-law had a massive fifth stroke from which he never regained consciousness. He was home with family and friends surrounding him as he drew his final breath. He was anointed and blessed before his journey. About six weeks later, my brother lost his year-long battle with lung cancer. I had the honor of spending some time with him before he died and while extremely difficult to see him in such dire circumstance, I would not trade those hours for anything. The second to the last night of his life I stayed with him, helped him in times of anxiety and agonizing pain and prayed over him. He received the anointing of the sick and was blessed by several other ministers from his community the day before he died. Nearly five months to the day later, my nephew lost his valiant struggle against the tumor that had taken him over. He, too, received final rites of the Church before his journey in this life ended. My sister's mother-in-law survived her grandson by about four months, but after ninety-seven years on earth she joined family members who preceded her in death. While my sister's daily responsibilities have been mercifully eased, real heartache remains with her, her daughter-in-law and her family, and her older son and his family.

Yet with all of the tragedy and hardships experienced just in our immediate family the past two years or so, I genuinely sense all of our family have remained faithful – because they each, in their own way have experienced God's love and mercy through these very difficult times. Is there loneliness and heartache over the losses? Absolutely. Is there still a real need to come to closure and move on? Most certainly. But in all these things there is great comfort in knowing our loved ones who have suffered here on earth will receive their eternal reward for lives well lived, that they will enjoy a perfect eternity. *Give thanks to the Lord for He is good, His love (and mercy) endures forever.*

I would like to offer two final thoughts. All of the suffering and heartache that surrounds us can be an overwhelming challenge. So many demands on our time, talent, treasure and – likely most draining of all – our emotions. How can we possibly juggle all of the competing demands? How can we endure the pain of losing those we love? Such competition goes to the heart of our human condition, just like joy and sorrow do. Henri J. M. Nouwen (1996), Dutch-born Catholic priest and spiritual author, in his book, *Can You Drink the Cup*, observes:

"The cup of life is the cup of joy as much as it is the cup of sorrow. Mourning and dancing are never separate. If joys could not be where sorrows are, the cup of life would never be drinkable. That is why we have to hold the cup in our hands and look carefully to see the joys hidden in our sorrows."

Another way of saying the same thing: there is no resurrection without the cross!

Again, I would like to reiterate the great wisdom and comfort in the message found in 2 Corinthians 1:3-5:

Blessed be the God and Father of our Lord Jesus Christ, the Father of compassion and God of all encouragement, who encourages us in our every affliction, so that we may be able to encourage those who are in any affliction with the encouragement with which we ourselves are encouraged by God. For as Christ's sufferings overflow to us, so through Christ does our encouragement also overflow.

What beautiful insights into the gift of God's mercy and our duty to shower mercy on those in need around us.

Reflection

VIII

Patron Saints – A History of Love and Mercy Outpoured

*For we do not have a high priest who is unable to sympathize with
our weaknesses, but one who has similarly been tested in every
way, yet without sin. So let us confidently approach the throne
of grace to receive mercy and to find grace for timely help.*

(Hebrews 4:15-16)

"Few practices of the Catholic Church are so misunderstood today as our devotion to patron saints. From the earliest days of the Church, groups of the faithful have chosen a particularly holy person who has passed on to intercede for them with God. Seeking the intercession of a patron saint does not mean that one cannot approach God directly in prayer; rather, it's like asking a friend to pray for you to God, while you also pray – except, in this case, the friend is already in Heaven, and can pray to God for us without ceasing." (Richert, 2018)

"Some Christians argue that patron saints detract from the proper emphasis we should have on Christ as our Savior. They ask questions, such as: Why approach a mere man or woman with our petitions when we can approach Christ directly? But such questions confuse Christ's role as *mediator* between God and man with the role of an *intercessor*. Scripture urges us to pray for one another; and, as Christians, we believe that those who have died still live, and therefore are capable of offering prayers as we do. In fact, the holy lives lived by the saints are themselves testimony to the saving power of Christ, without Whom the saints could not have risen above their fallen nature. It is the communion of saints, in actual practice . . . We must keep in mind that patron saints are intercessors, not mediators." (Richert, 2018).

The practice of adopting patron saints goes back to the building of the first churches in the Roman Empire, most of which were built over the graves of martyrs. The churches were then given the name of the martyr, with the hope and expectation the martyr would act as an intercessor for the Christians who worshiped there. Soon, Christians began dedicating churches to other holy men and women – saints – who were not martyrs. Today, we still place a relic of a saint inside the altar of each church, and often the church is dedicated to that saint. Early on that is what was meant by St. Peter's, or St. Luke's church.

Thus, the patron saints of churches, and more broadly of regions and countries, were generally chosen because of some connection of the saint to that place – he preached the Gospel there; he died there; some or all of her relics have been transferred there. As Christianity spread to areas with few martyrs or canonized saints, it became common to dedicate a church to a saint who was especially venerated by the founders of the church. In the United States, immigrants often chose as patrons the saints venerated in their native lands. By the Middle Ages, the practice of adopting patron saints had spread to include "the ordinary interests of the saint's life, his health and family, trade, maladies, and perils, her death, her city and country. The whole social life of the Catholic world before the Reformation was animated with the idea of protection by the citizens of heaven." (Catholic Encyclopedia). Saints were usually chosen as special patrons for occupations they worked in or had patronized during their lives. Thus, Saint Joseph became the patron saint of carpenters; Saint Cecilia, of musicians; etc. St. Patrick was chosen as the patron saint of Ireland and the patron saint of engineers. St. Gerard Majella was chosen as the patron saint of expectant mothers and of the pro-life movement because of his dedication to the protection of young lives. With a quick web search, you can easily find the special saint for the occupation, region, etc. in which you are interested.

The same line of thought is true of patron saints for diseases. These saints often suffered from the malady assigned to them or cared for those who did. For example – St. Damien and Leprosy. Sometimes, though, martyrs were chosen as the patron saints of diseases which were reminiscent of or connected to their martyrdom. For example, Saint

Agatha, who was martyred around the year 250, was chosen as the patron of those with diseases of the breast since her breasts were severed when she refused marriage to a non-Christian. Often, such saints are chosen, too, as a symbol of hope. The legend of Saint Agatha attests that Christ appeared to her as she lay dying and fully restored her body so she might die whole.

As Christians, we should adopt our own patron saints as intercessors – first and foremost the one whose name we carry or the one whose name we took at Confirmation. We should also have a special devotion to the patron saint of our parish, the patron saint of our country and the countries of our ancestors. The saints are powerful intercessors; in this day and age when they are so often neglected, we could use their prayers more than ever. In 1846, the bishops of our country chose Our Lady of the Immaculate Conception to be the patron saint of the United States. In 2020, our bishops rededicated our country to the protection of Our Lady.

There is one patron saint that has become a personal favorite quite recently – specifically, St. Peregrine, the cancer saint! I knew absolutely nothing about St. Peregrine until I was diagnosed with prostate cancer a few years ago. Only made sense to ask the patron saint of cancer victims to intercede on my behalf. Interesting how a saint I knew nothing about until recently is now very much a part of my prayer life. Maybe some of you know about St. Peregrine because of a cancer connection to a family member or friend. But if you have a loved one with cancer and did not know of this wonderful saint before, now might be the time to begin praying to him to intercede for your loved one(s). I choose to prepare for mass by praying the Pray to St. Peregrine in direct support of at least a half dozen friends and extended family who are currently battling some form of cancer or who are cancer survivors. By using this prayer as preparation, I am also instantly reminded to offer mass for those same loved ones.

St. Peregrine's story is remarkable. He was born Peregrine Laziosi (1265-1345) in Forli, Italy, the only son of well-to-do parents. In his teens, in a manner similar to St. Paul, he joined the enemies of the Pope in his hometown and soon became a ringleader of rebels against the Church. Because of significant unrest and defiance toward the Church, Pope

Martin IV placed Forli under a spiritual interdict which closed churches in the city, hoping to bring its citizens to their senses. That failing, he sent Philip Benizi, a priest of the Order of Servites (Servants of Mary), as his personal ambassador to try to bring peace to the angry rebels.

No welcome mat was spread for the papal delegate. While addressing crowds of malcontents, Philip was dragged off the rostrum, beaten with clubs and pelted with rocks. Young Peregrine, personally knocked Benizi down with a vicious blow to the face. Moments after, stricken with remorse, the youth cast himself at the feet of the bruised and bleeding priest and begged for his forgiveness. St. Philip granted it with a smile while offering the other cheek.

In the days that followed, Peregrine became a devoted disciple of Philip Benizi. He also heeded Philip's suggestion and often prayed in Our Lady's chapel in the local Cathedral. One day while kneeling in the chapel, he had a vision of the Blessed Mother holding in her hands a black habit (garment or robe) like the Order of the Servants of Mary (Servites) wore. "Go to Siena," Mary told the astonished Peregrine, "There you will find devout men who call themselves my servants. Attach yourself to them." Peregrine eagerly joined the Order and the Servites warmly welcomed him. He was ceremoniously clothed in his religious habit by Philip Benizi himself. Peregrine ultimately chose to focus his energy on the sick and needy.

Daily, Peregrine sought to become a more fervent religious man by working tirelessly for the poor and afflicted. He was a deeply introspective man and in tears would reflect on his sins and go to confession frequently. In reparation, he chose difficult and strenuous acts of penance, sometimes sacrificing by standing for prolonged periods of time. When tired he would support himself on a choir stall or a rock; when overcome by sleep, he preferred the bare earth to a bed. A special penance he imposed on himself was standing whenever it was not necessary to sit. Legend has it Peregrine once stood continuously for thirty years, and got what sleep he could by leaning against a wall. (More on that legend later.)

Some years after being ordained a priest, Peregrine was sent to Forli to found a Servite Monastery and to work among his own townspeople. His love for God and Our Lady fueled an active prayer life that included recitation of psalms, hymns and prayers, and to meditation on God's law. On fire with love for others, he devotedly served the poorest of the poor, comforting them by his presence, his words and his actions. Father Peregrine's favorite places to minister were the hospitals, prisons and homes of the poor. He lived his life pouring out love and mercy on those in need. Thanks to his hard work and loving dedication to others, he gained the well-earned reputation of being a model priest, much the same as St. John Vianney did centuries later. He preached passionately and as a confessor he was loving and wise. People began calling him the "Angel of Good Counsel" out of gratitude for his sage advice so freely given. Very simply, Peregrine lived the Spiritual and Corporal Works of Mercy every moment of every day.

While a life of poverty, penance and hard work began taking a toll on the aging Peregrine, he continued the same rigorous schedule of caring for the sick he had always kept. When a plague broke out in Italy and spread to Forli, no one was safe from the ravages of the disease as it spread. Peregrine's dedication to those in need did not diminish even though he was now a very tired sixty-year-old, barely able to stand. A painful cancerous sore developed on his lower leg and spread aggressively. While he suffered without complaint, his condition deteriorated. After consulting with the finest doctors in the area, all the friars agreed he had no other option – his leg would have to be amputated. Peregrine had struggled with his vow of obedience since the beginning of his ministry, and it was no different now. Fortunately, the Lord patiently waited for his servant to surrender, to obey!

Peregrine prayerfully asked his loving God to intercede, then with courage and humility, turned the entire matter over to Jesus and His Mother. Having surrendered, he knew he still needed to pray! He hopefully reasoned, if when he awakened from the operation the next day and was in the presence of Jesus and Mary, what better way to have prepared for the journey than in prayer?

The night before his surgery, Peregrine dragged himself to the chapter room of the monastery and sat in front of the crucifix. After hours of praying, he began to drift off. During a period of semi-consciousness, he thought he saw Jesus descend from the cross to heal his leg. He was so exhausted, though, he eventually dozed off. In his dream, he felt Christ touch and heal his foot and the thrill of that vision suddenly awakened him. There in the dim moonlight he saw his foot, carefully bandaged just a few hours before, miraculously and completely healed. When his surgeon arrived the next day to operate, he found neither a sign of the cancer, nor the remains of a wound.

His prayers had been answered, he got his miracle, the cancer was cured. But as wonderful as his physical healing was, Peregrine knew he had experienced an even greater healing through this trial – his heart had been softened. Most of us, too, from time to time, pray fervently for a need that lies close to our hearts – and so we should – because God cares deeply about our concerns. But no prayers please God more than ones pleading for an ongoing softening of our hearts.

Peregrine reinvigorated his energy in service of the Gospel and tirelessly continued his work for nearly twenty more years. Many of those he ministered to were healed of their ailments simply through the prayers he said for them. He died peacefully at age of eighty. An extraordinary crowd gathered for his funeral, many of whom were sick; some of them were even healed immediately through his intercession. Pope Paul V beatified Peregrine in 1609 and Pope Benedict XIII canonized him in 1726. The Church declared St. Peregrine the patron of persons with cancer, foot ailments, and any incurable disease.

I would like to go back and close the loop on my earlier reference that Peregrine reportedly stood for extended periods as a form of penance. James Foerster, Communications Director for the Friar Servants of Mary, commented, "The statement that St. Peregrine stood for three decades is a metaphorical way of attesting to St. Peregrine's devotion to penitence and asceticism." Whatever the exact amount of time he stood, the ever-penitent Peregrine was spending far too much time on his feet, and this practice would beget some serious medical issues. Eventually a huge ulcerative growth appeared on Peregrine's leg, exposed the bone and emanated the odor of gangrene. Peregrine was examined by the very best physicians of his time and all pronounced the lesion to be cancerous. Given the importance of his patronage and the urgency of the conditions under which his patronage applies, Saint Peregrine should be viewed "as a companion and friend to accompany them on their personal journey through sickness and suffering, wherever that journey may lead," even if it leads to one's mortality." One Servite friar, before succumbing to cancer in 2007 at the age of 61, commented that the "real miracle of St. Peregrine's life was the inner transformation that came from his total surrendering and conforming to the will of God."

Suffering is a gift that only the person who is suffering can give to God. When we understand its value, and offer it for the love of God and the good of others, we can find that suffering brings joy. Without question, good works are of great value, but pains and trials borne with love and patience are worth even more. Love can transform even the smallest pain into a worthy act of adoration. No one loves suffering for itself. But to suffer out of love, with an attitude of acceptance and trust, is to follow Jesus. St. Peregrine, the Cancer Saint, is an example of just such trust. We know Peregrine was a zealot, but he was first and foremost, a servant of God. Jesus said, *"Feed My lambs."* Peregrine did that with the last ounce of his strength. The same qualities he had shown as a brash young man, fighting against the Church, he used fighting for that same Church's people.

Praying this special intercession to St. Peregrine is a beautiful work of mercy we can loving offer for those suffering with cancer:

O great St. Peregrine, you have been called "The Mighty," "Wonder-Worker," because of the numerous miracles which you have obtained from God for those who have had recourse to you. For so many years you bore in your own flesh this cancerous disease that destroys the very fiber of our being, and who had recourse to the source of all grace when the power of man could do no more. You were favored with the vision of Jesus coming down from His Cross to heal your affliction. Ask of God and Our Lady, the cure of the sick whom we entrust to you.

(Mention those for whom you are praying)

Aided in this way by your powerful intercession, we shall sing to God, now and for all eternity, a song of gratitude for His great goodness and mercy. Amen.

St. Peregrine was a Paul-like oppressor of the Church who recognized the error of his youth, turned himself around, and devoted the rest of his life lovingly serving his *least brothers*. He gave every ounce of his being to help those in need, then gave more; bore excruciating pain without complaint; and had such unwavering faith in the healing power of God that he surrendered his sickness to Him. What an extraordinary link to our spiritual lineage. What an important part of the spiritual DNA that flows through our hearts. What an important intercessor for us to involve in helping our loved ones (and ourselves) suffering from all forms of cancer. The life of Saint Peregrine is a beautiful example (just one of many) of love and mercy poured out on the poorest of the poor, and sickest of the sick.

Reflection

IX

Through the Mercy and Grace of God

But God, who is rich in mercy, because of the great love he had
for us, even when we were dead in our transgressions, brought
us to life with Christ (by grace you have been saved.)

(Ephesians 2:4-5)

NO ONE IS PERFECT! Really. No one in human history has been perfect, except of course, Jesus and His mother, Mary. So why do we seem to think history should be portrayed as a smooth, clean, perfect story. To be useful, history should be a truthful and accurate account of what really happened and what was really said, as much as possible. How else can we, who live in the present, learn from the successes and failures of the past? Yet time after time we see attempts to rewrite history, either to *clean-up* the narrative of events that are somehow inconvenient or to eliminate events altogether because they are uncomfortable to some. There is a centuries-old aphorism, sometimes attributed to St. Teresa of Avila, that states, "God writes straight with crooked lines." One rightful interpretation of this comment could be that our spiritual growth is not a straight line between two points. Rather, getting from where we are at the present to where we need to be to get to heaven is likely going to be a bit of a tortuous path. Through God's grace and mercy, though, we can always get back on the right road moving toward salvation. Remarkably positive outcomes often result from painful events and misguided lives. Let me explain by way of a few examples from both secular society and from the community of saints.

A few years ago, a fairly significant bruhaha arose on the campus of the Oriel College at Oxford University. The focus of the protests was a statue of Cecil Rhodes and the desire by some black South African students to have the statue removed, even though the statue honors the generosity of Rhodes to Oxford. The students maintained that having to walk past that statue was an assault to their sensibilities and should be removed so that they would not have to deal with those offensive memories of the man. For those who might not be familiar with Cecil Rhodes, he is the guy responsible for the Rhodes Scholarships, the well-known and lucrative scholarships available only to 87 British, U.S. and German students per year. The rub cited by the students for the removal of the statue is that Cecil Rhodes was a strong supporter of British Imperialism, and while born in England, he lived most of his life and made most of his vast fortunes in Africa. He was well known for believing that whites were a superior race. Rhodes' fortune was made in agriculture and diamonds – he was the founder of DeBeers Diamonds, a company at one point responsible for 90 percent of the rough-cut diamonds mined and sold around the world.

A letter, likely written in exasperation by someone other than the President of Oriel College, to the protesting students attending Oxford as Rhodes Scholars – who were trying to get the statue of Rhodes removed – begins: "Dear Scrotty Students, Cecil Rhodes's generous bequest has contributed greatly to the comfort and well-being of many generations of Oxford students – a good many of them, dare we say it, better, brighter and more deserving than you . . . This does not necessarily mean we approve of everything Rhodes did in his lifetime – but then we don't have to. Cecil Rhodes died over a century ago. *Autres temps, autres moeurs.* If you don't understand what this means – and it would not remotely surprise us if that were the case – then we really think you should ask yourself the question: 'Why am I at Oxford?'" (For those not fluent in Latin, *Autres temps, autres moeurs* means literally, "Other times, other customs," and figuratively, "in other eras people behaved differently.")

Continuing from the letter, "This ludicrous notion you have that a bronze statue of Cecil Rhodes should be removed from Oriel College, because it's symbolic of "institutional racism" and "white slavery" – well even if it is – which we dispute – so bloody what? Undergraduates so feeble-minded that they can't pass a bronze statue without having their "safe space" violated really do not deserve to be here. And besides, if we were to remove Rhodes's statue on the premise that his life wasn't blemish-free, where would we stop? As one of our alumni, Dan Hannan, has pointed out, Oriel's other benefactors include two kings so awful – Edward II and Charles I – that their subjects had them killed. The college opposite – Christ Church – was built by a murderous, thieving bully who bumped off two of his wives. Thomas Jefferson kept slaves: does that invalidate the U.S. Constitution? Winston Churchill had unenlightened views about Muslims and India: was he then the wrong man to lead Britain in the war?"

At about the same time the letter appeared, BBC Radio broadcast an interview with Chris Patten (Lord Patten of Barnes), Chancellor of Oxford University. Patten's comments paralleled the sentiments of the letter. The (London) *Daily Telegraph* headline following the interview, was "Oxford will not rewrite history." Lord Patten commented "Education is not indoctrination. Our history is not a blank page on which we can write our own version of what it should have been according to our contemporary views and prejudices."

Having read about the Oxford incident, and about other incidents at numerous other venues – and reflecting on Lord Patten's observation that *our history is not a blank page on which we can write our own version of what it should have been according to our current societal views and prejudices*, it occurred to me that many of the saints, political and other leaders, and extremely influential figures of the past also had what could legitimately be called, *checkered* pasts, but have been responsible for much good later in their lives.

In our own country's recent history, a guy vilified as one of Richard Nixon's henchmen, Chuck Colson, spent the last several decades of his life ministering to prison inmates, not just across our country, but internationally as well. Should all the dubious deeds and escapades of his early life sully the accomplishments in his later years? I think not.

But way beyond recent political and public figures and their accomplishments, their individual pasts, etc., what about the legacy of those spiritual figures that influence us each and every day? For example, St. Peregrine (mentioned in Reflection VIII), patron saint of cancer patients, was a remarkably dedicated servant of God, especially to those with severe illnesses. But in his early life, he was a rounder. He was a rambunctious, rebel-rousing opponent of the Catholic Church and on one occasion actually decked the Pope's personal emissary, St. Phillip Benizi, with a blow to the face. Using some of the litmus tests of today, we could easily discount Peregrine's nearly sixty years of remarkable service to the sick and infirmed and instead concentrate on his numerous youthful indiscretions. To do so, however, would be beyond silly.

How about St. Augustine? In his formative years Augustine was not exactly a saint – in fact, very much the opposite. His dear mother, St. Monica, nearly wore out her knees praying for her son's conversion. He was so far off the rails, at one point, he was a staunch advocate of one of the major heresies against the Church of his time, a position that put a metaphorical dagger into Monica's heart. Eventually, though, his mother's prayers were answered, and Augustine did convert. For the rest of his life, he devoted his remarkable intellect and many talents to the growth of the Church. Nearly 1600 years after his death, Augustine's, *Confessions*, and, *The City of God*, are still widely read and intensely studied. St. Jerome, one of his contemporaries commented that Augustine "established anew the ancient Faith." Augustine developed his own approach to philosophy and theology, accommodating a variety of methods and perspectives. Believing that the *grace of Christ* was indispensable to human freedom, he helped formulate the doctrine of *original sin* and made seminal contributions to the development of *just war theory*. And the concept of the *Trinity*, as defined by the Council of Nicaea and the Council of Constantinople, closely aligned with Augustine's work entitled, *On the Trinity*. St. Augustine is one of the preeminent Doctors of the Church. So . . . once again, if we were to write history based only on the early actions and beliefs of Augustine, the work of this giant of our faith would have to be dismissed. As a result, some of the most important contributions he made to the life of the Church would be lost.

Another spiritual giant, with a bit of a checkered early life, was Saint Ignatius. But it was his insightful understanding of the human mind that ultimately led him to humbly acknowledged there were events in his past he could not change, even while he boldly hoped his Maker would accept him *as he is now*. Ignatius discovered in his own life that the Holy Spirit was able to use all the experiences that had shaped him, including all the traumas he endured and the mistakes he made along the way, to bring him to the love of Christ (Eden, 2012). Ignatius' writings have had a major impact on the development of Western Christianity and Western Philosophy as a whole.

Does it not seem extraordinarily odd that Michelangelo, one of the most talented sculptors of all time, would tackle the massive block of marble many of his contemporary sculptor buddies (and his artistic rivals as well) called, "The Giant," to create the remarkable seventeen-foot-tall statue honoring King David? Although David was God's chosen one, God allowed His blessed one (and all of us, as well) the ultimate freedom of choice, knowing that David would sin against Him. God allowed His beloved one to slide down the slippery slope, but before he completely vaporized, God held out His hand and allowed David to grab it. Remarkable – God loves unconditionally, yet we know David was a murder and adulterer. To be sure, though, he was not the only sinner in our spiritual family tree.

Many of the Church's canonized saints also had sullied and sordid life stories. But if we are intellectually honest, however, we must be able to celebrate both their blessedness and acknowledge the sinful things they did, all at the same time, because, in point of fact, we are all a combination of both.

St. Francis of Assisi, as a young man, was a rounder much like Peregrine and Augustine. Using language more familiar to modern society, Francis was a party animal. In fact, based on the wealth of his family, Francis might have been appropriately called a playboy. He was a young man of means, dressed in expensive clothes, lots of money in his pocket with which he could buy anything. Then came his encounter with Christ. Wow, what a turnaround! He physically returned all his possessions to his father, including the clothes from his back (in a public forum), symbolically denying all that was material, to take on life of poverty and service to "rebuild Christ's church." He is known for his tireless dedication to God's people and God's creatures. The first stanza of the popular hymn, "Prayer of St. Francis," is characteristic of him. "Make me a channel of your peace. Where there is hatred, let me bring your love. Where there is injury, your pardon, Lord. And where there's doubt, true faith in you." Pretty remarkable change of heart. We choose to celebrate the second half of his life versus dwelling on the first half.

St. Peter, the rock upon which Christ built His church, is another example of how a life can change when inspired by God's mercy and grace. Peter was coarse, thick-headed, quick-tempered, often spoke before he thought, and not the most intellectually astute of the apostles. Some might even have described Peter as rude, crude and impolite. He claimed to believe that Jesus was the Messiah, and said so, yet when Jesus asked him to walk to Him on the Sea of Galilee, Peter lost both focus and faith and began to sink, only to be pulled back to the surface by Jesus. Later he brutally assaulted one of the guards on Holy Thursday night, and publicly denied the man he called, "Messiah," not once or twice, but three times. Yet not long after all of that took place, Jesus appointed Peter to take the helm of what would become the most remarkable of God's enterprises – the very Church we hold dear – now two millennia old, and currently more than one billion strong and counting. Peter's leadership of the infant church was, frankly, remarkable. His power of persuasion, you will no doubt recall, resulted in the conversion of three thousand, pretty much on day one. Within a few short weeks, Peter transitioned from "denyer-chief" to "converter-in-chief." God smiled on Peter, and just like he did when assuring Abraham and Sarah about Isaac's arrival, asked, "Is there anything that is too hard for God?" God took the man who denied him three times and built His church on him. He used the untested one to lead His sheep. And by showering him with His mercy and grace, He took a man with many shortcomings and provided us an example of how we can and should live. Good thing for us God celebrated and gave responsibility to the man Peter became.

St. Paul did more than just deny Jesus – he encouraged and witnessed the martyrdom of many of the newly converted. Not sure if he actually personally killed any of the new believers, but he surely was complicit. Paul's personal conversion story, however, though well known, is proof positive that a person's past, while it cannot be denied, does not need to rule the present and future. Imagine the experience of merrily riding along on your horse headed for Damascus, then having some invisible force knock you to the ground and blind you. During the immediate aftermath of that experience, Paul was surrounded by and cared for by the nascent church. Then Barnabas arrived, spent time with Paul, instructed him, and converted the very man responsible for killing many. It is remarkable that Paul, a Jew, and a high ranking one at that, was ministered to by those who had chosen to follow Jesus the Christ, just like those he had martyred only days before. Paul's conversion was doubted by many of the disciples and was even a source of much debate, and rightfully so. How could the leaders of the infant church possibly trust someone who had so violently resisted what they knew to be God's truth? Yet, Barnabas interceded for Paul and finally convinced those in doubt, including Peter. The result was remarkable. The persecutor, Paul, became what many scholars claim to be the greatest of evangelizers, specializing in teaching, preaching and writing to the Gentiles. He was transformed from a persecutor of Christ into a vessel of His grace. Should we feel uncomfortable following the writings of one who acted against the very formation of our church? Or should we cherish them as the inspired words of a loving God to His people on earth? St. Paul's letters have clearly withstood the test of time – despite Paul's early violent acts.

So, what are the takeaway messages? Is it that the remarkable generosity of Cecil Rhodes, who funded countless scholarships for more than a century and provided for education facilities and other philanthropic enterprises, should be ignored and that we concentrate only on the highly prejudicial issues of his time? Is it that we should disregard the post-conversion evangelical energy that Chuck Colson devoted to ministering to hundreds of thousands of God's children who find themselves behind bars for whatever reason? Should the brilliance and insight of Augustine's philosophy and theology that was responsible for him be designated as a Doctor of the Church be dismissed because they might be tainted in some way by his pre-conversion passionate support of the Manichaeism and Neo-Platonism, heretical movements threatening the church of his day? Should Ignatian spirituality be ignored because as a young man,

Ignatius did not walk the straight and narrow path? Should we down-play the beauty and brilliance of the Psalms because the author of about half of them had sinned mortally against God. Should we decry forever the irreverence, hate and insolence of a youthful Peregrine Laziosi rather than concentrate on the sixty-plus years of his ministry to the extremely sick giving them hope in their hopelessness, and, in many cases, being God's agent in curing them of their sickness? Should we remove all statues of St. Francis from gardens around the world because they are concrete or stone reminders of a philandering young adult who squandered huge amounts of time and money? Should St. Peter be stripped of his sainthood, and the basilica in Rome be raised or renamed because so much of his life prior to the death of Jesus was spent stumbling along, being conspicuously absent in Jesus' time of need, and being intellectually and spiritually dishonest because he professed to Jesus that He, Jesus, was the Son of the Most-High God, but in practically the same breath denied three times he even knew Jesus? Should we dismiss the masterful writing of St. Paul because they came from a murder?

No, no, no, no, no, no, no, no and no!

Hopefully by now, you get the point. We each come to this very moment in time, influenced, shaped and formed not only by the good we do, but the not-so-good as well. Yes, Cecil Rhodes had controversial and ill-founded thoughts about imperialism and the primacy of the whites as the superior to others. But, in spite of his faults, he was an extraordinarily generous man, the fruits of his generosity showing up in some of the best and brightest of our times. Yes, Chuck Colson was guilty of some pretty shady shenanigans during his tenure in the Nixon White House and went to prison as a result. Interestingly, though, he went to prison for a crime he confessed to, rather than the crime for which he was accused. While in prison, he chose to use his time ministering to others about the Christianity he found in the months leading up to his imprisonment. The theology and philosophy of our Church, for more than a millennium and a half, has been significantly shaped by a guy whose mother prayed him to Rome. Monica's prayers were answered beyond her dreams. God is a cheerful and generous giver. Ignatius' zeal and dedication to Christ's

Church led to his starting the *Company of Jesus,* better known as the Jesuits. The impact of that 400-year-old company across the globe has been extraordinary. The story of David is instructional and inspirational on multiple levels and the beauty of the Psalms have touched the hearts and souls of billions, bringing comfort in time of sorrow, joy in time of grief, hope in times of despair and faith in times of doubt. If we concentrated on just David's sinfulness alone, we would have totally missed some of the most sacred passages of Scripture. The formative years of both St. Peregrine and Saint Francis were spent partying, having a good time and being wasteful of both time and money. Yet upon their conversions, at about the same age, both chose to turn their lives and energy to the service of the Lord, influencing countless in despair and loneliness. Franciscan priests, nuns and lay orders serve the kingdom of God around the world. Clearly, the influence of these two wonderful saints cannot be overstated. And if we choose to look only at the wrong, ill-conceived criminal or cowardly acts of Saints Peter and Paul, our beloved One, Holy, Catholic and Apostolic Church would not be Christ's legacy on earth as we know it.

God's covenant with us, His Church, is revealed to us in many different ways and through armies of people who have lived both lives of virtue, and those who, with the guidance of the Holy Spirit have taken their lives of sinfulness, then repented and reshaped their being to reflect God's plan for them. Once again, Newman's prayer is clear in its description of us: "God has created me to do Him some definite service. He committed some work to me He has not committed to another. I have my Mission."

Our history, really, is not a blank slate on which we can write our own version of what we think it should have been according to our current societal views and prejudices. History is a record of both evil and good, highs and lows, all of which God can use for His purpose. We cannot rewrite our spiritual journey, either, but we can learn and grow from acknowledging our failings. From personal experience, the more I deny the wrongs I have done, the more likely I am to repeat them. God intends for us to learn from the totality of our truthful past. And let not your heart be troubled, through His mercy and grace, there is remarkable hope for all, regardless of our personal history.

Reflection

X

The Bread of Mercy

Jesus said to them, "I am the bread of life; he who comes to me shall not hunger; and he who believes in me shall never thirst."

(John 6:35)

CATHOLIC AUTHOR, Flannery O'Connor, was one of the most gifted American authors of the twentieth century, and an absolute master of literary symbolism. She was taken by some friends one evening to a dinner party hosted by Mary McCarthy, a contemporary author of much greater fame than she. McCarthy, herself, had left the Church in her mid-teens fashioning herself a true intellectual. Late in the evening, the conversation among those at the gathering turned toward the Eucharist. McCarthy commented that when she was a child, she always considered receiving the Eucharist as receiving the "Holy Ghost," though now, she considered it a symbol – a "pretty good" symbol, but only a symbol. O'Connor, after not having said a word all evening, declared, "Well if it's a symbol, to hell with it." Later she added, the "[Eucharist] is the very center of existence for me: all the rest of life is expendable." As a lifelong Catholic, I believe without reservation, what O'Connor expressed – the Holy Eucharist truly IS the body, blood, soul and divinity of Christ – not a symbol of those realities.

Jesus instituted the Holy Eucharist at the Last Supper as His legacy to provide spiritual strength and nourishment for each of us. And even though the Eucharist is His gift to us, it is not intended just for us. As with everything else Jesus modeled for us while on earth, he expects us to take His gift and share it with others. Through the Eucharist, "We are

89

to become a living extension of Christ. His life is to 'take flesh' in us. Just as the lowly elements of bread and wine contain the magnitude of God's love, so too the humble conditions of our lives can become a liturgy of praise, adoration, and service. If we ask: where today is Jesus' smile, His words, His hands, His compassion, His voice, His face? The answer is; He lives in our charity…This means that our lives must be in harmony with the Eucharist. We, too, shall be broken for others and poured out, but it is Christ who is broken and poured out in us. We become the bread of mercy and intercession for others. We who have received healing become vehicles of healing." (Langford, 2018). We who have received mercy from God become vehicles of mercy to others.

The Holy Eucharist is at the very core of our Christian identity and the Church has always and continues to teach, that it is the source and summit of our faith. The Real Presence is central to those beliefs. In spite of this steadfast tenet of our faith, results of a recent Pew Forum (2019) survey indicated only one-third of all those who identify themselves as Catholics actually believe in the Real Presence. Quite surprising, only about two-thirds of those who attend Mass at least once a week believe in the Real Presence. While regular Mass-goers are twice as likely to believe this foundational teaching of the Church, compared to all who call themselves Catholics, still, one in three of them does not believe they are receiving the body, blood, soul and divinity of Christ when they receive Holy Communion. If the Eucharist truly is the *bread of mercy,* and I firmly believe it is, then many who claim to be Catholic are actually spiritually starving themselves, significantly hampering any inclination they may feel to minister mercy to those in need around them.

The scriptural foundation for all Christian belief in the Holy Eucharist is found in the Gospel of St. John, Chapter 6. As Catholics, we believe the words of John 6 are literally true. And while some Protestant denominations believe as we do, many denominations do not; instead, choosing to believe in several different interpretations. In essence, many believe that the Eucharist is more a symbol of Christ's body and blood, or that He is with the bread and wine. I am a practicing Catholic (and sinner) who tries hard to practice my faith in a manner consistent with Church teaching, and while I am no theologian, I would like to explain why I believe what I believe.

In John 6:35, Jesus said:

"I am the bread of life; whoever comes to me will never hunger, and whoever believes in me will never thirst."

Just a few verses later (verses 51-58), Jesus declares unequivocally:

"I am the living bread that came down from heaven; whoever eats this bread will live forever; and the bread that I will give is my flesh for the life of the world" The Jews quarreled among themselves, saying, "How can this man give us [his] flesh to eat?" Jesus said to them, "Amen, amen, I say to you, unless you eat the flesh of the Son of Man and drink his blood, you do not have life within you. Whoever eats my flesh and drinks my blood has eternal life, and I will raise him on the last day. For my flesh is true food, and my blood is true drink. Whoever eats my flesh and drinks my blood remains in me and I in him. Just as the living Father sent me and I have life because of the Father, so also the one who feeds on me will have life because of me. This is the bread that came down from heaven. Unlike your ancestors who ate and still died, whoever eats this bread will live forever."

In spite of the clarity of Jesus' words, even many of those who heard them directly from His lips found them difficult to swallow, so it is probably not hard to understand why these words continue to be the source of lively debate between Catholics and non-Catholics and cause for angst for many today. When taken literally, John 6:51-58, required a huge leap of faith many were (and are still) unwilling to make. John 6:60 is a simple but profound description of what happened when Jesus spoke to them:

Then many of his disciples who were listening said, "This saying is hard; who can accept it?"

While His closest disciples remained loyal to Him and to His teaching, many others did not. St. John described what the disbelievers did (John 6:66-69):

As a result of this, many [of] his disciples returned to their former way of life and no longer accompanied him. Jesus then said to the Twelve, "Do you also want to leave?" Simon Peter answered him, "Master, to whom shall we go? You have the words of eternal life. We have come to believe and are convinced that you are the Holy One of God."

A careful look at the Last Supper narrative, and the words Christ used when He instituted the Eucharist, reveals no equivocation. The exact same words are used in all three of the synoptic Gospels (Matthew 26:26, Mark 14:22 and Luke 22:19). Jesus said:

"This IS my body . . . "

Let me explain why I believe these four words are so critically important and why they should be taken literally. No doubt you have seen study-versions of the New Testament where Jesus' words are highlighted in a different color than the rest of the text so it is easy to find them. Many of those highlighted words are stories Jesus told or parables He used to teach His apostles privately or instruct publicly the large crowds that clamored to hear His message of redemption and eternal salvation. The descriptive words He used were (and are) extremely useful to help others learn and understand important concepts. At other times, Jesus used symbolic language to explain such things as "the kingdom of heaven is like a mustard seed" or ". . . like leaven." Symbolic language is also extremely useful for explaining unfamiliar or unknown concepts. But Jesus did far more than just teach and explain. As an example, the words He spoke to the blind man resulted in him regaining his sight. Similarly, the words He prayed over the deaf man resulted in the man being able to hear again. His assuring words to the pleading centurion caused his servant to be restored to full health. And, the words He spoke over Lazarus caused His dead friend to return to life. My point here is that many of Jesus' words are far more than just descriptive or symbolic, they are creative. He spoke, things happened. When God created the universe, He spoke and it came into being. King David, thought by many scholars to have been the author of Psalm 33, described the power of God's words (Psalm 33:6-9):

By the LORD's *word the heavens were made; by the breath of his mouth all their host. He gathered the waters of the sea as a mound; he sets the deep into storage vaults. Let all the earth fear the* LORD; *let all who dwell in the world show him reverence. For he spoke, and it came to be, commanded, and it stood in place.*

Using slightly different language, in a 2020 speech on the Real Presence, Bishop Robert Barron, said, "What God says, IS! What Jesus says, IS!"

When the Evangelists recorded Jesus' words from the Last Supper they did not say, "this is sort of my body and blood;" or, "this represents my body and blood;" or, "this is a symbol of my body and blood." And they did not say, "it is up to you to decide if you think it might be my real body and blood." Their words were unanimous, specific and unequivocal – Jesus said, "THIS IS MY BODY." The original twelve apostles; legions of the early Church Fathers (for example, Ignatius of Antioch, Polycarp, Justin Martyr, Irenaeus, Clement, Athanasius, John Chrysostom); scholars such as Augustine and Thomas Aquinas; participants in the Council of Trent prompted by the Protestant Reformation; and more recently Saint Pope Paul VI during the Second Vatican Council (to mention only a few), all affirmed the sacred truth of the Real Presence of Christ in the Holy Eucharist. The Church has always taught that the substance of the bread and wine are miraculously transformed into the Body and Blood of Christ during the Consecration at the Mass. The term used to describe that miracle is transubstantiation. No longer bread and wine – now the actual Body and Blood of Christ. The Magisterium of the Catholic Church has never wavered from the truth of transubstantiation. Christ is substantially (substance – to the core of its existence) present in the Holy Eucharist under the appearance of bread and wine. Divergence from this belief began with the teachings of Ulrich Zwingli, a Swiss priest and leader of the Protestant Reformation in Switzerland during the early sixteenth century. Some Protestant denominations adopted his beliefs immediately, and over time, others (but not all) did as well.

St. Dominic Barberi, an Italian-born, Passionist priest sent to England in the early 1840's, was ridiculed and scorned, mostly because of his ardent preaching about the truth of the Real Presence. One day, while walking down the street he was heckled by a non-Catholic minister who belittled him about his teaching. Eventually, Barberi turned to the man and calmly said: "Jesus Christ said over the consecrated elements: 'This is my body,' you say, 'No it is not His body.' Who then am I to believe? I choose to believe Jesus Christ." I believe it is important to understand that faith allows us to believe what we cannot see and what we cannot prove scientifically. When we truly open our hearts and minds to the Holy Spirit, we will be freely given the faith to believe. *"Faith is the realization of what is hoped for and evidence of things not seen."* (Hebrews 11:1). Jesus said it, IT IS!

What we, as Catholics, believe about the *bread of mercy* is not a frivolous abstraction; it is vitally important, because our beliefs drive what we think and do. Throughout Scripture, bread is frequently connected to acts of charity and mercy. For example, Abraham had his wife, Sarah, made bread to feed several hungry itinerant travelers. Those visitors were the ones who told them Sarah would bear a son, Isaac. God comforted the Hebrews with unleavened bread while escaping Egyptian captivity. He nourished them with manna during their decades-long journey to the Promised Land. Jesus fed the crowds of thousands who followed Him, hungry for His teaching about eternal salvation, with a few loaves of bread that miraculously yielded more leftovers after they ate than when they started. These and many other accounts of bread were all associated with acts of mercy. But when Jesus broke bread and distributed it at the Last Supper with the challenge to His apostles to, "Do this in memory of me," He created in that moment, the true sacred *bread of mercy*. Belief in the Real Presence is significant because the spiritual food provided by the Holy Eucharist is what spiritually nourishes us and provides the stamina for living our priestly responsibilities to serve those around us with love and mercy.

Cardinal Newman wisely taught, "We can believe what we choose, (but) we are answerable for what we choose to believe." So, believing what we read in Scripture and acting on those truths have positive, real consequences. To be sure, though, believing but not acting on, or simply choosing not to believe what we read has consequences as well.

Belief in the Real Presence is directly tied to the powers and privileges vested in the priesthood. Catholic priests are ordained by bishops who get their authority through a direct spiritual and historical continuity with the Apostles. Christ, Himself, empowered them. The grace a bishop receives at his own ordination allows him to ordain others. As Catholics, we believe that through the Sacrament of Holy Orders, our priests are empowered with the authority to change (consecrate) bread and wine into the Body and Blood of Christ through the validity of their ordination. While anyone can say the words of consecration, not everyone has the authority (faculty) to make the consecration happen. For example, if a person walks up to you on the street and declares he is arresting you, they have no authority to do so, so you are not arrested. If, by contrast, a police officer does so, you actually are arrested, whether you have done something wrong or not. Police have the authority to arrest. As Catholics, we believe the authority to consecrate the bread and wine into the Body and Blood of Christ lies solely with those properly ordained. Very simply, then, without the priesthood, we would not have the Real Presence of the Body and Blood of Christ at each Mass.

I am a cradle Catholic. During the first 61 years of my life, I had the honor of attending only one ordination, that of Matthew, now Father Joseph Van House. My wife and I were blessed to attend his celebration in Dallas, about a dozen years ago. The ceremony was beautiful – particularly special for us because we had known Matthew since he was a child. Adding to the joy, Father Joseph was the first man ordained into the Cistercian Order in more than 20 years. What a blessing for him and what a remarkable seed of rebirth for the Order. Even more beautiful is the reality that through their ordination into the priesthood, Father Joseph and other blessed men provide the continuation of the mystery of the Eucharist instituted by Christ at the Last Supper.

One year before his ordination to the priesthood, Matthew was ordained a "Transitional Deacon." We did not attend that ordination and frankly I was not aware of the full significance of the vows he professed then, and the promises he made during that ceremony. But about two years ago we had the honor of attending the ordinations of two other friends, Bill and Mark, one into the permanent diaconate, the other into the transitional diaconate. I clearly remember the moment when the

Archbishop looked into our friends' eyes and said, "Believe what you read. Teach what you believe. Practice what you teach." From the moment I heard those instructions I knew they were profound challenges being placed into their hearts and onto our friends' shoulders. These identical words had been spoken to Father Joseph when he was ordained to Transitional Deacon.

Explicit in the three simple-sounding sentences is the complex reality of the Gospel – specifically, that all of sacred Scripture is the Truth, God's truth. Reading, studying, reflecting on and contemplating Holy Scripture is critically important because the clergy share the same extraordinary responsibilities Jesus commissioned His followers to carry out just before His Ascension. Members of the clergy must know God's truth in order to speak and defend His truth and even though most Christians are not ordained, we must also know God's truth in order to fulfill our baptismal obligations as teachers and defenders of His truth. Believing what you read is the necessary first step.

Let's explore what it might mean to *believe what you read*. Philippians 2:1-11 says:

> *"If there is any encouragement in Christ, any solace in love, any participation in the Spirit, any compassion and mercy, complete my joy by being of the same mind, with the same love, united in heart, thinking one thing. Do nothing out of selfishness or out of vainglory; rather, humbly regard others as more important than yourselves, each looking out not for his own interests, but [also] everyone for those of others. Have among yourselves the same attitude that is also yours in Christ Jesus, Who, though he was in the form of God, did not regard equality with God something to be grasped. Rather, he emptied himself, taking the form of a slave, coming in human likeness; and found human in appearance, he humbled himself, becoming obedient to death, even death on a cross. Because of this, God greatly exalted him and bestowed on him the name that is above every name, at the name of Jesus every knee should bend, of those in heaven and on earth and under the earth, and every tongue confess that Jesus Christ is Lord, to the glory of God the Father."*

The truth of St. Paul's instruction plays out in countless ways, maybe the most important of which comes from knowing our happiness comes only from emptying ourselves for others, and never from concentrating on ourselves. A fool-proof roadmap to guiding our selfless giving is to live the Spiritual and Corporal Works of Mercy, which are all outwardly focused. The nourishment we need to do that work is provided by the Holy Eucharist, the bread of mercy. Matthew Kelly (2008) observed that we will never find happiness if the first question we ask is, "What's in it for me?" Rather, says Kelly, our happiness will be immediate the moment we ask instead, "How can I serve?"

We are assured our lives will be deeply enriched and given profound meaning when we follow Jesus' example, extending unconditional love and mercy to others. "How can I serve," leads to humility and the works of mercy. "How can I serve?", creates a mind- and heart-set that demonstrates the profound truth that even though Jesus is God, He did not insist on or equate Himself to God. Yet at the mention of His name, God the Father expects us to acknowledge Jesus' divinity by bowing, genuflecting or showing some other form of reverence.

Do you believe what you read about the Eucharist, particularly the passages in John 6? If so, do you teach others by way of example and explanation, even pushing back against attacks on the Eucharist when necessary? Do you use the grace received in the Eucharist to reach out mercifully to others? Knowing about the priceless gift of the Eucharist, do you take advantage of and receive Holy Communion as frequently as possible, nourishing both your body and soul? Or do you smother, hide or conceal the light of God's mercy?

God is the source and summit of love and truth and Holy Scripture describes those truths – one of the most important of which is the truth of the Real Presence of Christ in the Holy Eucharist. Although only priests have the faculty, though their ordination, to consecrate common bread and wine into the extraordinary gift of the Eucharist, the rest of us, as baptized Catholics, as Christians, as people of faith, share the responsibilities of living out our roles as priests, prophets and kings.

"We are to become a living extension of Christ. His life is to 'take flesh' in us . . . This means that our lives must be in harmony with the Eucharist . . . We become the bread of mercy and intercession for others. We who have received healing become vehicles of healing." (Langford, 2018)

Reflection

XI

Hail Holy Queen – Mother of Mercy

"When Jesus saw his mother and the disciple there whom
he loved, he said to his mother, "Woman, behold, your son."
Then he said to the disciple, "Behold, your mother."

(John 19:26-27)

ONE ASPECT OF Catholic teaching that confuses many who do not
share our faith tradition is our reverence for the Blessed Virgin Mary,
human mother of Jesus Christ. For those of us who are cradle Catholics,
and for those who have converted to Catholicism, the respect, admiration
and veneration we show the Blessed Mother is natural and, frankly, quite
sensible to us for many reasons. The most important reason, though, is
that she is the Mother of God – not just a mother, but THE Mother of our
Savior. Mothers of earthly kings, queens, presidents and other luminaries
are honored, simply because they bore their children. Seems logical that
Jesus' mother should be venerated as well, after all, Jesus Himself held
her in highest esteem. Early on, Mary seemed to know God had set her
apart for special service. Upon hearing her cousin Elizabeth's greeting,
she responded (Luke 1:46-49):

My soul proclaims the greatness of the Lord;
my spirit rejoices in God my savior.
For he has looked upon his handmaid's lowliness;
behold, from now on will all ages call me blessed.
The Mighty One has done great things for me,
and holy is his name.

The Blessed Mother is honored in numerous prayers in our Catholic faith tradition, including the *Hail Mary*. The first half of the prayer consists of two greetings – both taken directly from the first Chapter of St. Luke's Gospel – one from the Angel Gabriel, the other from her cousin, Elizabeth. The second half is an intercessory plea for Mary to pray to her Son for us now and at the hour of our death.

> Hail Mary, Full of Grace, The Lord is with thee. Blessed art thou among women, and blessed is the fruit of thy womb, Jesus. Holy Mary, Mother of God, pray for us sinners now, and at the hour of our death. Amen.

The *Memorare* is another prayer many use to ask for the Blessed Virgin's assistance to intercede for them during special times of need.

> Remember, O most gracious Virgin Mary, that never was it known that anyone who fled to thy protection, implored thy help, or sought thine intercession was left unaided. Inspired by this confidence, I fly unto thee, O Virgin of virgins, my mother; to thee do I come, before thee I stand, sinful and sorrowful. O Mother of the Word Incarnate, despise not my petitions, but in thy mercy hear and answer me. Amen.

Just why do Catholics (and some in other faith traditions) spend so much time praying to the Blessed Mother when they could simply go directly to the source of the assistance they seek? One of the most beautiful explanations I have ever found about why we revere and pray to Mary the way we do comes from Newman's, *Discourses for Mixed Congregations*, Discourse 18, written around 1849 and modernized slightly in 2019. While a bit lengthy, the beauty and genius of Newman is worth taking the time to reflect upon:

> "Blessed Mary has no chance place in the divine dispensation. The Word of God did not merely come to her and go from her. He did not pass through her, as He visits us in Holy Communion. It was no heavenly body which the Eternal Son assumed, fashioned

by the angels and brought down to this lower world. No, He imbibed, He absorbed into His Divine Person her blood and the substance of her flesh; by becoming man of her, He received her lineaments and features, as the appropriate character in which He was to manifest Himself of mankind. The child is like the parent, and we may well suppose that by His likeness to her was manifested her relationship to Him. Her sanctity comes, not only of her being His mother, but also of His being her son. "If the dough offered as first fruits is holy," says St. Paul, "so is the whole lump and if the root is holy, so are the branches" (Rom 11:16). And hence the titles which we are accustomed to give to her. He is the Wisdom of God; she therefore is the Seat of Wisdom. His presence is heaven; she therefore the Gate of Heaven. He is infinite mercy; she is the Mother of Mercy. She is the Mother of "fair love, and of fear, and of knowledge, and of holy hope" (Sir 24:24, Douay-Rheims (1899)). Is it wonderful then that she has left behind in the Church below an odor like cinnamon and balm, and sweetness like choice myrrh? (Sir 24:20, Douay-Rheims).

"Such, then, is the truth ever cherished in the deep heart of the Church, and witnessed by the keen apprehension of her children, that no limits but those proper to a creature can be assigned to the sanctity of Mary. Did Abraham believe that a son should be born to him of his aged wife? Then Mary's faith must be held greater when she accepted Gabriel's message. Did Judith consecrate her widowhood to God to the surprise of her people? Much more did Mary, from her first youth, devote her virginity. Did Samuel, when a child, inhabit the Temple, secluded from the world? Mary too was by her parents lodged in the same holy precincts, even at the age when children first can choose between good and evil. St. John the Baptist was sanctified by the Spirit before his birth; shall Mary be only equal to him? Is it not fitting that her privilege should surpass his? Is it wonderful, if grace, which anticipated his birth by three months, should in her case run up to the very first moment of her being, outstrip the imputation of sin, and be beforehand with the usurpation of Satan? Mary must surpass all the saints; the very fact that certain privileges are known to have been theirs persuades us, almost from the necessity of the case, that she had the same and higher. Her conception was immaculate, in order that she might surpass all saints in the date as well as the fulness of her sanctification.

"If the Mother of Emmanuel ought to be the first of creatures in sanctity and in beauty; if it became her to be free of all sin from the very first, and from the moment she received her first grace to begin to merit more; and if such as was her beginning, such was her end, her conception immaculate and her death an assumption; if she died, but revived, and is exalted on high: what is befitting in the children of such a mother, but an imitation, in their measure, of her devotion, her meekness, her simplicity, her modesty, and her sweetness? Her glories are not only for the sake of her Son, they are for our sakes also . . .

"What shall give us patience and endurance, when we are wearied out with the length of the conflict with evil, with the unceasing necessity of precautions, with the irksomeness of observing them, with the tediousness of their repetition, with the strain upon the mind, with our forlorn and cheerless condition, but a loving communion with her! She will show us her Son, our God and our all. When our spirit is excited, or relaxed, or depress, when it loses its balance, when it is restless and wayward, when it is sick of what it has, and hankers after what it has not, when our eye is solicited with evil and our mortal form trembles under the shadow of the tempter, what will bring us to ourself, to peace and to health, but the cool breath of the Immaculate and the fragrance of the Rose of Sharon? It is the boast of the Catholic religion, that it has the gift of making the heart chaste; and why is this, but that it gives us Jesus Christ for our food, and Mary for our nursing mother? Go to her for the royal heart of innocence. She is the beautiful gift of God, which outshines the fascinations of a bad world, and which no one ever sought in sincerity and was disappointed. She is the personal type and representative image of that spiritual life and renovation in grace without which no one shall see God."

For most of my life, at least since I was old enough to have learned how, I have prayed the Hail Mary. Our maternal grandmother taught my sister and me to pray the rosary, which is mostly repeating the Hail Mary, when we were small children. Whenever we visited her on the weekend, we prayed at least one rosary together with her, so over time, and, with reinforcement from our mother, the rosary became pretty familiar to us. Grandma prayed five rosaries each day – never missed a day and always prayed five. What a wonderful example of discipline, spirituality, and dedication. Over the years I continued saying this beautiful prayer, but unfortunately, the frequency, fervor, dedication and ease of saying the rosary faded. About twenty years ago, as part of our Christ Renews His Parish team formation process, we often gathered as teams of men and prayed the rosary in front of the tabernacle, usually for special intentions. As familiar as the prayerful ritual had been at various points in my life, I rediscovered the beauty and power of saying the rosary with my CRHP brothers. Unfortunately, as time passed, again my discipline waned, and I fell back out of the routine. Fortunately, God is kind and patiently waited for me.

About 12 years ago, a few months before the birth of our third grandchild, a boy, doctors told our daughter and son-in-law their baby had some issues that would need to be surgically corrected soon after his birth. Laurel and I decided we would commit to praying the rosary each day for our grandson's health and well-being. Then after the little guy was born safely, and the needed surgery completed successfully, we continued with our commitment and prayed the rosary to petition our loving Lord for a wide variety of intercessions, including thanking Him for our grandson's health. I will not claim we have prayed the rosary every day since then, but we have not missed very many days in the past 12 years. This account is not being made to impress you; rather, it helps provide the foundation for the major point I would like to make later.

The rosary, for those who may not know how to pray it, is a beautiful combination of prayers that includes reciting several familiar prayers, in a particular order: the Apostles' Creed, the Our Father, the Hail Mary, the Glory Be, the Fatima Prayer (may want to Google this prayer if you are not familiar with it), four series of Mysteries from the life of Christ and the Holy Family, and the Hail Holy Queen. Each time we pray the rosary, we say these same prayers, over and over. But, as many times as I have said the words, I must admit I cannot claim to have given all of them sufficient thought or reflection – particularly the Hail Holy Queen. Over my lifetime I have no idea how many times I have said this prayer. And even though most of the time I said the prayer with reverence, only recently, about 12 years ago, did the prayer take on a very different and significant meaning for me.

> Hail Holy Queen, Mother of Mercy! Our life, our sweetness, and our hope! To thee do we cry, poor banished children of Eve. To thee do we send up our sighs, mourning and weeping in this valley of tears. Turn, then, most gracious Advocate, thine eyes of mercy toward us and after this our exile show unto us the blessed fruit of thy womb, Jesus. O clement, O loving, O sweet Virgin Mary. Pray for us, O holy Mother of God. That we may be made worthy of the promises of Christ.

I would like to share some of my reflections on this prayer.

Hail Holy Queen – The opening words of this prayer are simply beautiful. I cannot think of a more fitting, and appropriate greeting for Mary than Hail Holy Queen. And Queen she is. In fact, the fifth and final Glorious Mystery is the declaration that Mary was Crowned Queen of Heaven and Earth. And holy, could not be a more apt descriptor – so holy, in fact, that Mary was the only human being (except for Jesus, himself) who was born free from original sin. Holy? Indeed. Queen? Absolutely, and the most glorious Queen ever. Unlike earthly queens that come and go, live their lives, then die – Mary is queen of heaven and earth for all eternity, actively advocating for us to her Son, actively showering us with her own mercy.

. . . *Mother of Mercy* – Mary has many titles, but Mother of Mercy may be one of the most comforting titles I can think of. How appropriate that Mary be called the Mother of Mercy – she is in fact the Mother of God, the source of all mercy. Not sure many of us, certainly not me, fully understand the complexity and dimensions of mercy, either as gift or as duty. But in simple terms, mercy is a virtue that includes gentleness, compassion, forgiveness and kindness. Mary, the Mother of Mercy, exemplifies each of these qualities. Her gentle spirit characterized her life. Her compassion for those who may be suffering, in any way, and her attention to the needs of all is a gift to all who are hurting. Her forgiving spirit is exemplary – it even extended to those who murdered her only Son. And, her genuine sense of kindness is evident by her actions – for example, visiting her cousin Elizabeth, intervening at the wedding in Cana, and interacting with everyone she encountered throughout her life on earth. But, even after her bodily Assumption into heaven nearly two millennia ago, the Blessed Mother continues to interact directly with us on earth, some of the most noteworthy human interactions in modern time being at Fatima, Lourdes, and Medjugorje. Sometimes her interactions with us are through answered prayers, other times through physical apparitions.

. . . *Our life, our sweetness, and our hope* – Mary is for us, the very source of our hope as human beings. She is fully human. She stepped up to the plate and accepted God's invitation to be the vessel that would bring His Son into the world and she did so without hesitation. Her *fiat*, her *yes*, to being the mother of the second person of the Blessed Trinity, is a genuine source of hope, especially when we see none. Can you think of another term for a mother that better describes the ideal than sweet?

. . . *To thee do we cry, poor banished children of Eve* – This plea to our Holy Mother is an admission that we are children of the first Eve, that we are sinners. In our cries for help, we are begging for consolation from our sorrow, not from our mother, Eve, but from our Holy Mother, the second Eve.

. . . *To thee do we send up our sighs, mourning and weeping in this valley of tears* – Who did you go to when you were a child and were hurt or in any kind of trouble or need? I usually went to my mother. Wouldn't we all do well to go to our Spiritual Mother in times of need: when we are down; when we need help; when we have lost hope; when we are sad and crying, both literally or figuratively. Throughout history, mothers have always been conduits to reach important people whether they were business leaders, politicians, people of influence – whatever. I find it fascinating how many people think Catholics pray *to* Mary, instead of *to* Jesus. Instead, with our Marion prayers, we are asking Mary to join us in our prayers to her Son. Many feel they want no one between themselves and God. But the honor we show Mary, when we ask for her intercession in our times of need, is exactly the same sort of honor that Jesus himself showed His Mother. What Jesus did, is exactly what we should do, too.

. . . *Turn, then, most gracious Advocate, thine eyes of mercy toward us* – This intercession to Mary is our direct plea to her to be our advocate with her Son, and to show her kindness, gentleness and compassion to us. Could we have a better advocate than the Mother of Jesus?

. . . *and after this, our exile* – Have you ever considered your life on earth as being in exile? Sounds like prison doesn't it? But compared to the eternal life God promises us, our life here is a prison of sorts. When we or a loved one is nearing the end of their life, this world and its pain, it's suffering surely does feel like a prison from which to be freed.

. . . *show unto us the blessed fruit of thy womb, Jesus* – The ultimate reward for a life well led here on earth, the goal for our lives as Christians, the focus of our spirituality, and God's purpose for us in eternity is to be with the fruit of Mary's womb in heaven.

. . . *O clement, O loving, O sweet virgin Mary* – What a wonderful term for the sweet virgin Mary – clement. Clement is not a word used much in our modern lexicon, and I must admit I had to do a little research to understand the full meaning of the word. As many times as I have prayed the term, I was not aware the word described the fullness of her love for us in its gentleness, softness, mildness and pleasantness.

. . . *Pray for us, O holy Mother of God* – Is there anyone else in the history of mankind that you would rather have intercede for you than the Mother of Christ?

. . . *That we may be made worthy of the promises of Christ* – And what must we do to be worthy of the promises of Christ? To live a life of love, service and devotion to God. One of the first questions in the old Baltimore Catechism was, "Why did God make me?" The answer still rings loud and clear, "To know, love, and serve Him in this life, and to be happy with Him for eternity in the next."

You might be wondering why have I spent so much time reflecting on this prayer. There is a reason, to me a good reason. My mother, and most of those who helped form my spirituality, were devoted to praying the rosary that concludes with the "Hail Holy Queen." Because she was so devoted to praying the rosary, I prayed it with her a number of times, particularly during the last few weeks of her life. In fact, about an hour and a half before she was called home, I prayed the rosary with her, or for her, or maybe both. She was sleeping, but I know she knew we were saying the rosary together.

In the time since her death, I have often thought of the last few hours I spent with her and the very last prayer I prayed with her. The phrases that keep coming back to me are:

Turn, then, most gracious Advocate, thine eyes of mercy toward us . . . and after this, our exile show unto us the blessed fruit of thy womb, Jesus . . . pray for us O holy Mother of God, that we may be made worthy of the promises of Christ.

Could there be a more beautiful invocation in life? Could there be a more magnificent plea to the Blessed Mother at the time of death? I don't think so. Whenever I think of my Mom, particularly her final hours, I cannot help but wonder just how much she must have been comforted by hearing the words (and I am quite confident she heard them) of this very familiar prayer. I only wish that I had had the insights about this prayer before Mother died. Having said that, what I do know is that the Virgin Mary is the Mother of Mercy. In our times of need, she enjoins her gift of mercy on us, with the boundless mercy of her Son and in so doing models just how we are to extend mercy to others.

Ridiculous Grace and Scandalous Mercy

Reflection

XII

Mercy at the Hour of Death – Spiritual Dreamers

Blessed are the clean of heart, for they will see God.
(Matthew 5:8)

F ROM TIME TO time, we all dream. Sometimes the dreams are pleasant, sometimes not so. Sometimes they are based on reality, other times not. Sometimes dreams can be messages from God, some conversations with Him. One well-known story of dreams taken from the Old Testament is the account of Samuel being awakened while he slept in the temple while under the tutelage of the prophet Eli. You may recall that the boy Samuel was awakened three times, each time thinking he heard Eli calling him. After the third time, however, Eli instructed the boy that if he heard the Lord calling him again, he should reply, "speak, Lord. your servant is listening." The story is rich in meaning as are other accounts of dreams in scripture.

In St. Matthew's gospel are four accounts of Joseph's dreams. The first was when Joseph was told by an angel not to be afraid of taking Mary for his wife, that her pregnancy was not by man but by the power of the Holy Spirit. By taking Mary as his wife, he became Jesus' earthly father. The second was to warn Joseph to take Mary and the infant Jesus and flee to Egypt because they were in grave danger of being killed. After Herod died, Joseph had another dream letting him know it was safe to return to Israel; but on the way home, his fourth specifically instructed him to take his family to the town of Nazareth, in the region of Galilee. Based on his dreams, Joseph made life-altering decisions, leading to radical actions. Spiritually, too, much can and does happen to us through our dreams.

In 1865, John Henry Cardinal Newman wrote the poem, *The Dream of Gerontius*, the prayer of a dying man and what he mentally, emotionally and spiritually goes through in the moments immediately before and after death. It was written after Newman's conversion from Anglicanism to Roman Catholicism during the Victorian era in England. At that time, the Anglican Church did not accept the concept of purgatory. Newman used this literary vehicle to explore his newly-held Catholic beliefs about our journey from death, through final purification in Purgatory, to eternal reward in Paradise with God. The poem follows Gerontius (a wise old man) as he nears death, and then, reawakens as a soul outside of his body, preparing for judgment, following one of the most important events any human can experience: death. Newman's insight into God's love, mercy and compassion is beautifully described through his intellectual genius and mastery of language.

Newman uses the death and judgment of Gerontius as a way of helping us contemplate our own fear of death and sense of unworthiness before God. Although few have even heard of this work today, the poem was widely acclaimed in the late nineteenth century in both religious and literary circles. Edward Elgar, at the turn of the twentieth century, was commissioned to compose a score for orchestra and chorus that included the text of the entire poem. Elgar's composition has been recorded numerous times, over the years, by some of the world's finest orchestras and choruses.

I would like to share portions of the poem with you, including my narrative of events as they occur. My comments are italicized and Newman's original text are in normal font. I have preserved Newman's spelling, punctuation, capitalizations, etc.

Lying on his death bed, Gerontius prays:
JESU, MARIA - I am near to death,
And Thou art calling me; I know it now.
Not by the token of this faltering breath,
This chill at heart, this dampness on my
brow, — (Jesu, have mercy! Mary, pray for me!)
'tis this new feeling, never felt before,
That I am going, that I am no more.

Pray for me, O my friends; a visitant
Is knocking his dire summons at my door,
The like of whom, to scare me and to daunt,
Has never, never come to me before;
'Tis death, —O loving friends, your prayers! — 'tis he!
As though my very being had given way,
As though I was no more a substance now,
O horror! this it is, my dearest, this;
So pray for me, my friends, who have not strength to pray.

Without even knowing of Gerontius' private plea, his friends in the room are already praying:
KYRIE eleison, Christe eleison, Kyrie eleison.
Holy Mary, pray for him.
All holy Angels, pray for him.
Choirs of the righteous, pray for him.
Holy Abraham, pray for him.
St John Baptist, St Joseph, pray for him.
All ye Saints of God, pray for him.

In a very surreal way, Gerontius, not sure if he is dead yet, says to himself:
ROUSE thee, my fainting soul, and play the man;
And through such waning span
Of life and thought as still has to be trod,
Prepare to meet thy God.
And while the storm of that bewilderment Is for a season spent,
And, ere afresh the ruin on thee fall, Use well the interval.

All the while His friends continued to pray:
BE merciful, be gracious; spare him, Lord.
Be merciful, be gracious; Lord, deliver him.
From the sins that are past;
From Thy frown and Thine ire;
From the perils of dying;
From any complying
With sin, or denying
His God, or relying, On self, at the last;

From the nethermost fire;
From all that is evil;
From power of the devil;
Thy servant deliver,
For once and for ever.
By the Spirit's gracious love,
Save him in the day of doom.

Sensing death, Gerontius furiously reaffirms his beliefs, leaving nothing to chance:
Firmly I believe and truly God is Three, and God is One;
And I next acknowledge duly Manhood taken by the Son.
And I trust and hope most fully In that Manhood crucified;
And each thought and deed unruly Do to death, as He has died.
Simply to His grace and wholly Light and life and strength belong,
And I love, supremely, solely, Him the holy, Him the strong.

And I hold in veneration,
For the love of Him alone,
Holy Church, as His creation, And her teachings, as His own.
And I take with joy whatever Now besets me, pain or fear,
And with a strong will I sever All the ties which bind me here.
Adoration aye be given,
With and through the angelic host, To the God of earth and
heaven, Father, Son, and Holy Ghost.

A fierce and restless fright begins to fill
The mansion of my soul. And, worse and worse,
Some bodily form of ill
Floats on the wind, with many a loathsome curse
Tainting the hallowed air, and laughs, and flaps
Its hideous wings,
And makes me wild with horror and dismay.
O Jesu, help! pray for me, Mary, pray!
Some angel, Jesu such as came to Thee
In Thine own agony . . .
Mary, pray for me.

Joseph, pray for me.
Mary, pray for me.

His friends, now sensing death is imminent, pray:
RESCUE him, O Lord, in this his evil hour,
As of old so many by Thy gracious power: (Amen.)
Isaac, when his father's knife was raised to slay; (Amen.)
Moses from the land of bondage and despair; (Amen.)
Daniel from the hungry lions in their lair; (Amen.)
And the Children Three amid the furnace-flame; (Amen.)
David from Golia and the wrath of Saul (Amen.)
—so, to show Thy power, Rescue this Thy servant in his evil hour.

There is a priest present and he offers final anointing and his blessings:
Go forth upon thy journey, Christian soul!
Go from this world! Go, in the name of God
The omnipotent Father, who created thee!
Go, in the name of Jesus Christ, our Lord,
Son of the living God, who bled for thee!
Go, in the name of the Holy Spirit, who
Hath been poured out on thee!
And may thy dwelling be the Holy Mount
Of Sion:—through the Same, through Christ, our Lord.

His Body and Spirit are separated now but the soul of Gerontius is confused, not knowing if he is alive or dead:
I went to sleep; and now I am refreshed.
A strange refreshment: for I feel in me
An inexpressive lightness, and a sense
Of freedom, as I were at length myself
And ne'er had been before. How still it is!
I hear no more the busy beat of time,
No, nor my fluttering breath, nor struggling pulse;
Nor does one moment differ from the next. I had a dream;
yes: — someone softly said, "He's gone;" and then a sigh
went round the room.

I cannot make my fingers or my lips
By mutual pressure witness each to each,
Nor by the eyelid's instantaneous stroke
Assure myself I have a body still.

Another marvel; someone has me fast
Within his ample palm; 'tis not a grasp
Such as they use on earth, but all around
Over the surface of my subtle being,
As though I were a sphere, and capable
To be accosted thus, a uniform
And gentle pressure tells me I am not
Self-moving, but borne forward on my way.
And hark! I hear a singing; yet in sooth
I cannot of that music rightly say
Whether I hear or touch or taste the tones.
Oh what a heart-subduing melody!

He now hears his Guardian Angel say softly:
    My work is done,
    My task is o'er, And so I come,
    Taking it home,
    For the crown is won,
    Alleluia,
    For evermore.

    This child of clay
    To me was given,
    To rear and train
    By sorrow and pain
    In the narrow way,
    Alleluia,
    From earth to heaven.

The reality of his earthly death has settled on Gerontius' soul and he observes:
    IT is a member of that family
    Of wondrous beings, who, ere the worlds were made,

Millions of ages back, have stood around
The throne of God: —he never has known sin;
But through those cycles all but infinite,
Has had a strong and pure celestial life,
And bore to gaze on th' unveiled face of God
And drank from the eternal Fount of truth,
And served Him with a keen ecstatic love,
Hark! he begins again.

*Again, his Guardian Angel speaks, worships the Father, and pleads for
mercy to Him for his charge:*
O LORD, how wonderful in depth and height,
But most in man, how wonderful Thou art!
With what a love, what soft persuasive might
Victorious o'er the stubborn fleshly heart,
Thy tale complete of saints Thou dost provide,
To fill the thrones which angels lost through pride!

Then was I sent from heaven to set right
The balance in his soul of truth and sin,
And I have waged a long relentless fight,
Resolved that death-environed spirit to win,
Which from its fallen state, when all was lost,
Had been repurchased at so dread a cost.

How should ethereal natures comprehend
A thing made up of spirit and of clay,
Were we not tasked to nurse it and to tend,
Linked one to one throughout its mortal day?
More than the Seraph in his height of place,
The Angel-guardian knows and loves the ransomed race.
ALL praise to Him, at whose sublime decree
The last are first, the first become the last;
By whom the suppliant prisoner is set free,
By whom proud first-borns from their thrones are cast;
Who raises Mary to be Queen of heaven,
While Lucifer is left, condemned and unforgiven.

Now knowing his body has breathed its last, Gerontius' soul, naively says:
    I WILL address Him. Mighty one, my Lord,
    My Guardian Spirit, all hail!

His Guardian Angel then gently advises:
    THOU art not let; but with extremest speed
    Art hurrying to the Just and Holy Judge:
    For scarcely art thou disembodied yet.
    Divide a moment, as men measure time,
    Into its million-million-millionth part,
    Yet even less than that the interval
    Since thou didst leave the body; and the priest
    Cried *"Subvenite,"* and they fell to prayer;
    Nay, scarcely yet have they begun to pray.

    Of years, and centuries, and periods.
    It is thy very energy of thought
    Which keeps thee from thy God.

Gerontius asks his angel companion:
    Dear Angel, say,
    Why have I now no fear at meeting Him?
    Along my earthly life, the thought of death
    And judgment was to me most terrible.
    I had it aye before me, and I saw
    The Judge severe e'en in the Crucifix.
    Now that the hour is come, my fear is fled;
    And at this balance of my destiny,
    Now close upon me, I can forward look
    With a serenest joy.

To which his Angel responds:
    It is because
    Then thou didst fear, that now thou dost not fear.
    Thou hast forestalled the agony, and so
    For thee the bitterness of death is past.
    Also, because already in thy soul

The judgment is begun. That day of doom,
One and the same for the collected world –
That solemn consummation for all flesh,
Is, in the case of each, anticipate
Upon his death; and, as the last great day
In the particular judgment is rehearsed,
So now too, ere thou comest to the Throne,
A presage falls upon thee, as a ray
Straight from the Judge, expressive of thy lot.
That calm and joy uprising in thy soul
Is first-fruit to thee of thy recompense,
And heaven begun.

At this point Gerontius and his Guardian Angel begin their journey toward the seat of heaven for his judgement. Along the way, Gerontius observes:
But hark! upon my sense
Comes a fierce hubbub, which would make me fear,
Could I be frighted.

His Guardian Angel, knowing the way, informs his charge:
We are now arrived
Close on the judgment court; that sullen howl
Is from the demons who assemble there.
It is the middle region, where of old
Satan appeared among the sons of God,
To cast his jibes and scoffs at holy Job.
So now his legions throng the vestibule,
Hungry and wild, to claim their property,
And gather souls for hell. Hist to their cry.

In horror, Gerontius replies:
how uncouth a dissonance!

At this point in his journey, the demons begin to taunt Gerontius' soul, mocking him, and tempting him with the notion that it is still not too late for him to abandon and deny God. Some of their taunts are the same as those that befell Adam and Eve – you, too, can be better than God – all you need to do is deny Him in this present moment.

In the midst of these demons and final temptations, Gerontius observes:
    HOW impotent they are! and yet on earth
    They have repute for wondrous power and skill;
    And books describe, how that the very face
    Of the Evil One, if seen, would have a force
    Even to freeze the blood, and choke the life
    Of Him who saw it.

To which his Guardian Angel reassuringly responds:
    In thy trial-state
    Thou hadst a traitor nestling close at home,
    Connatural, who with the powers of hell
    Was leagued, and of thy senses kept the keys,

    But when some child of grace, angel or saint,
    Pure and upright in his integrity nature, meets the demons on
    their raid,
    They scud away as cowards from the fight.

Getting past the demons, Gerontius anxiously asks:
    SEE not those false spirits; shall I see
    My dearest Master, when I reach His throne?
    Or hear, at least, His awful judgment-word
    With personal intonation, as I now
    Hear thee, not see thee, Angel? Hitherto
    All has been darkness since I left the earth;
    Shall I remain thus sight bereft all through
    My penance time? If so, how comes it then
    That I have hearing still, and taste, and touch,
    Yet not a glimmer of that princely sense
    Which binds ideas in one, and makes them live?

Still doing his/her angelic duties, the Angel advises Gerontius:
    So will it be, until the joyous day
    Of resurrection, when thou wilt regain
    All thou hast lost, new-made and glorified.
    How, even now, the consummated Saints

118

See God in heaven, I may not explicate.
Meanwhile let it suffice thee to possess
Such means of converse as are granted thee,
Though, till that Beatific Vision thou art blind;
For e'en thy purgatory, which comes like fire,
Is fire without its light.

As Gerontius gets closer and closer to the moment of judgment, even though he has lived a good life, his soul laments:
His will be done!
I am not worthy e'er to see again
The face of day; far less His countenance,
Who is the very sun. Nathless, in life,
When I looked forward to my purgatory,
It ever was my solace to believe
That, ere I plunged amid th' avenging flame,
I had one sight of Him to strengthen me.

His Guardian Angel replies:
NOR rash nor vain is that presentiment;
Yes,—for one moment thou shalt see thy Lord.
Thus will it be: what time thou art arraigned
Before the dread tribunal, and thy lot
Is cast forever, should it be to sit
On His right hand among His pure elect,

What thou dost ask: that sight of the Most Fair
Will gladden thee, but it will pierce thee too.

Trying desperately to take it all in, Gerontius says to his Guardian Angel:
THOU speakest darkly, Angel; and an awe
Falls on me, and a fear lest I be rash.

Gerontius and his guardian, now passed the final temptations by the demons, continue their journey to the place of judgment. As they proceed, they pass five choirs of angels, each singing glorious messages of encouragement.

Passing the first choir, his Guardian Angel advises:
WE now have passed the gate, and

119

The House of Judgment; and whereas earth
Temples and palaces are formed of parts
The very pavement (of this place) is made up of life—
Of holy, blessed, and immortal beings,
Who hymn their Maker's praise continually.

Continuing, His Guardian Angel loving instructs:
WHEN then—if such thy lot—thou seest thy Judge,
The sight of Him will kindle in thy heart,
All tender, gracious, reverential thoughts.
Thou wilt be sick with love, and yearn for Him,
And feel as though thou couldst but pity Him,
That one so sweet should e'er have placed Himself
At disadvantage such, as to be used
So vilely by a being so vile as thee.
There is a pleading in His pensive eyes
Will pierce thee to the quick, and trouble thee.
And thou wilt hate and loathe thyself; for, though
Now sinless, thou wilt feel that thou hast sinned,
As never thou didst feel; and wilt desire
To slink away, and hide thee from His sight;
And yet wilt have a longing aye to dwell
Within the beauty of His countenance.
And these two pains, so counter and so keen,—
The longing for Him, when thou seest Him not;
The shame of self at thought of seeing Him, —
Will be thy veriest, sharpest purgatory.

And then the Angel tells Gerontius:
We have gained the stairs
Which rise towards the Presence-chamber; there
A band of mighty angels keep the way
On dither side, and hymn the Incarnate God.

At the foot of the stairs, a Choir of Angels sing:
FATHER, whose goodness none can know, but they
Who see Thee face to face,

By man hath come the infinite display
Of Thine all-loving grace;
But fallen man—the creature of a day—
Skills not that love to trace.
It needs, to tell the triumph Thou hast wrought,
An Angel's deathless fire, an Angel's reach of thought.

It needs that very Angel, who with awe,
Amid the garden shade,
The great Creator in His sickness saw,
Soothed by a creature's aid,
And agonised, as victim of the Law
Which He Himself had made;
For who can praise Him in His depth and height,
But he who saw Him reel in that victorious fight?

Gerontius cannot contain himself:
HARK! for the lintels of the presence-gate
Are vibrating and echoing back the strain

The final choir of Angels announces:
O loving wisdom of our God!
When all was sin and shame,
A second Adam to the fight
And to the rescue came.
O wisest love that flesh and blood
Which did in Adam fail,
Should strive afresh against the foe,
Should strive and should prevail;

And that a higher gift than grace
Should flesh and blood refine,
God's Presence and His very Self;
And Essence all divine.

O generous love! that He who smote
In man for man the foe,
The double agony in man

For man should undergo;

And in the garden secretly,
And on the cross on high,
Should teach His brethren and inspire
To suffer and to die.

As the two arrive at heaven's gates, Gerontius' Guardian Angel lovingly says to his charge:
THY judgment now is near, for we are come
Into the veiled presence of our God.

To which Gerontius responds:
I HEAR the voices that I left on earth.

The Guardian Angel then explains to Gerontius the experience he has just traversed:
IT is the voice of friends around thy bed,
Who say the "*Subvenite;*" with the priest.
Hither the echoes come; before the Throne
Stands the great Angel of the Agony,
The same who strengthened Him, what time He knelt
Lone in the garden shade, bedewed with blood.
That Angel best can plead with Him for all
Tormented souls, the dying and the dead.

The time of judgment has arrived and the angel attending the seat of judgement prays:
Jesu! spare these souls which are so dear to Thee,
Who in prison, calm and patient, wait for Thee;
Hasten, Lord, their hour, and bid them come to Thee,
To that glorious Home, where they shall ever gaze on Thee.

Fearfully, Gerontius then pleads with his Guardian Angel:
GO before my Judge, Angel

The Guardian Angel reassuringly advises:
Praise to His name!
The eager spirit has darted from my hold,

And, with the intemperate energy of love,
Flies to the dear feet of Emmanuel;
O happy, suffering soul! for it is safe,
Consumed, yet quickened, by the glance of God.

There at the gates of heaven, knowing he has passed the ultimate tests, Gerontius realizes that even though forgiven, he is not sufficiently clean to enter the ultimate joy of the Beatific Vision, so he pleads with his Guardian Angel to take him away to be fully cleansed:

TAKE me away, and in the lowest deep
There let me be,
And there in hope the lone night-watches keep,
Told out for me.
There, motionless and happy in my pain,
Lone, not forlorn,
There will I sing my sad perpetual strain,
Until the morn.
There will I sing, and soothe my stricken breast,
Which ne'er can cease
To throb, and pine, and languish, till possest
Of its Sole Peace.
There will I sing my absent Lord and Love:
Take me away,
That sooner I may rise, and go above,
And see Him in the truth of everlasting day.

Hearing and understanding his plea, Gerontius' Guardian Angel takes him to purgatory for that final cleansing:

NOW let the golden prison open its gates,
Making sweet music, as each fold revolves
Upon its ready hinge. And ye great powers,
Angels of Purgatory, receive from me
My charge, a precious soul, until the day,
When, from all bond and forfeiture released,
I shall reclaim it for the courts of light.

And as he completes his angelic task for the Prince of Peace, Gerontius' guardian says his temporary goodbye to his charge:

SOFTLY and gently, dearly-ransomed soul,
In my most loving arms I now enfold thee,
And, o'er the penal waters, as they roll,
I poise thee, and I lower thee, and hold thee.

And carefully I dip thee in the lake,
And thou, without a sob or a resistance,
Dost through the flood thy rapid passage take,
Sinking deep, deeper, into the dim distance.
Angels, to whom the willing task is given,
Shall tend, and nurse, and lull thee, as thou liest;
And (HOLY) Masses (offered for you) on the earth and
prayers in heaven,
Shall aid thee at the Throne of the most Highest.

Farewell, but not forever! Brother dear,
Be brave and patient on thy bed of sorrow;
Swiftly shall pass thy night of trial here,
And I will come and wake thee on the morrow.

The End

Could the power of God's love, mercy and compassion at the hour of death be described any more beautifully?

Reflection

XIII

The Duty of Mercy

"Amen, I say to you, whatever you did for one of these least brothers of mine, you did for me."

(Matthew 25:40)

ABOUT 50 YEARS ago in St. Louis, Missouri, a six-year-old African-American boy by the name of Maurice Nutt was in a really tough place. His mother was in the hospital giving birth to his third sibling. Down the hall from his mom lay his dad, being treated for advanced cancer. His mom gave birth to a healthy baby boy, but the outcome for his dad was terminal. Maurice's family was in dire straits. His mother was now a single parent with four children under the age of six. Mrs. Bea Nutt was a remarkably strong young woman of great faith. While she knew what she needed to do she did not necessarily know how to go about it. With a newborn to care for and three other small children, going to work outside their home would be really hard, but with a total of five mouths to feed she had no choice. In spite of everything, she had faith that God would get her (and them) through.

Within a couple of years, Maurice began to stretch his wings and started playing with a group of boys who were not blessed with parents who cared for them as his mother did for him. The group wandered the streets of the neighborhood and while they got into mischief, none of their shenanigans got them into any serious trouble. One day, the boys came upon a down-on-her-luck woman who lived wherever she could find shelter. The boys quickly picked up on the street-lady's vulnerability and began taunting her with unkind comments. One day, they found the lady searching for food in nearby garbage cans, and so they decided to up the ante with their insults. Although uncharacteristic of his upbringing,

Maurice joined in the boy-chorus shouting at her, "Dirty, Stinky, Smelly, Sally, why don't you climb in the garbage can?" Their insulting name for her became routine for them, so every time they saw her, they screamed, in unison, "Whatcha doin' Dirty, Stinky, Smelly Sally?" Day after day, week after week they mocked and insulted the poor woman.

One Saturday morning, Maurice was looking out the window of his bedroom in the second-floor walk-up apartment he shared with his family, and saw Sally again scrounging in the garbage for something to eat. He opened the window, stuck his head out and shouted, "Hey Dirty, Stinky, Smelly, Sally, what are you doing in our trash?" Over and over, he ridiculed her. And then, with a cold chill that instantly overcame him, he realized his mother was standing behind him. He pulled his head back into the room and slowly turned around to face his mom. Bea gave him *one of those looks* that all kids have gotten from a parent at some point along the way; only after looking into Maurice's eyes, she looked and pointed heavenward. Maurice knew he was in big trouble, but the upward look confused him. He wasn't sure if he was going to die at that moment, or whether his mother was looking for inspiration on how to discipline her son. Fortunately for him, she was looking for guidance. After firmly telling him never to speak disrespectfully to Sally or anyone else again, she assigned him a long list of household chores to do that day.

As had become a custom for the Nutt family, the following Saturday morning, Bea prepared a large breakfast for her brood consisting of pancakes, sausage and fruit. But when Maurice arrived at the table there was an extra person there, sitting in his normal seat. He thought he recognized the woman, but she was dressed in one of his mother's Sunday church dresses, her hair was neat and clean and she was surrounded by a delicate, pleasant fragrance. Maurice's mother informed him that it would be his job to serve their breakfast guest, with the greatest of kindness, insuring she had plenty to eat. Only after he had served her, and assured she had all she needed, including refreshing her coffee, would he be allowed to join the rest of the family and their guest to eat his own lovingly prepared breakfast. Unbeknownst to Maurice, his mom had graciously invited their guest to bathe in their apartment, helped her wash and style her hair, then gave her clean underclothes, shoes and one of her best dresses to wear.

After breakfast, Maurice was told it would also be his job to clean up and wash the dirty dishes, while his mom and their guest would go to the living room to talk. Before Maurice completed his kitchen duties, the guest graciously thanked Mrs. Nutt and left their apartment. As Maurice was cleaning the last of the silverware, his mom returned to the kitchen and asked her eldest if he knew who had eaten breakfast with them. Maurice knew exactly who had been there. Quite sheepishly, he started to say, "Dirty, Stinky, Smelly Sally," but his mother gently put her index finger to his lips to keep him from speaking, and said, "Our breakfast guest this morning was Jesus Christ."

A half century later, Father Maurice Nutt, C.Ss.R, a Redemptorist priest, continues to tell this story because, he says, "It was the first moment I realized I might have a vocation to the priesthood." Father Nutt served as a parish priest for several decades, taught theology and homiletics to seminarians, and is an in-demand director of parish missions, revivals, and retreats all over the United States. He has also authored numerous spiritual publications including four books.

So why have I shared this story? Hopefully, the point is clear. As children of God, we must treat everyone we come in contact with as a fellow child of God. We must be kind to them, be respectful to them despite their situation, and in doing so, hopefully, begin to understand the loving brilliance Mrs. Nutt conveyed to her son when she told him, "Our breakfast guest this morning was Jesus Christ." Everyone we encounter, whether they are well dressed and clean or in tattered dirty cloths and smell like the garbage they sift through looking for food, must be loved unconditionally and treated with dignity. If they are hungry, we need to give them something to eat. If they are thirsty, it's our job to give them something to drink. If they need clothes, we need to clothe them. If they are homeless, we need to help them find shelter. If they are sick, we must care for them. If they are in prison, we should visit them. And when they die, we should insure they are buried with dignity and respect. Bea Nutt understood to the core of her being the Corporal Works of Mercy, and lovingly taught them to Maurice, not with her words, but more importantly by her actions. All of these are acts of love. All of these acts of love are, in fact, acts of mercy! They are the path to holiness in our everyday lives.

The mercy we show to those who are vulnerable must go beyond what are called the Corporal Works, it must also include the Spiritual Works of Mercy. And to be sure, Jesus modeled all of them for us during His public ministry. We must do our very best to instruct those who do not know about God by teaching the faith that has been shared with us. For those in doubt or ignorance, we must counsel them with wisdom and patience. For those who have done wrong, we are obliged to let them know of their transgressions, particularly when teaching our children. We must be patient with those who have wronged us and willingly forgive offenses and not hold grudges. We must comfort those in pain of any sort. And we must regularly pray for both the living and the dead.

Pope Francis, in his call to action for the universal church during the recent *Extraordinary Jubilee Year of Mercy*, rightly pointed out, that for most of us, practicing the Spiritual Works of Mercy tend to be more difficult than the Corporal Works, mostly because the Corporal Works are more obvious and up-front than the Spiritual Works. When we see someone who is in tattered clothes, it is easy to recognize the need and do something about it. By contrast, when we have been wronged by another, forgiving them is often not quite so simple – and not holding a grudge against someone who has hurt us is also difficult. But Matthew Kelly (2017) points out, "We are all writing the story of our lives. Are you satisfied with the story you are writing with your life?" One very important way to insure we are writing a story with the glorious ending God intends for us is by living the Spiritual and Corporal Works of Mercy. Not sure if you have ever thought about it, but living the works of mercy is a real way of growing in holiness – and we are all called to holiness.

Virtually all of what you have read in this volume thus far has focused on the gifts of God's love, mercy and compassion – that He give us without condition. But as observed earlier, the gifts we unconditionally receive from God are just one dimension of His gifts. In return, having received, we are now obligated to return His gifts, not to Him, but rather to those in need around us. In Matthew 5:14-16, Jesus declared:

You are the light of the world. A city set on a mountain cannot be hidden. Nor do they light a lamp and then put it under a bushel basket; it is set on a lampstand, where it gives light to all in the house. Just so, your light must shine before others, that they may see your good deeds and glorify your heavenly Father."

Extending unconditional love, mercy and compassion to those around us is a direct response to living the beatitudes and the Spiritual and Corporal Works of Mercy. There are no secrets about the *what* of living these, rather the challenge is the *how*.

Early in His public ministry, Jesus found Himself in the midst of a crowd, so he went up the mountain, sat down and began to teach. Matthew 5:3-10, the transcript of what Jesus taught, is often called the Sermon on the Mount. These are the Beatitudes:

Blessed are the poor in spirit, for theirs is the kingdom of heaven.
Blessed are they who mourn, for they will be comforted.
Blessed are the meek, for they will inherit the land.
Blessed are the clean of heart, for they will see God.
Blessed are the peacemakers, for they will be called children of God.
Blessed are they who are persecuted for the sake of righteousness,
  for theirs is the kingdom of heaven.
Blessed are they who hunger and thirst for righteousness, for they
  will be satisfied.
Blessed are the merciful, for they will be shown mercy.

In his book, *Heaven in Our Hands*, Father Benedict Groschel, C.F.R. (1994), describes just what it means to live the Beatitudes, and in so doing, receive the blessings we long for. He observed the Beatitudes *do not give specifics* about the *how* to do something, rather they *indicate* the way, and carry within them the power to form and transform us. Groschel adds, "In some mysterious way the Beatitudes not only *tell* us the way, they *pull* us along the way. Like an airport conveyor belt, they pick us up and carry us along with the power of the Spirit. Like an unseen force, they draw us closer to God, like a magnetic field draws metal."

Living the Beatitudes requires our full-time attention to love, mercy and compassion. To be sure, though, extending mercy to others actually does have a cost, we must be prepared to pay the price. But, Groeschel points out: "mercy does not mean being a fool. New York (where Groschel lived) is an especially difficult place to practice mercy because all sorts of crooks want to cheat you out of everything. The most merciful thing you can do for those trying to cheat you is to not let them succeed. But how can you tell the difference. How can you be sure which of the panhandlers lining the streets of Manhattan seriously need food, and which of them want money to support their drug habit?"

Groeschel's solution is one of the most sensible I have found – it not only shows us how to be merciful to those in need, it also deals with the reality that we can sometimes be swindled. "One of the most sinister and awful advantages of life in New York is that many of the impoverished look so thoroughly destitute that they can't be acting. Trying to help an obviously needy person requires only a few moments. A brief pause allows us to exchange a kindly word and ask how the person is doing, to make a small contribution, or to buy a little food to ease the physical hunger that constantly plagues the poor. These are acts of mercy. And they cost us something, either in time or in money or both…[But] what if you suspect that someone might be abusing your charity? Decide once and for all not to let it bother you in the least, and then live by that conclusion. Better to take the chance of being cheated than to neglect mercy. Merciless people never have to worry about being cheated; they just don't help anybody. Foolish people, on the other hand, help everybody! Those who decide to be merciful in an intelligent way should probably expect about a 12 to 15 percent loss on the investment. This is the amount I figure will go to charlatans or crooks or people who could be helping themselves a bit more than they are."

Many of us want to be merciful to those around us but are paralyzed by the possibility of being scammed. If that's you, take stock of your resources, decide how you want to help others and the amount you are willing to give, then simply step out in faith. If you are actually cheated, take heart, it's not the first time you have been taken advantage of and likely not the last!

People in need are not a new social phenomenon. The poor have been around for all of recorded history. Sharing with the poor is not new either.

While there are likely earlier citations in Scripture, Isaiah 58:7-10 is pretty clear about our spiritual-social obligations to those less fortunate than ourselves. The Lord said to His servant:

> *Is it not sharing your bread with the hungry, bringing the afflicted and the homeless into your house; clothing the naked when you see them, and not turning your back on your own flesh? Then your light shall break forth like the dawn, and your wound shall quickly be healed; your vindication shall go before you, and the glory of the LORD shall be your rear guard. Then you shall call, and the Lord will answer, you shall cry for help, and he will say: "Here I am!" If you remove the yoke from among you, the accusing finger, and malicious speech; if you lavish your food on the hungry and satisfy the afflicted; then your light shall rise in the darkness, and your gloom shall become like midday.*

The Church has long taught, "The Church's love for the poor...is a part of her constant tradition." (CCC #2444). This love is inspired by the Gospel of the Beatitudes, of the poverty of Jesus, and of His concern for the poor. This love is, in fact, the very foundation of Catholic social teaching.

Love for the poor is even one of the motives for the duty of working so as to "be able to give to those in need." It extends not only to material poverty but also to the many forms of cultural and religious poverty (CCC #2444).

The works of mercy are wonderful guidelines to help us focus our energy to serving others. They are charitable actions by which we come to the aid of our neighbors in their spiritual and bodily needs. Among all these, giving alms to the poor is one of the chief witnesses to fraternal charity: it is also a work of justice pleasing to God. In James 2:15-16, we hear:

> *If a brother or sister has nothing to wear and has no food for the day, and one of you says to them, "Go in peace, keep warm, and eat well," but you do not give them the necessities of the body, what good is it?*

The CCC (#2448) highlights this passage and points out:

"In its various forms – material deprivation, unjust oppression, physical and psychological illness and death – human misery is the obvious sign of the inherited condition of frailty and need for salvation in which man finds himself as a consequence of original sin. This misery elicited the compassion of Christ the Savior, who willingly took it upon himself and identified himself with the least of his brethren. Hence, those who are oppressed by poverty are the object of a preferential love on the part of the Church which, since her origin and in spite of the failings of many of her members, has not ceased to work for their relief, defense, and liberation through numerous works of charity which remain indispensable always and everywhere."

Even though showing mercy to our neighbors is not complicated, frankly, it is not always easy. Jesus knew this from the outset; after all, He gave us everything. Yet in the presence of His graciousness, we often choose callously to go our own way, violating the laws He provided for our happiness. Then, because He loved us so much and so unconditionally, He became like us to suffer and die for our redemption. Jesus' public ministry was about teaching us what it takes to live happy productive lives. He did so by modeling how we need to live to truly be in His image and likeness. To that end, part of what He taught in the Sermon on the Plain (Luke 6:27-36) was:

But to you who hear I say, love your enemies, do good to those who hate you, bless those who curse you, pray for those who mistreat you. To the person who strikes you on one cheek, offer the other one as well, and from the person who takes your cloak, do not withhold even your tunic. Give to everyone who asks of you, and from the one who takes what is yours do not demand it back. Do to others as you would have them do to you. For if you love those who love you, what credit is that to you? Even sinners love those who love them. And if you do good to those who do good to you, what credit is that to you? Even sinners do the same. If you lend money to those from whom you expect repayment, what credit [is] that to you? Even sinners lend to sinners, and get back the same amount. But rather, love your enemies and do good to them, and lend expecting nothing back; then your reward will be great and you will be children of the Most High, for he himself is kind to the ungrateful and the wicked. Be merciful, just as [also] your Father is merciful.

Be merciful, just as your Father is merciful. Show kindness to others, because kindness has been (and continues to be) shown to you. Love others unconditionally, because (from your conception) you are loved unconditionally. Be merciful because you have already (and will always) be showered with His mercy!

Jesus shared a profound message with St. Faustina (1981). He said: "I am giving you three ways of exercising mercy toward your neighbor: the first – by deed, the second – by word, the third – by prayer. In these three degrees is contained the fullness of mercy, and it is an unquestionable proof of love for me."

The remainder of this work is dedicated to reflecting on some of the important ways we can carry out our mission as agents of mercy to those around us. Several of the reflections examine practical ways to live the works of mercy and the beatitudes, and, several explore ways to exercise *non-traditional* works of mercy. However, the essence of all these is simply looking at how Jesus lived his earthly life, then committing ourselves to doing likewise.

Reflection

XIV

Mercy Is About Being "Others-Focused"

"Therefore, as God's chosen people, holy and dearly loved, clothe yourselves with compassion, tenderness, kindness, humility, gentleness and patience."

(Colossians 3:12)

MERCY REQUIRES US to be others-focused. Being others-focused requires humility. And, humility requires unconditional love. These linkages provide a simple, but profound, basis for understanding just how we must act in order to fulfill our duty of being merciful to others. By contrast, pride and its first cousin arrogance are insidious forces that cause us to be self-centered, thus preventing us from loving others unconditionally. So, a conversation about pride and pridefulness is in order because it is at the heart of our unwillingness or reluctance to exercising works of mercy to those around us.

In speaking of the human condition, twentieth-century intellectual giant, C.S. Lewis (2001 edition, originally, 1952) observed, "there is no fault which makes a man more unpopular, no fault which we are more unconscious of in ourselves, and no fault that the more of we have in ourselves, the more we dislike it others – than PRIDE." He states categorically, "According to Christian teachers, the essential vice, the utmost evil, is Pride." Lewis also poetically observed that "unchastity, anger, greed, drunkenness, and all that, are mere fleabites in comparison – it was through pride the devil became the devil – pride leads to every other vice, it is the complete anti-God state of mind."

Lewis was a professed atheist during his early adult life but became a devout Christian when the results of his own research, discernment and reflection on just why he was *right* in denying the existence of God, disclosed the absurdity of his denial. His journey back to Christianity was deeply influenced by the writings of G. K. Chesterton and by his personal friendship with J. R. R. Tolkien. While Lewis was Anglican by faith tradition, nearly all of his observations on issues of morality are fully consistent with Catholic moral theology. I have often mused that had he lived a few more years, he might have made his way to Rome, in much the same way his fellow countryman John Henry Cardinal Newman had done about a century earlier.

Lewis' intellectual prowess as a professor and writer at Oxford University was legendary. Most of his very finest writings are deeply religious, deeply moralistic. Some titles that might be familiar: *The Screwtape Letters* (likely my most favorite), *The Four Loves*, *The Great Divorce*, *The Tales of Narnia* (the series), *The Problem of Pain*, and my second most favorite, *Mere Christianity*.

Mere Christianity is a remarkable literary work. Like both of my previous books, which never started out to be books, Lewis never intended *Mere Christianity* be one either. (By the way, that single comparison is the only valid one between my work and his!) Let me explain. During the darkest hours of World War II, when Hitler's Luftwaffe relentlessly rained bombs on England, the Director of Religious Broadcasting for the BBC invited C. S. Lewis to deliver a series of radio broadcasts he hoped would raise the morale of the country. Lewis attempted to instill a genuine sense of hope for Britain during times when all seemed hopeless by explaining to his listeners how their faith in God could be applied to living through the horrors and challenges of the war. The talks were so popular a grass-roots demand quickly bubbled up for the transcripts to be published. As early as 1942 some of his talks began showing up in print. A decade later, however, the entire collection was compiled and published under the title, *Mere Christianity*. While the language of mid-twentieth century England can be a bit stodgy for many, Lewis' messages are profound. One chapter of *Mere Christianity* entitled, "The Greatest Sin," is frequently used as a reference to explain the folly of pridefulness.

In, *Live Humbly, Serve Graciously,* I dedicated a great deal of time exploring pride and its antidote, humility, so you might logically expect me to have a decent grasp of this topic. But recently I reread, *Mere Christianity,* and rediscovered some brutal truths about pride that pointed to additional, deep chinks in my own spiritual armor that continue to be significant moral challenges for me. I was reminded of the remarkable beauty of humility, and the power it has over pride – I seem to need to be reminded periodically as I inch my way along on my own spiritual journey. Why is pride such a problem? It is a problem because it creates a barrier to so many virtues such as mercy. Mercy is about serving others unconditionally. Serving unconditionally requires humility (the opposite of pridefulness). Humility requires unconditional love, which is others-centered. Pride by definition is self-centered. The foundation of all meaningful service and all genuine love, mercy and compassion is being others-centered. So, if all you can concentrate on is the image looking back at you from the mirror, there is no real foundation for turning your love toward others.

Pride, frankly, leads to every other vice. If that seems an overstatement or gross exaggeration, think it over. Lewis observed the more pride one has, the more he/she dislikes pride in others. Quoting Lewis:

> "How much do I dislike it when other people snub me, or refuse to take any notice of me, or shove their oar in, or patronize me, or show off. The point is that each person's pride is in competition with everyone else's pride. It is because I wanted to be the big noise at the party that I am so annoyed at someone else being the big noise. Two of a trade never agree. Now what you want to get clear is that pride is essentially competitive – is competitive by its very nature – while the other vices are competitive only, so to speak, by accident. Pride gets no pleasure out of having something, only out of having more of it than the next man. If everyone else became equally rich, or clever, or good-looking there would be nothing to be proud about. It is only the comparison that makes you proud: the pleasure of being above the rest. Once the element of competition has gone, pride is gone."

By way of confession, I must tell you, I am a proud man – I am proud of being smarter and better looking than you. My counsel is wiser and advice more useful than yours. I am more talented than you and a better writer and storyteller. While I am at it, I am also holier than you, more devout in my faith – and without doubt, humbler than you! And…in case you are wondering, I am very, very proud of my humility. Clearly, these claims are made for effect with my tongue deeply imbedded into my cheek. But in truth, these kinds of claims are not really rare. In fact, they are far too present in our society today, often hidden in flowery language.

So why would people behave in ways that substantiate such claims – either consciously or unconsciously. The reality is, the desire for *power* is what pride really relishes. If you doubt this assertion, I would simply ask you to reflect on the behavior, for example, of so many already in the political arena and those currently seeking office. What makes a politician go on and on, demanding more and more power? It is pride. We have all heard the now famous quote by Lord Acton from the late 19th century, "Power tends to corrupt and absolute power corrupts absolutely." Well, it is true – spiritually and otherwise. Very simply, pride is the unhealthy pursuit of power.

Lewis remarked that because pride is competitive by its very nature, it tends to feed on itself. "If I am a proud man, then, as long as there is one man in the whole world more powerful, or richer, or cleverer than I, he is my rival and my enemy." Interestingly, pride always means enmity, not only between two humans, but enmity between us and God, Himself.

Lewis brilliantly observed, "In God you come up against something which is in every respect immeasurably superior to yourself. Unless you know God as that – and, therefore, know yourself as nothing in comparison – you do not know God at all. As long as you are proud you cannot know God. A proud man is always looking down on things and people: and, of course, as long as you are looking down, you cannot see something that is above you."

In thinking about Lewis' assertion, it occurred to me that when I pray, "In the Name of the Father, the Son, and the Holy Spirit. Amen," I am making a simple but profound statement about the relationship among the Trinity; but I am also declaring my desire to be in that relationship as well. So, by extension, how can I claim to belong to the Lord, if I am solely focused on myself?

Mark 10:35-45 (a commentary very similar to this one appears in Matthew 20:20-28) is useful in furthering our understanding:

James and John, the sons of Zebedee, came to Jesus and said to him, "Teacher, we want you to do for us whatever we ask of you." He replied, "What do you wish me to do for you?" They answered him, "Grant that in your glory we may sit one at your right and the other at your left." Jesus said to them, "You do not know what you are asking. Can you drink the cup that I drink or be baptized with the baptism with which I am baptized?" They said to him, "We can." Jesus said to them, "The cup that I drink, you will drink, and with the baptism with which I am baptized, you will be baptized; but to sit at my right or at my left is not mine to give but is for those for whom it has been prepared." When the ten heard this, they became indignant at James and John. Jesus summoned them and said to them, "You know that those who are recognized as rulers over the Gentiles lord it over them, and their great ones make their authority over them felt. But it shall not be so among you. Rather, whoever wishes to be great among you will be your servant; whoever wishes to be first among you will be the slave of all. For the Son of Man did not come to be served but to serve and to give his life as a ransom for many.

Can you imagine what the other ten felt when they found out James and John were trying to get themselves elevated to the most prominent positions in His Kingdom? They must have been both angry and disappointed. And can you just imagine what James and John must have felt when Jesus responded to their question,

"whoever wishes to be great among you will be your servant; whoever wishes to be first among you will be the slave of all. For the Son of Man did not come to be served but to serve and to give his life as a ransom for many."

Remarkable. The Son of Man came to serve, not be served. We, too, were anointed to serve in Jesus' image and likeness, through our baptism. Our role was cast when the celebrant made the sign of the cross on our forehead with holy oil and anointed us priest, prophet and king. We are thus equipped to follow Jesus' lead as servant. Are we serving the way God planned for us, or are we choosing to do our own will?

Lewis aptly observed,

"Whenever we find that our religious life is making us feel that we are good – above all, that we are better than someone else – I think we may be sure that we are being acted on, not by God, but by the devil. The real test of being in the presence of God is, that you either forget about yourself altogether or see yourself as a small, dirty object. It is better to forget about yourself altogether."

There is an insidious, frankly seldom recognized aspect of pride to which most of us are oblivious, specifically, that pride often smuggles itself into the very center of our spiritual lives. So prideful people are not just those who live in the secular world, but also those of us who are active in the Church. While painful, we should not be surprised. The lust for power over others stirs even religious leaders and dedicated servants of the Church to prideful behavior. One warning from the Old Testament, Proverbs 16:18, is clear:

"Pride goes before disaster, and a haughty spirit before a fall."

There are actually more than 50 passages in Holy Scripture warning against what St. Paul refers to as *vainglory pride*. The message seems pretty simple.

But that the devil would attack us in our spirituality means that we must remain constantly aware of such temptations in all aspects of our life, particularly in those areas that might represent our greatest talents. Dorothy Sayer (1949), in her book, *Creed or Chaos?*, commented that of the seven deadly sins, pride is the only one that Satan acts on us in our strength, all the other six deadly sins he attacks us on our weaknesses.

The wickedness of pride shows up almost everywhere we look. I frequently see it in myself. As much as I like to think I am working to erase pridefulness in my thinking and behavior, every time I honestly look, I must admit I see it – again and again. But let's be clear about one thing, as much as it might be nice to think that humility, the cure for pride, is a destination, it is not – it is a journey. In fact, if you think you have become a truly humble person, look again, it is your pridefulness that makes you believe so! Funny how *old dirty face* even uses our progress in areas of spiritual growth to set us up for the true spiritual cancer of pride. While that sounds pretty harsh, keep in mind pride eats up the possibility of unconditional love, contentment or even common sense. Pride is self-centered and blocks inclinations for being merciful to others in their misery.

The *I am better than you* flavor of political discourse; of social media exchanges; of the dog-eat-dog clawing many experience to advance in their careers; of the insistence that it is *my way or the highway* attitude in leaders; and many other expressions of my superiority over you all point to the reality that the devil has his hooks deeply imbedded into us, our society, and, yes, our church as well.

Please understand that being delighted for being praised or recognized for an accomplishment is not the vainglory kind of pride I have been speaking about. Nor is that warm feeling that comes from seeing your child, grandchild or great grandchild succeed beyond your expectations. And, pride in your alma mater, your parish or community for its accomplishments is not either, unless in expressing that pleasure, we take on an air of superiority that intends to put others down. The warm feelings that my wife and I feel when we watch our grandchildren do well in sports or academics is also not a sinful form of pride – that is, unless those feelings stimulate words and actions that intend to raise ourselves up by putting others down.

The final paragraph of Lewis' chapter on "The Great Sin," he observes the following:

> "If anyone would like to acquire humility, I can, I think, tell him the first step. The first step is to realize that one is proud. And a biggish step, too. At least, nothing whatever can be done before it. If you think you are not conceited, it means you are very conceited indeed."

Matthew Kelly, for much of his public ministry, has talked and written a great deal about "Being the Best Version of Yourself." He's even copyrighted the phrase. But in recent years, while he still encourages us to become the best version of ourselves, he has come to recognize that some very well-intentioned, hardworking people find such a challenge to be overwhelming. In his relatively new and very popular book, *Perfectly Yourself* (2017), Matthew talks about becoming a better version of yourself, with the implication that if we constantly strive to be better, we will actually move toward being the best version of ourselves. The best version, after all is about the journey, not an achievable destination. When we strive to become a better version of ourselves, God is fully aware of our effort and our journey. He is also acutely aware of our journey toward humility. We only become the best version of ourselves with God's help. And . . . We grow in humility only with God's help.

Humility is about being close to the earth. The root word for humility is humus, that is, being close to the earth. We act humbly when we lift others up and show them the dignity that God intends us to show them. Let me be clear, lifting another up is not the same as lowering ourselves so that, relatively speaking, they are higher than we. Recall what Jesus said in Luke 12:37:

> *Blessed are those servants whom the master finds vigilant on his arrival. Amen, I say to you, he will gird himself, have them recline at table, and proceed to wait on them.*

The master (Jesus) humbled himself and lovingly lifted the servants up, showing them levels of dignity not normally accorded servants in His time and culture. He demonstrated, by role-modeling for them, what they, too, must do. Our journey toward humility is not achieved by lifting ourselves up, or by telling others how humble we are. We move forward, with God's help, when we lift others up – and that is done most effectively by showing them unconditional love, mercy and compassion.

So, what are some examples of prideful behavior from today's world? Could there be more obvious battles for power than what we see in our political system? Whether at the local, state or federal level, the rhetoric between and among candidates is vitriolic. Seldom, if ever, do we see campaigns stick entirely to the high road. Instead, what we usually see is a constant barrage of personality attacks (the *I am better than you*, as just one example) with the intent of one candidate or party doing their best to destroy the other's character, reputation, etc. Recent hearings for confirming Supreme Court Justices were ugly examples of just how bad it can get.

In industry, we see corporate entities working to destroy their competition and senior executives clawing their way past colleagues in search for the power at the top. But it is not just big wigs that do such stuff, there is plenty of that same sort of power grabbing in the lower ranks as well.

In academia we see unsavory rivalries between and among professors and non-teaching researchers, in pursuit of the power that comes from winning the big, prestigious research project or academic chair.

Having spent nearly four decades in government, I must say the same nonsense goes on there as well. In all honesty, I have been guilty of such search for power as I advanced in my own career. Would love to relive those times, hopefully getting it right the second time around.

Sadly, such behavior happens in our families as well, and when it does, the very fabric of our lives is torn, the result impacting all of society.

And it should be no surprise that in our own beloved Catholic Church (and in other faith traditions, as well), even some of our church leaders fall prey to the evil one's temptations. Surely, the lust for power is the true root of the deadly sin of pride. Lest we forget, it was pride, the yearning for power, that drove Lucifer to declare, "I will not serve."

I'd like to take a stab at explaining what all of this means. We were each created for a truly unique purpose. By deduction, there is some service we must fulfill that no one else can. Such service, inspired by the Holy Spirit, leads to decent, charitable, useful and meaningful outcomes. Some of those outcomes might be noteworthy on a large scale, but most are meaningful on a smaller scale – but they are meaningful outcomes just the same. Inspired merciful service must have as its foundation a humble spirit, a genuine sense of doing for others simply because of their inherent dignity. We put ourselves into the appropriate state of heart when we continually struggle to become better versions of ourselves, in search of becoming the best version of ourselves.

My engineering mentality seems to be fed by mental images, diagrams or pictures, if you like, to explain what I am thinking. Such an image for what I have just described could be visualized by a simple small building. The roof represents the service that God created uniquely for each of us. That roof structure must be supported by the body of the building which is humility. And the foundation that supports the building, represents the beautiful, unconditional love that Jesus perfectly modeled for us. What about mercy? I see mercy as the shingles on the roof – but not asphalt shingles with a twenty- or thirty-year guarantee. Mercy, instead, is more like slate shingles that are constantly exposed to the elements yet remain competent for millennia!

Let's regroup for a moment and tie all of this together. Pride, according to many theologians, is the greatest sin, but even if not the greatest, it is still one of the seven deadly sins. The only treatment for pride is humility. Our baptism requires that we serve others, and in so doing fulfill our exclusive role as a servant, becoming an integral part of God's intricate and mysterious plan for the universe. We cannot serve unless we humble ourselves in that service. But in order to be humble we must love, and we must love unconditionally. That beautiful *agape* form of love is others-centered rather than self-centered. The lust for power, however, is self-centered. If we are focused on power, we are focused on ourselves. If we are centered on ourselves, we will be unable to love unconditionally. If we are unable to love unconditionally, we will be unable to develop a humble spirit, and if we are short on humility, our service will lack the necessary ingredients for meaningful participation in God's plan for us. Therefore, when we lack a loving spirit toward others, we will focus instead on ourselves and all the power we can muster. In extreme cases of self-centeredness, we see others as a distraction or as an object to use. Even God Himself becomes less and less our focus. Taken to its logical conclusion, our focus on self and power will eventually destroy us spiritually and severely restrict our ability to show mercy to those in need.

St. Paul provided a beautiful roadmap in his letter to the Ephesians 4:1-6, that if we follow it, will prepare us to reach out to those in need with mercy, while protecting ourselves from the moral decay that would otherwise lead us to sinful pride.

I, then, a prisoner for the Lord, urge you to live in a manner worthy of the call you have received, with all humility and gentleness, with patience, bearing with one another through love, striving to preserve the unity of the spirit through the bond of peace; one Body and one Spirit, as you were also called to the one hope of your call; one Lord, one faith, one baptism; one God and Father of all, who is over all and through all and in all.

As a way of putting an exclamation point on this reflection, I'd like to share a story that Dr. Scott Hahn often tells during talks he gives around the country. It seems he traveled back to Pittsburg to visit a friend who was in the hospital with little time left to live. Hahn had lived in Pittsburg some years before and while he knew his way around, he did not really have sufficient detail in his memory to find Mercy Hospital. After driving around for more than twenty minutes, he finally succumbed to do what men have an aversion to doing – he stopped and asked for directions! The response he got turned out to be not only great directions to get to the hospital, it was also a remarkably strong lesson for life. The stranger told Hahn to continue down the street they were on to the next intersection, then turn right off of *Pride* and he would quickly find *Mercy*. A great lesson for us all!

Reflection

XV

Stewardship – The Essence of Mercy

"I tell you truly, this poor widow put in more than all the rest."
(Luke 21:3)

THE VERY FAMILIAR story found in Luke 21:1-4, offers remarkable insight for guiding our personal stewardship, our merciful reaching out to others:

> When Jesus looked up he saw some wealthy people putting their offerings into the treasury and he noticed a poor widow putting in two small coins. He said, "I tell you truly, this poor widow put in more than all the rest; for those others have all made offerings from their surplus wealth, but she, from her poverty, has offered her whole livelihood.

The primary lesson to learn from this passage is about *how* we should give, not about *how much* to give. Are we giving generously, or is our giving essentially skimming some cream off the top? Do we give from our excess or from our poverty? The essence of our choice gets to the heart of extending mercy to others. Even though our stewardship goes well beyond any financial sacrifices we might make, this simple message from St. Luke's Gospel serves as a wonderful framework for reflecting on the whole of our stewardship, our dedication to reaching out to others in love, mercy and generosity.

Throughout His ministry on earth, Jesus spoke frequently about what we need to do in order to share in His kingdom. For example, in His Sermon on the Mount (Matthew 5:10), Jesus tells us:

Blessed are they who are persecuted for righteousness, for theirs is the Kingdom of Heaven.

If there is a kingdom, there must be a *King*. Jesus, Christ the King, clearly was neither talking about an earthly kingdom or earthly king, nor are the words of earthly kingship prayed over us at our Baptism. The kingdom spoken of here is principally about our stewardship, our spirituality, our living the Gospel, using all the gifts we have been given to love others and to show them mercy by serving their legitimate needs. In short, to live the kingship of Jesus, we must imitate, to the best of our ability, the whole of the life He modeled for us. Only by imitating Him do we truly model for others the gift of mercy He extends to us. Only by imitating Him do we truly live our baptismal responsibility of royal kingship.

One of the most beloved passages in the New Testament is Paul's first letter to the Corinthians Chapter 13, where he described what love is, and what it is not. In the preface to that letter, 1 Corinthians 12:1, 7-11, St. Paul tells us:

Now in regard to spiritual gifts, brothers, I do not want you to be unaware. To each individual the manifestation of the Spirit is given for some benefit. To one is given through the Spirit the expression of wisdom; to another the expression of knowledge according to the same Spirit; to another faith by the same Spirit; to another gifts of healing by the one Spirit; to another mighty deeds; to another prophecy; to another discernment of spirits; to another varieties of tongues; to another interpretation of tongues. But one and the same Spirit produces all of these, distributing them individually to each person as he wishes.

With regard to our God-given gifts, Newman was spot-on when he taught that we are each created to do God some definite service that no one else was created to perform. When we choose not to live our mission, not to accept the opportunities we are afforded to reach out to others mercifully, those situations are lost for all time. Knowing that, we need to be open to the urgings of the Holy Spirit at all times and be willing to act on them.

The Church normally asks us to reflect on our personal stewardship during the fall of the year (leading up to Advent), but the reality is that now, not tomorrow, not next week or next month is the perfect time to reflect on the goodness of His glory, the greatness of His mercy and generosity, and what our response should be to Him in all things. God has blessed every one of us with unique gifts He expects us to use in serving others. The question we must each frequently ask ourselves is, "Am I doing what He asks of me and am I doing it graciously and with charitable intent?"

To be sure, charity goes well beyond financial giving and sacrifice. In fact, almsgiving includes the full testament of our Catholic Christian stewardship and is the personal expression of our spirituality, the generous use of our time, talent and treasure. The Corporal and Spiritual Works of Mercy are accurate road maps that speak directly to our stewardship and how we are to carry it out. A point missed by many is that charitable acts are merciful acts, and merciful acts are always charitable.

Although using our financial treasure for good is probably the most visible and frequently talked about form of almsgiving, throughout the New Testament we read about people who needed food, shelter and clothing. We also are told of the many who were crippled, blind and otherwise unable to care for themselves, sitting and begging, often outside the doors of the synagogue waiting for the generosity of others. These are not just stories of the needy in Jesus' time and before, these same needs exist today. Even today, in wealthy countries like ours, such needs are not fully met by the government; but fortunately, there are numerous organizations that dedicate much time and money to help mitigate those needs. One such organization is the St. Vincent de Paul Society. At our parish, the Vincentians collect financial donations monthly and many parishioners contribute regularly via electronic giving. Even within our parish, most do not have a real clear understanding of the impact their generosity (small or large) has on the less fortunate in the surrounding community. The impact of the help received by SVDP clients, frankly, is often quite transformational. So, if you do not currently donate regularly to St. Vincent de Paul, or a similar organization (like Catholic Charities), consider doing so soon. If you would rather your contributions be used for food, maybe you would prefer donating a $25 or $50 food card each month from a local grocery. But if you are simply wanting to help others, regardless of their need, a monthly cash contribution could help with rent, utilities, etc., based on caseworker evaluation. Even when the St. Vincent Council at our parish is short on funds to help with critical necessities, they are always willing to provide food to those in need, in the form of food cards or from our food pantry – fully consistent with Catholic social teaching. If a man is hungry, give him a fish, then teach him to fish, so he can provide for himself and his family.

Visiting the sick or imprisoned; volunteering to drive someone to a doctor's appointment or to church; participating in a Habitat for Humanity build; volunteering with a wide range of other charitable organizations dedicated to helping others; or spending quality time, particularly spiritual time with our children, or grandchildren, or godchildren are just a few examples of ways we can give of our time. Extra time in prayer, particularly on behalf of others, is another wonderful way to give of ourselves. Even participating in parish instructional programs and social events are expressions of our stewardship, hence our mercy, because as Christians we are known through community.

"Glorifying God through our deeds" means a willingness to use the best talents God has given us to help others. But, the intent of our doing is critical. Am I looking for some sort of compensation, or is my service – to family, neighbor, parish, community or someone in need – my free gift to them? Our talents are freely given gifts; hopefully, our use of those gifts is equally generous.

Many wonderful stories of almsgiving, and the freedom that results from generous giving, are recorded in Holy Scripture. One such story is that of the Samaritan woman at the well whom Jesus engaged in conversation while He asked her for a drink. He then offered her *living water* so that she would never thirst again. His gift profoundly changed her life. Another is the story of Jesus giving sight to a man who had been blind from birth. Giving him sight was remarkable, but Jesus did more than just restore his physical sight, He also gave him the ability to see Jesus as the Christ, the savior of all mankind. Many came to believe as they witnessed the events of that day.

Not surprising, many of us feel overwhelmed by what God is asking us to do. If true of you, take a slow, deep breath. Exhale. Now think about the Blessed Virgin Mary and the way she surrendered herself to God's call. What a remarkable challenge, to give up everything to become the new Arc of the Covenant. What about St. Joseph's leap of faith? On several occasions, he took life altering steps based on dreams. Think, too, about the apostles and the day of Pentecost. They must have been overwhelmed knowing they were being equipped in that moment to execute *The Great Commission*. So, if you are overwhelmed, you are in good company. You might want to do what Mary and Joseph and the apostles did – ask for divine help to give you the confidence you need to do what you have been led to do. The Holy Spirit loves when we turn to Him and is more than happy to give us all we need to fulfill our calling.

So, what does all this have to do with stewardship? Well, very simply, stewardship is all about the way we respond to God's call in our lives, as uniquely defined by our spirituality, and is reflected in how we practice the works of mercy and live the Beatitudes. Stewardship is the way we fulfill our baptismal obligations as priest, prophet and king.

How do I share the gifts God has given me? How do I use my time each day? How do I give my financial resources to support the Church and those in need? All such tough questions require thought before answering. And in case the thought might have crossed your mind – there is no age limit on our responsibility to be generous stewards of the gifts we have been given. So we must give generously, then give again.

In the opening words of their pastoral letter on Stewardship in 2013, the U.S. Catholic Bishops said, "Once one chooses to become a disciple of Jesus Christ, stewardship is not an option." The bishops further instruct, "As Christian stewards, we (must) receive God's gifts gratefully, cultivate them responsibly, share them lovingly in justice with others, and return them with increase to the Lord."

At our parish, when the topic of stewardship is discussed, the three T's mentioned are time, talent and treasure. Many (or most) people hear only *treasure* and immediately roll their eyes and think, "Oh great, here comes the request for money." Interestingly, though, few of us make the connection between stewardship and mercy. If that sounds like you, consider that stewardship is simply the offering of our entire selves to God. We have the choice to live self-centered lives, or Christ-centered lives. Choosing to live Christ-centered lives is choosing to be *others-centered*. Knowing that God gives us all of our time, talent and treasure, does it not seem logical we should return to Him the first fruits of these gifts? After all, God gave us His first fruits, His Son!

One measure of giving is a term that causes many Catholics to shudder – *tithing*. Tithing is referred to specifically in Leviticus 27:30 and 2 Corinthians 9:7. Both the narrative in Mark 12:41-44, and the one found in Luke 21:1-4 quoted earlier, speak directly to what it means to give sacrificially, the essence of tithing:

> *"Amen, I say to you, this poor widow put in more than all the other contributors to the treasury. For they have all contributed from their surplus wealth, but she, from her poverty, has contributed all she had, her whole livelihood."*

Are we called to abandon all of our earthly possessions like St. Francis of Assisi did? Not necessarily. Are we asked to live in the desert and survive on locusts and honey as John the Baptist did? No. But, we are asked to extend mercy to others. We are called to give of ourselves as the widow did, to give from our livelihood which is in the form of our time, our talent and our treasure. In Matthew 25:31-46, Jesus is quite clear about how we are to treat the least of our brothers – and how we will be judged if we do not. As you recall, Jesus talked about reaching out to the homeless, hungry, thirsty, imprisoned, naked and the stranger – the needy of His time.

> *When the Son of Man comes in his glory, and all the angels with him, he will sit upon his glorious throne, and all the nations will be assembled before him. And he will separate them one from another, as a shepherd separates the sheep from the goats. He will place the sheep on his right and the goats on his left. Then the king will say to those on his right, 'Come, you who are blessed by my Father. Inherit the kingdom prepared for you from the foundation of the*

world. For I was hungry and you gave me food, I was thirsty and you gave me drink, a stranger and you welcomed me, naked and you clothed me, ill and you cared for me, in prison and you visited me.' Then the righteous will answer him and say, 'Lord, when did we see you hungry and feed you, or thirsty and give you drink? When did we see you a stranger and welcome you, or naked and clothe you? When did we see you ill or in prison, and visit you?' And the king will say to them in reply, 'Amen, I say to you, whatever you did for one of these least brothers of mine, you did for me.' Then he will say to those on his left, 'Depart from me, you accursed, into the eternal fire prepared for the devil and his angels. For I was hungry and you gave me no food, I was thirsty and you gave me no drink, a stranger and you gave me no welcome, naked and you gave me no clothing, ill and in prison, and you did not care for me.' Then they will answer and say, 'Lord, when did we see you hungry or thirsty or a stranger or naked or ill or in prison, and not minister to your needs?' He will answer them, 'Amen, I say to you, what you did not do for one of these least ones, you did not do for me.' And these will go off to eternal punishment, but the righteous to eternal life.

Today, to this list of His children in need, Jesus would surely add the shooting victim, the bullied, the addicted, the sexually abused, the isolated, the undocumented, the doubting, the confused, the victims of human trafficking, the mentally ill. While our ability to do much directly for many of these modern-day needy might be limited (and for legitimate reasons), there are always (small) things we can do in service to others in our local community. Such kindnesses could be as simple as providing a small gift at Christmas for someone who would not otherwise get one; helping someone get to church that might not have transportation; sharing a kind word with a stranger; spending a few extra minutes praying for a sick friend; or giving a few more dollars to a charitable organization that directly helps those in need. Regardless, do something! Agape, charity, tithing is about giving up, giving to, and giving of one's heart. It is a priceless expression of mercy. It is a priceless labor of love.

In Luke 6:38 Jesus tells us:

Give and gifts will be given to you; a good measure, packed together, shaken down, and overflowing, will be poured into your lap. For the measure with which you measure will in return be measured out to you.

While tithing is most often associated with financial giving, it also applies to the generous giving of our time and talent. When tithing our time, just like with tithing our financial resources, we are asked to give 10 percent to God. Ten percent of 24 hours is two hours and 24 minutes – a day! Sounds like a lot, doesn't it? For those who believe tithing of our income means 10 percent after taxes, they would likely say something like, "but I sleep eight hours a day, so shouldn't I get a break and only have to give one hour and 36 minutes to God?" I am not going to wade into that debate. However, regardless of whether we give two hours and 24 minutes or one hour and 36 minutes per day, it is still a lot of time. There are many ways we can give our time in service and dedication to the Lord – including praying, reading or studying Scripture, meditating, or visiting the sick, helping a neighbor or volunteering our time to a ministry that helps the poor. For many, particularly parents of young children, finding blocks of time for prayer, scripture reading, etc., can, frankly, be a real challenge. But that being said, the opening Mass prayer (Collect) for the 20th Sunday in Ordinary time should offer us some consolation:

O God, who have prepared for those who love you good things which no eye can see, fill our hearts, we pray, with the warmth of your love, so that, *loving you in all things and above all things*, we may attain your promises, which surpass every human desire. Through our Lord Jesus Christ, your Son, who lives and reigns with you in the unity of the Holy Spirit, one God, for ever and ever.

Loving you in all things and above all things . . . We might each want to do an inventory and assess where we are. If you are short on the time you give God like I am, try to start adding small manageable increments of service beyond what you currently give.

What about tithing our talent? Giving what constitutes a tenth of our talent is not as easy to quantify as with time and money – but that's okay. Actually, tithing our talent simply means willingness to offer the very best talents we have, to share our first fruits. Doing so might include joining the choir and sharing the voice God gave you. Maybe it is time to consider stepping up to the plate and use your spirituality, insight and education to teach CCD (or Sunday school or a bible-study class.) Maybe your ability to listen compassionately could be put to good purpose as a volunteer St. Vincent DePaul caseworker. There are lots of opportunities to give of your first fruits.

In Luke 12:48 Our Lord lovingly advises us:

Much will be required of the person entrusted with much, and still more will be demanded of the person entrusted with more.

Tithing serves two fundamental purposes. First it supports the Church, but second, and frankly more importantly, a tithe is a symbolic gesture of the reality that all we have in this world really belongs to God. To show the way, God the Father gave us His first fruit, to die on the cross for us. We imitate the Father's love for us by giving to Him the best we have to offer.

Stewardship, in all of its forms, has the power to shape and mold our understanding of our lives and the way we live them in relation with others. Giving is important, but even generous giving without noble intent is very much like the candy coating from an M&M peanut, without the peanut and chocolate, it is an empty shell. If I shower my wife with physical gifts, but do not love her, my gestures are empty. If she loves the gifts more than she loves me, her actions are equally empty. Giving God our skill and wealth without giving of our self is meaningless.

Tithing our treasure, without giving God our talent, and perhaps more valuable, our time, is empty, just like a father who gives his children *stuff*, but never spends time with them. Time is one of those gifts that we never seem to have enough of, yet when we give it away in service to others, even if only for fellowship and building quality relationships, we always seem to have enough of it. The importance of giving our time generously can be highlighted by borrowing a thought from a homily I heard a couple of years ago – consider that *time* was the very first of God's creations. Genesis 1:1 is very clear, "*In the beginning…*" Before God decided to create the heavens and the earth, He created time for us!

As reinforcement, we are advised in James 2:26:

> *For just as a body without a spirit is dead, so also faith without works is dead.*

In his book, *Life's Greatest Lesson – What I've Learned from the Happiest People I Know,* Allen Hunt (2013) narrates a semi-fictional autobiography about his own growing up and the marvelous things he learned primarily from his grandparents and parents. My favorite character in the story is his grandmother, whom he named, *Lavish Grace.* Throughout the story, Hunt tells of the remarkable love, struggles and generosity of Lavish as she lived out her seemingly ordinary life. She wore a bracelet much like the ones popular in recent years – WWJD – What Would Jesus Do? But his grandmother's bracelet had the letters L E G and S. While he remained curious about the bracelet and often asked questions, she seemed determined to tell him the meaning of the four letters over time, as he matured and was able to understand the concepts behind each. Without retelling the whole story, I will simply tell you that *LEGS* had nothing to do with the lower body parts that move us around. Rather, *L* stood for the simple message to *Love* as much as you can; *E* was to remind ourselves to *Earn* as much as you can; *G* was an admonition to *Give* as much as you can; and, the *S* was a bit of a circular challenge to *Save* as much as you can, with the unwritten message that the savings would then be given away or used to fuel a long-term legacy for future giving. Hunt's fictional grandparents lived their entire lives based on that acronym and did so mostly by flying under the radar of those around them. In the story, as he matured, Allen adopted the *LEGS* way of living, but let it lapse during his college years. Sound familiar? As he prepared to marry, though, his fiancée somehow sensed the spirit of Lavish, and so the couple began their lives together, doing as his grandparents had done before them. In short, their philosophy of generosity was to live and give, rather than to be seen and highlighted by others.

At times, we find it much too easy to ignore spiritual realities, denying that religion plays a fundamental role in shaping human and social values. We rationalize our relationship with God as a very private matter, so practicing our religion is private. But such logic is flawed. While our relationship with God is private, the practice of our religion, living out our stewardship, is anything but private. How we practice our faith tradition is a very important and visible sign of who and what we are. As Catholics, we live in the mainstream of American society and experience many of its advantages; but we also live in a secular society that bombards us with temptations and adversely influences what we think, say and do. Accepting the challenge of Christian stewardship, rather than giving in to the temptations of self-centeredness and greed, can be quite overwhelming; so, we must make extraordinary efforts to understand the true meaning of stewardship and live accordingly. Each member of the Church has her or his own special God-given role to play. Once we choose to become a disciple of Jesus Christ, stewardship is no longer an option and neither is living the works of mercy.

So, how will I answer His call? How might I focus or refocus my energies to love and shower mercy on those in need? How will I accept the challenges issued by our current and two former Popes to "always step outside myself?" Answers to these and other similar questions will guide how we respond to the mission of mercy God has created uniquely for each of us.

Reflection

XVI

No Room for Benchwarmers in Practicing Mercy

What good is it, my brothers, if someone says he has faith
but does not have works? Can that faith save him?

(James 2:14)

STAGECOACHES WERE ONE of the first forms of mass transportation in the United States. Tickets could be purchased by class, much like airline tickets are today. First-class, second-class, or third-class tickets were available for your journey. Needless to say, provisions and conditions were different for each class. With a first-class ticket, you got a seat on the stagecoach, and if the stage broke down, you got to remain in your seat, regardless. If your ticket was second class, you got a seat, but if the coach broke down, you would be asked to get out and simply stand aside while repairs were made or physical obstacles (such as water, mud or downed trees) were handled. But, if you could only afford a third-class seat, when difficulties occurred, even as a passenger, you were required to exit the coach and help the driver and shotgun rider to get it back in motion, even if it meant helping lift the carriage, push it out of mud, remove a downed tree, repair broken wheels, axles, etc. – whatever it took. It sounds pretty hard, doesn't it? Here is our reality as Catholic Christians – we are not given the opportunity to buy first- or second-class tickets for our journey through this life to eternity. The only tickets available are third class. We don't have the opportunity to be on the sidelines. Sitting on the bench is not an option.

Newman (1848), spoke of this very same thing at the conclusion of his, *Meditations on Christian Doctrine, Hope in God – Creator, The Mission of My Life:*

> If I am in sickness, my sickness may serve Him, in perplexity, my perplexity may serve Him; if I am in sorrow, my sorrow may serve Him. My sickness, or perplexity, or sorrow may be necessary causes of some great end, which is quite beyond us. He does nothing in vain; He may prolong my life; He may shorten it; He knows what He is about. He may take away my friends, He may throw me among strangers, He may make me feel desolate, make my spirits sink, hide the future from me – still He knows what He is about.

The bottom line meaning in all of this, to me, is we must remain actively engaged in our vocations as Catholic Christians, no matter what. Our involvement must be about loving and serving others, or said a different way, we must devotedly extend mercy to everyone we encounter. As third-class ticket holders, we must be *part of the solution.* Beginning with our Baptism, our life's purpose must be to serve others, helping to bring them to Christ by what we think, in all we feel, in all we say, in all we do – to live the mission God has created uniquely for us. We cannot delegate this responsibility. Oh, and by the way, the reflections presented here were not written by someone who is an expert; quite the opposite, they were written by someone who struggles with all of these challenges every day, likely more than you. Showing mercy to others by serving them is hard work.

In James 2:14-17, we are told:

> *What good is it, my brothers, if someone says he has faith but does not have works? Can that faith save him? If a brother or sister has nothing to wear and has no food for the day, and one of you says to them, "Go in peace, keep warm, and eat well," but you do no give them the necessities of the body, what good is it? So also faith of itself, if it does not have works, is dead.*

The issue of living our faith by what we do is addressed in the *Catechism of the Catholic Church*, paragraph 1969:

> *The New Law practices the acts of religion: almsgiving, prayer and fasting, directing them to the 'Father who sees in secret,' in contrast with the desire to 'be seen by men.'*

During the *Year of Faith* (November 2012 to October 2013), Pope Benedict XVI called for the entire universal Church to renew and grow in the knowledge of their faith so all could fully participate in the very same new evangelization in which St. John Paul II challenged us to be involved. No matter if we are young, old, large or small, we have the responsibility to get ourselves to heaven. But each of us also has the obligation to help get others to heaven (to evangelize). If you are husband or wife, parent or grandparent, you have the responsibility to teach those coming along behind you and help your spouse and children get to heaven. Even though the use of the word evangelization makes many Catholics shudder, none of this is really new – Jesus actually challenged each of us to evangelize while He was on earth two thousand years ago. Matthew 28:16-20 is often referred to as *The Great Commission*:

> *The eleven disciples went to Galilee, to the mountain to which Jesus had ordered them. When they saw him, they worshiped, but they doubted. Then Jesus approached and said to them, "All power in heaven and on earth has been given to me. Go, therefore, and make disciples of all nations, baptizing them in the name of the Father, and of the Son, and of the Holy Spirit, teaching them to observe all that I have commanded you. And behold, I am with you always, until the end of the age."*

Pope Francis's 2013 Apostolic Exhortation entitled *Evangelii Gaudium* (*The Joy of the Gospel*) deals extensively with the importance of preaching the gospel. He uses very clear language directed to the clergy about their responsibility for preparing and preaching quality homilies, and all of that is as it should be, and frankly, what I expected he would teach. However, Pope Francis is quite clear about the massive responsibilities the laity has for spreading the gospel: constantly being in missionary mode and being ever vigilant for opportunities to evangelize. St. Francis is attributed with saying we have the responsibility of preaching the gospel always and, when necessary, use words. One way we preach the Gospel is by being merciful to all we encounter in our journey through life.

The Pope's message closely parallels St. Francis's call to action. Specifically, referring to *The Great Commission*, Francis says:

> In virtue of their baptism, all members of the People of God have become missionary disciples. All the baptized, whatever their position in the Church or their level of instruction in the faith, are agents of evangelization . . . The new evangelization calls for personal involvement on the part of each of the baptized . . . Every Christian is a missionary to the extent that he or she has encountered the love of God in Christ Jesus.

Pope Francis lovingly reminds us that even in John 4:

> "The Samaritan woman became a missionary immediately after speaking with Jesus and many Samaritans came to believe in him 'because of the woman's testimony.'"

At the very real (and significant) risk that you might angrily close this book right now, and not read another word; I am compelled to tell you that all of what you have read so far in this reflection is a *preamble*, hopefully, providing appropriate background for the message of mercy which is the point of this reflection. If you choose to continue, be aware, there is more background, so please be patient.

A couple of years ago, my wife and I vacationed in Alaska with two dear friends. I could bore you with a *what we did on our summer vacation* story, but I won't. I would, however, like to share a small piece of our journey, that, from start to finish, actually took place in under two minutes, yet left an indelible mark on my memory and on my heart. But before I get down to the details of those couple of minutes, I still need to provide a bit more context.

Due to a reservations error that was completely my fault and no one else's, we had to return our rented motorhome to the rental outfit a full day early. The reservation I made required us to return the motorhome on Saturday morning, yet our flight home was not until early Sunday night, the next day. So . . . What to do?

We were able to get two rooms in a bed and breakfast for our last night in Anchorage. While that took care of where to sleep, we still had issues related to our luggage and ground transportation. Fortunately, our B&B host allowed us to drop our stuff off before we actually checked in and before returning the motorhome. A rental car was going to be very expensive for the day and half we needed it, so instead we chose to use cabs, shuttles, buses, etc. to get around the last day and a half. Ride-share services had not yet made it to Anchorage.

After a pleasant day in downtown Anchorage, we had the joy of going to the Saturday afternoon vigil mass at the Cathedral of the Holy Family, one of several churches in the Diocese of Anchorage with doors that had been designated as *Holy Doors* for the *Extraordinary Year of Mercy*. The Mass was beautiful, music lovely, congregation welcoming, and after mass we had the honor and privilege of receiving a personal blessing from a newly ordained priest, freshly assigned as parochial vicar at the Cathedral.

On Sunday morning after breakfast at the B&B, we took a cab to the airport and did a very early check-in of our baggage for the trip home. Fortunately, the easiest and cheapest way to get from the airport to downtown Anchorage was by bus. After dropping our bags, we bummed around downtown, had lunch, then late Sunday afternoon, went back to the airport for our flight home.

So . . . you are probably wondering by now, "I thought he was not going to do a *what we did on our summer vacation* story." Well, you would be justified in making that statement, but all the background I have provided is necessary to frame the REAL STORY.

During the back and forth between the airport and downtown, I was taught a most wonderful lesson in evangelization as I witnessed a simple yet beautiful act of mercy, one that I neither expected, nor one I will soon forget. No doubt, you are puzzled. Here is what happened.

As we were leaving the airport at 11:00 AM to go downtown, we had purchased day-pass bus tickets and were seated on the bus. Across the aisle from me was a mid-40ish-aged woman who was likely native Alaskan. As we waited for the bus to leave, a young man, probably in his mid-20s got on the bus. The driver told him the cost of the fare, about day passes, and that exact change was necessary. But no matter how hard he tried, the young man was totally unable to understand what the driver was saying about fares, etc. Other passengers tried to assist, but all of them failed as well. The language barrier was a real issue. The woman sitting across from me, seeing the dilemma, and getting a bit nervous about the delayed departure, got up out of her seat, opened her purse, walked to the front of the bus and paid the young man's fare. With no fanfare whatsoever, she returned to her seat, sat down, and we headed to downtown. I sat there, frankly quite paralyzed as I watched the woman generously get involved in helping a perfect stranger in trouble. It was clear to me she had absolutely no expectation that she would be recognized or repaid for her kindness – those things did not matter to her.

I leaned over and said to her, "What a wonderful act of love." She replied, with a bit of an accent, "I was worried we would be delayed, and I can't be late for Mass." Quickly putting the pieces together, I asked her if she was headed to noon mass at the Cathedral, and she assured me she was.

As it turned out, with very broken English spoken by the last passenger on the bus, and other passengers doing their best to talk with him participating in a sometimes-humorous charades-type of conversation, we discovered the young man had just arrived from Prague, did not know a great deal of English, that all he had with him was in a stuffed backpack and the only cash he had was in $20 bills, fresh from the ATM. All he knew at the time was he needed to get to downtown. His smile at the Good Samaritan lady near me spoke volumes of gratitude. Such a small act, such a small amount of money ($3, I think), but what a quick and unreserved call to action, what a small but transformational work of mercy. As much as I thought I knew about evangelization; as much as I know about the need to reach out and help others in need; as awkward as the moment was before our fellow passenger sprang into action; I sat there, hands folded on my lap, unable to quickly process the events of the moment, unable to do anything, frankly, but watch – then admire the beauty of a fellow member of the body of Christ unselfishly inserting herself into that young Czech man's life. I learned a remarkably beautiful, remarkably simple, remarkably loving lesson in living my faith, or should I say I learned a real lesson in practical evangelization through a very simple corporal work of mercy (not one of the normal list of seven).

This might seem like the logical end to the story, but it is not. After spending the rest of Sunday afternoon downtown, we climbed back on the bus to return to the airport for our trip home and rather mindlessly took our seats. Just as I was about to sit down beside my wife, I unconsciously looked at the person sitting in the row behind us – and yep, much to my surprise, there was the Good-Samaritan-teacher-lady from the morning bus ride, the one who had taught me such a beautiful lesson by her actions! I smiled and asked her if she had gotten to church on time, and, with a warm smile on her face, she told me she had gotten there a few minutes before Mass started. Then, looking straight into her eyes, I said, "Thank you for the beautiful lesson in evangelization you taught me this morning!" Her answer actually caught me by surprise, although it should not have (please note, I do not claim to be the sharpest knife in the drawer). With the loveliest of expressions on her face, she responded, "To Him give all the glory." Not only did she teach me a lesson in charity on the morning bus ride, she taught me a second lesson on the afternoon trip – this time a lesson in genuine humility – she wanted to take no credit at all – To HIM give all the glory.

Has any of what I have shared with you so far seemed like a big deal? Probably not. Did that small act of kindness, in the big scheme of things, really matter? Again, not too likely. Was the woman's kindness lessened by her nervousness about being late for mass? Maybe, but the clock showed there was nearly an hour before mass time and only about a 20-minute bus ride. So . . . what's the big deal? Well, for me-the-paralyzed-bystander, the really big deal was the Good Samaritan's unhesitating willingness to help a perfect stranger, preaching the Gospel loudly – without fanfare – and without words, then giving the credit to the Lord – that was the BIG DEAL. With two, almost incidental encounters with her within just a few hours, she demonstrated two of the most important characteristics of a devoted follower of Christ – love and humility. What quickly came to mind there in that bus was the advice given by St. Teresa of Calcutta – we should not worry about doing "big" things, but doing "lots of little things" with great love.

Having watched, and hopefully, learned a giant lesson from that simple act of mercy, done with such unconditional love, I would simply hope if I ever find myself in a similar situation again, I would have the presence of mind, the courage, and generosity to do what was demonstrated for me that Sunday morning.

What a beautiful realization and demonstration of what it means to live our lives with aggressive humility – the passionate, unconditional loving service of others. Such actions are the real backbone of living the Spiritual and Corporal Works of Mercy. What a compassionate demonstration of solidarity (helping one another because we are *all in this together*) and subsidiarity (aiding others in the right measure – not too little and not too much).

Pope Francis told 1.6 million young people gathered in Krakow, Poland, in July, 2016, for World Youth Day, that they are not called to be couch potatoes living boring lives; rather, they should leave their mark in history and not let others determine their future. Like a soccer match, the Pope said, "Life only takes players on the first string and has no room for benchwarmers. Today's world demands that you be a protagonist of history because life is always beautiful when we choose to live it fully, when we choose to leave a mark." The Pope warned the massive gathering not to fall into a "paralysis that comes from confusing happiness with a sofa." The sofa that promises comfort, safety and relaxation, instead is an "insidious form of paralysis" that makes young men and women become "dull and drowsy." The Pope's message to the youth is equally valid to people of all ages. The involvement Pope Francis was urging the young people to engage in is often called evangelization – actively reaching out to others, willingly showing those in need the mercy that we ourselves have each been granted. Living these challenges are enormous responsibilities we share as members of Christ's Mystical Body.

Let me put this reflection into perspective. During the *Extraordinary Jubilee Year of Mercy*, just a few years ago, Pope Francis, and other Church leaders, not only invited, but also challenged each of us to be involved. We were urged to reach out and serve others, particularly those in need, and we were counseled to do so by practicing the Spiritual and Corporal Works of Mercy. What better way to evangelize than practicing these works of mercy on at least a daily basis – loudly preaching the Gospel without using words.

So, I guess I must (at least rhetorically) ask myself, did I learn anything during the recent *Jubilee Year*? I would like to think so. But maybe one of the most important lessons I learned, I learned from a perfect stranger, in the company of mostly perfect strangers. I simply cannot help but smile each time I recall that experience on our last day in Alaska. A beautiful trip, good friends, beautiful scenery, friendly people, and a lovely lesson in sharing the Gospel with others.

Bottom line: there is no room for benchwarmers when it comes to being merciful to all we encounter. Our job is to make history in the lives of others.

Reflection

XVII

Feed the Hungry and Give Drink to the Thirsty

*For I was hungry and you gave me food, I was
thirsty and you gave me drink.*

(Matthew 25:35)

GOD'S DEDICATION TO feeding His people is highlighted throughout all of Judeo-Christian history. For example, roughly two millennia before the birth of Christ, we are told the story (Genesis 18:1-8) of our father in faith, Abraham, and his wife Sarah welcoming three strangers into their home, offering them customary hospitality of water to wash their feet, a meal to fill their empty stomachs and milk to quench their thirst.

The LORD appeared to Abraham by the oak of Mamre, as he sat in the entrance of his tent, while the day was growing hot. Looking up, he saw three men standing near him. When he saw them, he ran from the entrance of the tent to greet them; and bowing to the ground, he said: "Sir, if it please you, do not go on past your servant. Let some water be brought, that you may bathe your feet, and then rest under the tree. Now that you have come to your servant, let me bring you a little food, that you may refresh yourselves; and afterward you may go on your way." "Very well," they replied, "do as you have said."

Abraham hurried into the tent to Sarah and said, "Quick, three measures of bran flour! Knead it and make bread." He ran to the herd, picked out a tender, choice calf, and gave it to a servant, who

169

quickly prepared it. Then he got some curds and milk, as well as the calf that had been prepared, and set these before them, waiting on them under the tree while they ate.

Providing for the physical needs of others is simply the right thing to do, and we have known this for thousands of years. Today is no different.

Six hundred or so years later, the Israelites were in the midst of their exodus from Egypt. In one of the most iconic stories in the Old Testament we are told of their harrowing escape from Pharaoh; the parting of the Red Sea and their miraculous crossing of it on the sea floor; and the 40-year long journey across the desert on their way home to the Promised Land. During that epic ordeal, God's chosen people began to complain bitterly to Moses and Aaron about their *wretched food*. The Lord heard their pleas and for nearly 40 years lovingly, graciously and mercifully provided bread and meat to nourish them (Exodus 16:13-15):

"In the evening, quail came up and covered the camp. In the morning there was a layer of dew all about the camp, and when the layer of dew evaporated, fine flakes were on the surface of the wilderness, fine flakes like hoarfrost on the ground. On seeing it, the Israelites asked one another, "What is this?" for they did not know what it was. But Moses told them, "It is the bread which the LORD has given you to eat."

More than a millennium later, according to the Gospels, Jesus fed two large crowds who were following him. The narrative of His feeding a crowd of five thousand is recorded in all four Gospels. In a similar story recorded in the Gospels of Mark and Matthew, Jesus fed four thousand. These may be the same story, but maybe not; regardless, Jesus modeled substantial graciousness and mercy by feeding the hungry during his public ministry. Matthew 14:15-21 is a very familiar narrative:

When it was evening, the disciples approached him and said, "This is a deserted place and it is already late; dismiss the crowds so that they can go to the villages and buy food for themselves." [Jesus] said to them, "There is no need for them to go away; give them some food yourselves." But they said to him, "Five loaves and two fish are all we have here." Then he said, "Bring them here to me," and he ordered the crowds to sit down on the grass. Taking the five loaves and the two fish, and looking up to heaven, he said the blessing, broke the loaves, and gave them to the disciples, who in turn gave them to the crowds. They all ate and were satisfied, and they picked up the fragments left over —twelve wicker baskets full. Those who ate were about five thousand men, not counting women and children.

Providing food for the hungry and drink to the thirsty are two of the easiest and most obvious acts of mercy we can show to the vulnerable around us. Very simply, food and water are necessary to sustain our physical existence, so having adequate amounts of both (and, of course, clean air to breath) are essential to maintain our health and vitality. Pope Francis (2018) commented that, "Hunger and thirst are intense experiences, since they involve basic needs and our instinct for survival." While each of us from time to time gets hungry and thirsty, the majority of people in our country have never been debilitatingly hungry like those who are truly starving, and never truly been thirsty like those who do not have safe, clean water to drink. While these two statements are mostly true, in the United States there are far too many people, especially children, who either go to bed hungry, or if they have enough to eat, do not have adequate nutrition. Sadly, according to *Feeding America*, a nonprofit funded by a *Who's Who* of Fortune 500 partners and foundations, "In the U.S., hunger is caused by the prevalence of poverty, not food scarcity. Stable food access is often blocked for low-income families that struggle to balance the need for food with other basic necessities. [Interestingly] we have enough food to feed every man, woman and child, yet 72 billion pounds of safe, edible food goes to waste each year. In fact, an estimated 25 – 40 percent of food grown, processed and transported in the U.S. will never be consumed. And more food reaches landfills and incinerators than any other single material in municipal solid waste. [The] long-term effects of hunger and poor nutrition can be devastating. That's why it's not enough to just provide families with food. They need a healthy variety of foods, such as fresh fruits and vegetables, whole grains, low-fat dairy and lean protein." (*Feeding America*, 2016)

Even though we live in the world's wealthiest country, remarkably more than ten percent of our people are undernourished, and tragically, roughly thirty percent of those undernourished are children. As sad as this situation is, when looking at hunger in other parts of the world, the need is substantially greater there, in staggering proportions. Pope Francis, in his Apostolic Exhortation, *Laudato Si* (2015), pleaded with the Church to take seriously the need to mitigate the hunger suffered by so many, in so many parts of the world and to provide potable water to areas that have shortages.

The Pope frequently begs passionately for the needs of the poor – in his homilies, in his public audiences, in his Apostolic Exhortations (such as, *Laudato Si*), and in documents sent to world and Church leaders. For example, in a letter to the Food and Agricultural Organization of the United Nations, for *World Food Day 2019*, Pope Francis emphasized:

"The battle against hunger and malnutrition will not end as long as the logic of the market prevails and profit is sought at any cost, with the result that food is relegated to a mere commercial product subject to financial speculation and with little regard for its cultural, social and indeed symbolic importance. Our first concern should always be the human person: men, women and children, especially those who lack daily food and have a limited ability to manage family and social relationships (see *Laudato Si*, paragraphs 112-113). When priority is given to the human person, humanitarian aid operations and development programs will surely have a greater impact and will yield the expected results."

While hunger seems to exist no matter where we look in our communities, those needs are actively being addressed by many individuals, organizations and programs. Throughout our country, governmental programs, like the federally funded and locally administered Supplemental Nutrition Assistance Program (SNAP) (formerly, the Food Stamp Program), provide financial assistance for food to nearly forty million low-, or no-income people. Many recipients of these benefits also receive federally funded support through free, or reduced cost, breakfast and lunch programs through schools. Yet in spite of the government-backed programs, hunger is not fully abated. To bridge the unfilled gap, many community and church-operated food banks provide much needed assistance. Grass-roots programs that help feed the elderly and homeless, such as *Meals on Wheels* and community and church-sponsored soup kitchens, food pantries and night shelters, help fill real needs, and organizations such as St. Vincent DePaul Society and Catholic Charities also serve many clients in need. Volunteering to assist with feeding the poor can be done in many ways, including getting involved with the generous organizations mentioned here and others. Regular, monthly contributions to your favorite group is a positive, disciplined way to tithe part of your financial resources.

Helping feed the poor is not just for adults. Parents should encourage their children to get involved as well, because the lessons they can learn from giving of themselves are valuable life experiences and lessons. Most schools require students to do *service hours,* and many parishes require children preparing for Confirmation to do the same. Helping feed the hungry is one of the most noble ways of doing such service. Parents would be well-advised to use each such experience as a valuable teaching moment for their children. Parents modeling merciful, loving, generous hearts to their kids is a great way to show them what Jesus did for us during His public ministry.

There are many creative ways to address hunger around us. For example, one way some people choose to help people they encounter who are hungry is to actually take the person(s) to a nearby restaurant, and let them order what they want, have the wait-staff know they are paying and they will cover the cost of what the person(s) orders. Is this a big deal? Not really, because it does not really cost very much; however, for the hungry person(s), it is a really big deal. We prefer to ensure that the person asking for food is really getting the food they need.

Encouraging local grocery stores to donate their excess or outdated food to local food banks is remarkably useful, particularly in light of the enormous amount of food that is landfilled or incinerated. That edible food is the single largest commodity deposited in municipal landfills is an outrageous tragedy.

Donating food and water for storm or other disaster relief efforts fills an often-critical need for those affected. My sister and her family have been recipients of such donations on several occasions in the aftermath of Gulf Coast hurricanes, such as Katrina. Natural tragedies such as tornados, hurricanes and floods bring out the best in people. Tons of food are donated by various churches, civic groups and community food- and water-collection drives. Likewise, man-made tragedies, such as the disaster of 9/11, call into action the love, charity and compassion of many who simply want to do something to help those in need. Without question, feeding the hungry, however it is done, is a vital work of mercy.

Jesus used a *drink of water* as a teaching moment many times. Two such times are:

"And whoever gives only a cup of cold water to one of these little ones to drink because he is a disciple—amen, I say to you, he will surely not lose his reward." (Matthew 10:42)

And,

A woman of Samaria came to draw water. Jesus said to her, "Give me a drink." (John 4:7)

Giving drink to the thirsty takes on a bit different character than feeding the hungry. In most parts of our country, getting a drink requires only a short walk to the nearest water faucet. While this statement is not completely accurate, few parts of our country are without safe drinking water. Having said that, the distribution of water across the landscape is not even, and the cycle of shortage and excess can be problematic. Having spent a significant portion of my adult life working in the field of water resources, I would be remiss if I did not make a strong appeal for responsible water conservation and mindful respect for water quality. While we have adequate supplies of water in our country, safe drinking water is not free, and it is not limitless, so each of us has an obligation to use water responsibly. Many people simply are not aware how much water they waste. Simply keeping plumbing maintained, turning off water while brushing your teeth, being prudent in length of showers and similar sensible conservation awareness saves significant water. Granted water that simply runs down the drain is not lost, but treating and purifying water requires energy, so wasting the water wastes energy, which in turn creates other environmental domino-effects. The point here is that common-sense awareness of what we do with water and how we do it can make a huge difference.

Potable water is not a *given* in many parts of the world. Many underdeveloped countries are plagued with inadequate safe drinking water. Because human health is dependent on safe drinking water, many NGO's (Non-Governmental Organizations) have been established to help develop methods for purifying water and providing long-term safe supplies for communities without potable water. Clever, innovative and inexpensive means for installing simple water supply wells have been developed over the past few decades, but more work still needs to be done. Generosity to such organizations is, in a very real way, an act of mercy toward those who benefit.

In conclusion, much could be suggested for other ways to provide food for the hungry and drink for those who are thirsty. These two critical human needs are at the heart of our physical health and vitality. I would like to add a couple of more thoughts as a way of emphasizing the need to make these two Corporal Works of Mercy part of our consciousness and daily life. Throughout His public ministry, Jesus mercifully fed the large crowds that followed Him. In the time between Jesus' resurrection and His Ascension, He appeared to the apostles while they were unsuccessfully fishing a hundred yards from the shore. At His instruction, the apostles cast their nets to the other side of the boat and they were filled to point of bursting. They dragged the full nets to the shore, where Jesus had prepared a charcoal fire to cook the fish for their breakfast. Feeding them in their hunger was in the forefront of His thinking. During breakfast, Jesus asked Peter, three times, if he loved Him. Each time, Peter affirmed he did, but he was hurt by the repetition of the question. To two of Peter's three, "you know I love you," responses, Jesus replied, "Feed my lambs," and once, "Feed my sheep." I believe Jesus' frequent and consistent message of feeding cannot be ignored. Being fed (or eating) is fundamental to maintain our physical life. But the most important event in all of history illuminating the need for feeding the hungry and giving drink to the thirsty, was Jesus' institution of the Eucharist. At the Last Supper, Jesus took bread, blessed it, broke it and gave it to the apostles and instructed them to take and eat. Similarly, He took wine, blessed it and gave it to them, instructing them to take and drink. Take and eat, take and drink. "This is my body," "This is my blood." Symbolic? Absolutely not. While the physical essence of the bread and wine clearly satisfy our physical hunger and thirst, the consecrated bread and wine, transformed into His sacred body and blood, are life-giving nourishment to our souls. When we follow Jesus' example by feeding the hungry and giving drink to the thirsty, we are showing mercy to our brother(s) and sister(s) in a real, tangible way. These works of mercy, truly, are holiness in action.

Reflection

XVIII

Clothe the Naked and Shelter the Homeless

*Amen, I say to you, whatever you did for one of
these least brothers of mine, you did for me.*

(*Matthew 25:40*)

MOST OF YOU reading this book very likely have never been wanting for clothes to cover yourself or needed a roof to provide adequate shelter. I certainly have not – I have been greatly blessed. While you may have not been happy about the clothes you wore, the reason(s) had more to do with not liking your mother's choices for you, or because your family simply did not have sufficient disposable income to afford the labels you thought you wanted to wear, so you could fit in with those around you. Hand-me-downs might not have fit quite right, and the knees might have been a tad worn. Styles, too, might have changed a bit since your older sibling or cousin wore them. But being dressed in truly ragged clothes was only a reality you observed, not lived. Similarly, you likely never wore the same clothes day-after-day, week-after-week, month-after-month, to the point that you began to realize people avoided you or gave you wide berth because you smelled so bad. Sadly, those so poor that they have no change of clothes also have no simple way to bathe or deal with the most basic of personal hygiene needs. So much is taken for granted by most of us.

The poor who either do not have shelter, or their shelter is grossly inadequate, are often the same poor souls who need clothes on their backs and food in their stomachs. Most large cities in the United States have homeless populations that range into the tens of thousands, and granted, some choose to live their lives that way, but most are the victims of tragic circumstances, some of their own making, but most often not. Yes, there are homeless shelters for those who have no place to lay their heads, but most shelters operate only at night, even during the harsh winter. During cold weather, especially, there is not enough space to accommodate all of those who need a place to sleep.

In the poor countries of Central and South America, parts of Africa and in many areas of the Middle East, conditions are even worse. I have had the blessing of participating in three mission trips to Comayagua, Honduras, and can attest to the tragic levels of poverty and suffering there. So many of God's children would actually be naked were it not for the clothes donated by generous benefactors in other parts of the world – go anywhere and you see adults and children alike wearing t-shirts from across the globe! Homes there are very rickety, often made of scavenged materials that rarely provide adequate protection from the weather. Floors are bare dirt, and furniture to sleep on, sit on, or eat from simply does not exist. Running water and sanitation are mostly nonexistent. Refugee camps, particularly in many parts of the Middle East, are severely overcrowded, and often lack basic facilities. Yet people in dire straits, through the grace of God, find ways to survive.

While the number of those who need clothes and shelter today is staggering, such needs are not new. Throughout recorded history, the human family has suffered shortages of these basics while some looked on and did nothing. Some simply ignored the realities in their midst, while others opened their hearts and gave. During Jesus' public ministry, He constantly held up the poor and treated them with dignity and respect. He repeatedly pled with those who had much to share with those who had little or nothing. He frequently taught about the mercy and compassion we should shower on those in need. Pope Francis also makes similar and frequent pleas for the poor of the world. He stressed the many, many needs of the poor in his apostolic exhortation, *Amoris Laetitia (2016),* highlighting the need for pastoral care of families.

In our country, there are virtually none who are literally naked, but there are many who are inadequately clothed, particularly during cold weather. Many do not have warm coats, gloves, shoes, boots, scarfs or hats to keep themselves warm, nor do they have the resources to buy them. We are cautioned in James 2:1-6 we must not judge others by their appearance or what they have on their backs:

> *My brothers, show no partiality as you adhere to the faith in our glorious Lord Jesus Christ. For if a man with gold rings on his fingers and in fine clothes comes into your assembly, and a poor person in shabby clothes also comes in, and you pay attention to the one wearing the fine clothes and say, "Sit here, please," while you say to the poor one, "Stand there," or "Sit at my feet," have you not made distinctions among yourselves and become judges with evil designs? Listen, my beloved brothers. Did not God choose those who are poor in the world to be rich in faith and heirs of the kingdom that he promised to those who love him? But you dishonored the poor person.*

While in Scripture we are told that we must clothe the naked and shelter the homeless, there are important modern-day society complications, particularly with housing. These complications should not be used as a way of ignoring the problem; rather, they should be used as a way to scope out what and how aid can be provided to those who really need the help. Let's face it, many of the poor, even many of the *working poor*, in our country cannot afford a decent place to live that is dry, warm and, maybe most important of all, safe. In spite of Section 8 housing, municipal public-housing projects and other forms of local low- or controlled-rent housing options, many still cannot afford the cost, do not qualify for whatever reason, are on lengthy waiting lists, or somehow, they simply fall through the cracks. Regardless the reason, they have no safe place to live. Most people would be surprised to know that even many of our courageous veterans, when they muster out of the military after returning home, having sacrificed much during war-zone deployments, tragically end up living in their cars, often with a spouse and children.

So much poverty, so many people, so many needs – what can we do? Fortunately, there are many well-organized groups that collect *slightly used* clothes and distribute them to people in need. Some collect clothes and sell them at thrift stores with the proceeds used to assist the poor. In our part of the world, in the December – January timeframe, a ministry at our parish collects coats and blankets to assist the many in our community who need to stay warm. Having helped to collect those donations, I am always amazed to see how generous people can be. From our relatively small parish, there are usually a couple of vans full of warm clothes and blankets given each year. Keep in mind even the smallest donations of clothes, shoes, coats, etc. for the needy is a beautiful way of practicing mercy.

Several years ago, my wife and I, both retired, made a household rule that when an article of new clothing came into our house, a similar article from the closet or drawer must be given away. Is this a big deal? Clearly not. Yet every time we choose to buy something, someone else benefits in a small way. Maybe we all should do a closet- and chest-of-drawers-purge of things we have not worn for a year or two! When there are so many people in need, does it make sense to continue holding on to clothes we no longer use? How about you? Are there things in your closet that would help others? Is there a coat, blanket or sweater you no longer need? Someone else clearly does, and finding a charity to donate to is not difficult. Remarkable how liberating such giving can be.

Sheltering the homeless in today's society is a multifaceted problem, and maybe it has been throughout history. But safety and security, unfortunately, are real issues, particularly when considering providing shelter to someone in-need, in our homes. Maybe thinking creatively is in order. In Luke 10:29-37, we read the beloved account of the Good Samaritan. While the Samaritan did not take the beaten man to his own home, he did bind the man's wounds, put him on his donkey and take him to a nearby inn, paid the innkeeper to house and take care of him and offered to reimburse for additional expenses. While we might not be able to do the exact same thing, there may be opportunities to do similar caring for someone in need.

Two organizations that my wife and I are involved with (St. Vincent DePaul and Catholic Charities) offer assistance to those in need of shelter on a temporary basis. Sometimes that help is in the form of paying for a week or two in an extended stay hotel. Other times the assistance is in the form of augmenting or paying their rent during financial crises. Occasionally, the assistance is for single individuals, but most of the time families (single- and two-parent) are the ones struggling to make ends meet. So often, the need results from a working parent getting sick, not being able to work, not having health insurance and not being paid for the missed time. When funds are tight and the choice is food or rent, rent ends up on the short end of the stick. Eating, obviously, must always take priority over paying rent!

Maybe offering to house the friend-of-friend in need of a place to stay overnight as they are passing through town would lighten their financial load. One of my favorite Gospel passages is actually read twice within a short period of time in the two weeks following Easter. Saint Luke (24:13-35) provides the moving account often referred to as, "The Appearance on the Road to Emmaus."

Now that very day two of them were going to a village seven miles from Jerusalem called Emmaus, and they were conversing about all the things that had occurred. And it happened that while they were conversing and debating, Jesus himself drew near and walked with them, but their eyes were prevented from recognizing him. He asked them, "What are you discussing as you walk along?" They stopped, looking downcast. One of them, named Cleopas, said to him in reply, "Are you the only visitor to Jerusalem who does not know of the things that have taken place there in these days?" And he replied to them, "What sort of things?" They said to him, "The things that happened to Jesus the Nazarene, who was a prophet mighty in deed and word before God and all the people, how our chief priests and rulers both handed him over to a sentence of death and crucified him. But we were hoping that he would be the one to redeem Israel; and besides all this, it is now the third day since this took place. Some women from our group, however, have astounded us: they were at the tomb early in the morning and did not find his body; they came back and reported that they had indeed seen a vision of angels who announced that he was alive. Then some of those with us went to the tomb and found things just as the women had described, but him they did not see." And he said to them, "Oh, how foolish you are! How slow of heart to believe all that the prophets spoke! Was it not necessary that the Messiah should suffer these things and enter into his glory?" Then beginning with Moses and all the prophets, he interpreted to them what referred to him in all the scriptures. As they approached the village to which they were going, he gave the impression that he was going on farther. But they urged him, "Stay with us, for it is nearly evening and the day is almost over." So he went in to stay with them. And it happened that, while he was with them at table, he took bread, said the blessing, broke it, and gave it to them. With that their eyes were opened and they recognized him, but he vanished from their sight. Then they said to each other, "Were not our hearts burning [within us] while he spoke to us on the way and opened the scriptures to us?" So they set out at once and returned to Jerusalem where they found gathered together the eleven and those with them who were saying, "The Lord has truly been raised and has appeared to Simon!" Then the two recounted what had taken place on the way and how he was made known to them in the breaking of the bread.

In a genuine gesture of love and friendship, Cleophas and his companion asked Jesus to stay with them overnight because it was getting late, and He needed a place to sleep. Clearly at that moment, the two did not know they were offering the Risen Christ a place to lay His head. Only after He agreed to stay with them did they recognize, in the *breaking of the bread,* the supreme honor they had received. They offered kindness to a stranger, and in turn were blessed to have their Savior as their guest. Even though Jesus did not actually spend the night with them, the important point to me is that He, a stranger, was invited. So, maybe one way we could imitate the hospitality of Cleopas and his companion in this story is to offer to have someone visiting our town or parish spend the night at our home. We have actually had the opportunity of hosting several such visitors, who at the time we offered them shelter, were strangers to us. Each of them was a genuine blessing to us. One was a highly educated gentleman who, through a series of unfortunate circumstances, found himself in a strange town, with no job, almost no money, and no place to live. He stayed with us for several months, ate at our table, and enlightened us with his native culture and customs and good nature. During the time he was with us, he got back on his feet financially, and maybe more importantly, regained his emotional strength. The second was a priest visiting our church to deliver a parish mission. The week he spent with us can only legitimately be described as a treasured gift. Daily conversations about a myriad of topics left my wife and me enriched in ways we are still discovering many years later, including the seeds he planted in our hearts about the beauty of "praying the Psalms," the Liturgy of the Hours. Took several years before those seeds germinated, but they finally did. One major lesson we learned from opening our home to both of these guests is this – in giving we received (Sirach 35:13)!

For He is a God who always repays
and will give back to you sevenfold.

Practicing the works of mercy truly does return God's favor.

Almost 50 years ago, Linda and Millard Fuller founded a non-governmental, nonprofit organization, *Habitat for Humanity*, to bring people together to build homes, communities and hope. Homes are built using volunteer labor and Habitat makes no profit on the sales. Thus far, Habitat has helped more than 29 million people in all 50 states and seventy countries construct, rehabilitate or preserve homes. As of 2013, Habitat was the largest not-for-profit builder in the world. In the aftermath of 9/11, the *Tunnels To Towers Foundation* was established to honor Steven Siller, a New York firefighter who lost his life rescuing many trapped in the World Trade Center. The goal of this organization is to provide mortgage-free homes for the families of first responders and veterans disabled or killed in the line of duty to country and community. More than a thousand such families have been aided thus far. With a similar purpose, about 15 years ago another group calling themselves *A Soldier's Journey Home*, comprised mostly of current and retired firefighters and retired veterans began working on a variety of disaster relief construction projects. Their focus has now morphed to ignite communities to come together to build homes specially adapted for the needs of severely disabled veterans who have suffered much in defending us. Volunteers from the local community, working alongside the first responders and retired veterans from more than a dozen states, typically complete their builds in two weeks or less, sometimes in cooperation with the *Tunnels*

To Towers Foundation. Many of the volunteers give up their vacation time to participate. Donating to, or even better, participating in a build with one of these groups is a beautiful way of extending mercy to families in need.

I would be remiss if I did not mention the importance of being open to housing members of our family or extended family when needs present themselves. Yes, there can be complications, and yes, doing so is not always convenient. Yet the notion of *agape* starting at home seems to be a critically important principle to consider. Clearly issues of codependency and tough love must be taken into account, but whenever the good of the person needing shelter is best served by opening our home to them, we should try to make it happen.

There are many ways *clothing the naked* and *sheltering the homeless* can be practiced and clearly only a few have been mentioned here. But, the important part of both works of mercy is maintaining an open and generous heart for the poor and those in need, sharing as much as we are able with them. While their needs are typically year-round, warm clothes, blankets and shelter are absolutely critical during cold weather and could easily be the difference between life and death. Such simple ways to make life-altering differences in someone's life.

James 2:12-13 clearly advises:

So speak and so act as people who will be judged by the law of freedom. For the judgement is merciless to one who has not shown mercy; mercy triumphs over judgement.

Reflection

XIX

Extending Mercy to the Sick, Incarcerated and the Deceased

'When did we see you ill or in prison, and visit you?' And the
king will say to them in reply, 'Amen, I say to you, whatever you
did for one of these least brothers of mine, you did for me.'

(Matthew 25:39-40)

SOMETIMES WE NEED to do things, that frankly, may not be in our comfort zone. For many, the idea of going to visit a friend or loved one in the hospital or any other type of health-care facility is a challenge. At the risk of sounding trite, when people are in the hospital for an extended period, they are there because they are sick, really sick, and seeing someone in that condition is hard for many of us. And if hospital stays are not bad enough, some illnesses, surgeries or other procedures require even longer stays in rehab or skilled nursing facilities. Extended stays can result in loneliness and sometimes even depression for the person confined, so visiting her/him is truly a merciful thing to do. But it takes time to get dressed, drive to the facility, go through the visitor protocols, find the room, etc., all of which might take a couple of hours just for a 10- or 15-minute visit. Then there is the return trip home. From start to finish you might easily be tied up for three hours or more. But keep in mind that while all of this is time consuming, the sacrifice on your part to make that short visit possible almost surely will make your loved one, friend, etc. feel special. Your visit might very well be the single most important thing in their not-so-fun day – and you might be the only person they interreacted with all day that they really know well. Going to visit someone sick at their home, even though logistically simpler, can be just as time consuming.

So, why should we make the effort? We do not need to look too hard in the New Testament to find evidence that visiting the sick was something Jesus frequently did. He cleansed the lepers. Returned sight to the blind. Healed the crippled. Cured a woman who had been hemorrhaging for a long time, and raised many from the dead. He healed Peter's mother-in-law, the boy with epilepsy, the centurion's servant, and restored hearing to the deaf man. While these events did not actually take place in a hospital setting, or even in someone's home, nonetheless, Jesus took time to minister and give comfort and healing to each of these, and more. We also know of at least one woman who was healed by simply reaching out in faith and touching His garment as He passed by. Our visiting the sick is not on par with the many healings Jesus performed; however, the healing our presence can have for those who are unable to be up and out and about, is very real. Healing their spirit with our presence is real healing and should never be underestimated.

There are occasions when a friend or loved one is sick or injured and cannot have visitors. In such situations, a quick call to say hello, or sending them a card to offer a word of encouragement, can be very meaningful. Even when calling is not possible, prayers offered directly for them is always the right thing to do – in fact, prayers should be offered even if you are able to visit or call. From personal experience, I know that praying with or over a sick friend or relative during a hospital visit is a powerful testament of our love for them. And just as Jesus offered mercy to the sick and lame he encountered, we can too.

The Church from her founding has devoted significant energy to caring for the sick. In fact, in 2010, more than a quarter of all health-care facilities in the world were managed by entities of the Catholic Church. While that number might be slightly different today, regardless, the Church has always taken seriously Jesus' instruction to care for the sick. Although visiting is not the same thing as healing the sick, taking the time to visit can be a valuable and powerful part of a person's healing process – and is one in which we can all be involved.

Visiting the sick provides all sorts of opportunities to serve and show kindnesses to those who are sick or recovering. For example, without any fanfare, cutting their grass, shoveling their snow, caring for minor children, cleaning their house or watching their home while they are away are all things we can do in the spirit of visiting the sick. From personal experience, covertly cutting someone's lawn is really quite fun, especially when the person never finds out who did it. Recognition is not the issue; providing kindness and mercy are.

Most hospitals have *auxiliaries* that raise money for them, and those same organizations also provide lots of opportunities for volunteerism. The value of volunteering our time and energy to hospitals and their patients cannot be overstated. Similarly, many neighborhoods and many parish ministries have organized ways of providing meals when someone in the household is sick.

Personally taking care of a loved one or friend after surgery or serious illness is a noble way of extending mercy to someone. Caring for a parent or family member in declining health over an extended period can be even harder, but doing so is a remarkably beautiful and generous way of showering love and mercy on them.

Donating blood, platelets and plasma, even visiting an elderly friend or neighbor, or filling in for a caregiver to give them respite, are all important ways to show mercy to the sick. Regular monthly donations to organizations such as Shriner's Hospital for Children, St. Jude Children's Research Hospital and Wounded Warrior Project are worthwhile efforts dedicated to curing, rehabbing and equipping the very sick and heavily injured or disabled. If for some reason, these are not your favorite charities, find one or two that you can support and share with them each month.

In short, anything we might be able to do to reduce the burden of those who are sick or those who are caring for the sick are merciful acts, and each is in its own way, an imitation of what Jesus would (or did) do.

I have visited someone in jail on only two occasions, but I would have to say, doing so is much more difficult than visiting someone who is sick. Most likely, the really difficult part of visiting someone in jail is the environment. People in hospitals or other health-care facilities are there because they do not have a choice, they are sick. A person in jail, by contrast, is usually there because of a specific choice they made that violated a law or ordinance. Committing time to visiting someone incarcerated also takes time, but the whole institutional experience is different. There is very little smiling, very little small talk, just the facts and only the facts, then wait until you are ushered to a booth. That booth has a window separating you from the person you are visiting; communication is usually via a telephone-type device; and, the visit is terminated the second the timer *dings*. The atmosphere is often cold and impersonal. Having said that, though, the impact of the visit on the incarcerated person is usually very uplifting, and often profound.

While I have no real way to evaluate my next comment, my guess is that a very small percentage of adults have ever visited someone in jail. In fact, I suspect the majority in our society has never even known someone who has been in jail. So, how might we take up the charge to visit the imprisoned?

In many respects, we might need to use a bit of ingenuity and imagination. One way we could show mercy to a person in prison is to reach out to their family and help them. We also have the opportunity, no matter what, to pray for the imprisoned, their family and for a just outcome of their legal issues. Some parishes have prison ministries that work directly with inmates, pray with them and offer them encouragement and hope. Volunteering for such ministries, while frightening for some, is a comfortable opportunity for others to offer the face of Christ to those in trouble.

Another less personal, but still important way we can help the imprisoned is to promote the passage and enforcement of laws that ensure justice to the accused regardless of their skin color, national origin, gender, social preference, etc. The United States' tradition of "innocent until proven guilty" is frankly pretty straightforward and should be a simple way to help defend and support those who have been accused. Unfortunately, with our 24-hour news cycles, cell-phone cameras and videos, and the court of public opinion, our national tradition concerning innocence and guilt has been severely tarnished. As much faith as we might have in our legal/judicial system, it is a human institution so mistakes have been, are and will continue to be made. We must have the courage to stand up and defend our fundamental constitutional rights with regard to law enforcement, even when it is not comfortable to do so. While few of us will ever be in a position to defend someone accused of a crime on the public square, we can and should do so, in private and small group conversations. Until proven guilty by a jury of their peers, the accused is innocent.

What else might we do? How about supporting efforts to ensure humane living conditions in our jails, which should go without saying. As hard as it might be for many of us to do, reaching out to and offering a person who has just been released from jail a job, or simply the hand of friendship, are important. Bottom line is that anything we can do to give comfort and assistance to the person incarcerated or to their family is important merciful work.

Finally, I believe practicing this Corporal Work of Mercy requires at least one other thing of us. As people who believe in the sanctity of life, we must stand up and loudly oppose capital punishment. If we object to abortion at any stage of life from the moment of conception on, and oppose assisted suicide for any reason, by extension, we must support life until natural death in all cases. Capital punishment is not natural death any more than abortion or assisted suicide are!

Burying the dead is an important final tribute to a person's life. Traditions for funerals, burial, etc. vary among different cultures around the world and within cultures, and while they have evolved over time, the essence of respectfully disposing of the body of a loved one or friend (or even a stranger for that matter) is a beautiful way to show the deceased person dignity. As a child of God, each of us deserves to be shown such respect.

For centuries, the traditional mode of burial in western society has been in a casket in a cemetery. Cremation, while available for millennia, was once frowned on by the Church; but over the past few decades, those views have been relaxed somewhat. The Church's primary concern about the disposal of the remains is that it be done in a dignified way, and for Catholics, that includes following a few simple rules. For example, when cremation is chosen, the Church prescribes that the ashes be interred as soon as possible after the funeral or memorial service. Such burials can be in a columbarium or in the ground as done with caskets. Note: The Church does not condone scattering of cremains.

Attending funerals and memorial services is an important way to show our respect for the person who died. Likewise, our presence is also comforting to those left behind and shows them our ongoing love and support of them in their time of grief. For some, another way to show our support is by volunteering to help host a reception following the funeral or memorial service. Doing so is a merciful way to help the family and all those attending the ceremony celebrate the life of the person who died.

Probably the most important aspect of practicing all three of the works of mercy reflected upon here is simply our having a genuine awareness of the physical, emotional and spiritual needs of those who are sick, incarcerated or deceased and their families. And, an important reality to keep in mind is that the need to support those who have lost someone dear is not a single event, it is ongoing.

Unconditional love directed toward those in need is the essence of mercy.

Reflection

XX

Using Our Minds and Hearts to Guide Others

Those with insight shall shine brightly like the splendor of the firmament,
and those who lead the many to justice shall be like the stars forever.

(Daniel 12:3)

I THINK IT IS safe to say that each of us, at some time or another, has had moments of doubt in our faith journey. Similarly, no matter how well we might have been catechized or how highly educated we might be in morality, philosophy and theology, there are occasions when we simply do not have credible, understandable, useful and timely answers to important questions. My point here, is that sometimes, we simply have to go searching for answers. Occasionally, we can find those answers on our own, but often, we may need to tap into the wisdom of others.

Fortunately, we do not exist in a vacuum – we live within a framework of community, we are surrounded by others. In that context, we might naturally reach out to them in our quest for answers. By extension, though, others in our community might reach out to us! Internalizing that reality could be uncomfortable or frightening to many. But God has created each of us with unique talents, intellect, insights and sensibilities, so all of us bring something special to the table. Willingness to share our uniqueness is an important part of what it means to live in community with others. As Christians, we are community.

Many of us, by the very nature of our vocations, jobs, family relationships, friendships, etc., have special instructional and counseling responsibilities – for example, parents, teachers, priests, catechists and counselors. While such roles have obvious connections to both teaching and counseling, others might not be quite so clear. Actually, as baptized Catholic Christians, we all share responsibilities in these tasks; and, as members of the Mystical Body of Christ, we have the obligation to provide both counseling and instruction to others, but equally importantly, we must be sufficiently humble to seek the help of others in our personal spiritual growth journey.

The importance of asking for and providing helpful guidance is clearly outlined in Wisdom 7:13-14:

Sincerely I learned about her, and ungrudgingly do I share – her riches I do not hide away; for she is an unfailing treasure; those who gain this treasure win the friendship of God, being commended by the gifts that come from her discipline.

Underlying the rightful fulfilment of our responsibility to both counsel and teach is the critical need for developing a well-formed conscience. The Catechism of the Catholic Church (#1777) says that a moral conscience:

". . . bears witness to the authority of truth in reference to the supreme Good to which the human person is drawn, and it welcomes the commandments. When he listens to his conscience, the prudent man can hear God speaking."

Having a strong well-formed conscience is not accidental. Developing one requires reading, searching, asking questions, praying and reflecting on the moral and theological teachings of Christ and His Church over a long period. But just knowing whether a thought, word or action is right or wrong is not sufficient; our choices, that is our actions, must reflect our conscious decision to do the right thing. A note of caution – when we have a question about a choice we are about to make, simply saying, "I was never taught that so and so was wrong," is not sufficient defense for doing it. If we have questions, we need to seek out legitimate answers.

One of the lesser-known books of wisdom in the Old Testament is the Book of Sirach (sometimes called the book of Wisdom of Ben Sira, or simply Ben Sira). One passage I find remarkably insightful and rich is Chapter 6:33-37:

> If you are willing to listen, you can learn; if you pay attention, you can be instructed. Stand in the company of the elders; stay close to whoever is wise. Be eager to hear every discourse; let no insightful saying escape you. If you see the intelligent, seek them out; let your feet wear away their doorsteps! Reflect on the law of the Most High, and let his commandments be your constant study. Then he will enlighten your mind, and make you wise as you desire.

Seeking genuine wisdom from credible sources is a never-ending, life-long part of what it means to develop a strong moral conscience. Choosing to do otherwise, arguably could be likened to the half-hearted commitment to the "lukewarm" faith referred to in Revelations 3:16. Our Lord wants all of us to be fully committed to the faith. Another word of caution is worth adding here – If you are approached with a question or situation you do not know the answer to or how to provide real help, you would be well advised to let the person who has approached you know you do not have a definitive answer, but would be willing to help them look for one. Often when people approach us with a question or problem, they are not expecting an immediate reply; rather, they feel the need to engage in a conversation hoping the dialogue with us will provide useful ideas. When you help someone research an answer, not only are they enlightened, you will be as well!

To me, *instructing the ignorant* has an oddly negative tone. The word ignorant has multiple meanings, many of which have off-putting connotations. Some examples include: discourteous or rude; lacking knowledge or awareness in general; uneducated or unsophisticated; lacking knowledge, information, or awareness about a particular thing. But synonyms include uneducated, unknowledgeable, illiterate, unread, uninformed, unscholarly, backward, impolite, ill-mannered, uncivil, crude uneducated, unknowledgeable, etc. Using theses definitions as context, though, I believe this call for mercy actually has only positive connotations: namely, we use our God-given gifts to assist those who do not share the same gifts or level of knowledge or experiences we do. It is an act of pure love when we help others learn the truths they need to know to save their souls. All of us are called to share and teach the faith passed on to us. But this means that we must know our faith and what the Church really teaches. To be sure, the best way to instruct and to teach is by the way we live our lives.

For parents, opportunities for instruction are virtually endless. They are the first and most important teachers of their children, and as such, have life-forming responsibility to instruct their children in the faith. During the Sacrament of Baptism, parents (and Godparents, alike) are specifically reminded of the importance of their influence on the spiritual and moral development of their child. But let's be clear, to be effective teachers of their children, parents themselves must be dedicated to life-long spiritual growth and learning. Sadly, many parents feel they are not adequately equipped to teach their children the truths of the faith, so they avoid doing so. But here is the reality, even if that is true, committing to teach your children is the very best way to learn yourself. Parents must be the role models for learning.

As mother and father of two and grandmother and grandfather of four, my wife and I have lifelong responsibilities for influencing the spiritual development of our children (and their spouses) and grandchildren. Our responsibilities, however, do not end there. We are also aunt and uncle to many, and great aunt and great uncle to still more young family members. Being a positive role model to all of them is never ending. The way we live our lives and the way we communicate with each of them matters a great deal. Not surprising, our responsibilities do not stop with family alone, they actually extend to all we touch. So, if we align ourselves with the teachings of Christ and His Church, we will actively practice both of the works of mercy related to instruction and counseling.

To that end, there are a myriad of ways we can extend mercy to others in the spirit of *instructing the ignorant*. Angelo Stangaro (2018), in an article entitled, *89 Practical Recommendations for the Spiritual Works of Mercy*, published in *The National Catholic Register*, provides a list of practical ways we can live this spiritual work of mercy. Related to *Instruct the Ignorant* he suggests that we:

- Read the Catechism of the Catholic Church. It's not as difficult as you might think, and you might learn something.

- Support organizations that support religious freedoms.

- Actively learn about your Catholic faith and share your understanding with others.

- Don't be shy about evangelizing. As Pope Francis reminds us, either the Faith grows or we need to invest in mothballs.

- Volunteer to assist at a parish retreat.

- Make sure your children and grandchildren are properly catechized. Catholic school tuition might be a burden for some, but the education and spiritual formation it provides is well worth it.

- Read good literature and encourage others to do so also.

- Share your insights, knowledge and spirituality with others.

- Be patient with those who are only beginning to master new skills.

- Go on a service trip or short-term mission trip.

- Support others on their own service/mission trips.

- Invite an unchurched friend or family member to attend Mass with you. Even if they refuse, your invitation will give them something to think about. They will be less likely to turn you down the next time you ask.

This list is clearly not exhaustive; however, it does provide a worthwhile framework for understanding some of the ways we can dedicate ourselves to serving others by instruction. While some might be a bit timid about reaching out to others in the ways listed, Sirach 4:23-24 urges:

Do not refrain from speaking at the proper time, and do not hide your wisdom; for wisdom becomes known through speech, and knowledge through the tongue's response.

Every one of us has had doubts and questions about our faith, including the saints. St. Teresa of Calcutta was plagued with doubts. She often spoke of her *dark nights of the soul*, described originally by St. John of the Cross in his book by that name. Even in the midst of her heroic showering of love and mercy on the poorest of the poor, her heart was troubled with doubts. *Counseling the doubtful* should remind us how very important it is for us to walk closely with others going through transitions, losses and tragedies, holding them up in prayer and companionship.

While some might think this spiritual work advises us to solve other people's problems, such is not the intent. That being said, we might actually solve or resolve their issue as a natural result of helping them. But our real intent ought to be helping them find solutions themselves, in much the same way parents teach their children to solve problems on their own whenever possible, or the way executive coaches help their clients resolve issues. If in helping others we are primarily focused on solving *the problem*, we are actually acting inwardly. When we help others find their solution by guiding them, they become the focus, and they are far more likely to successfully work through the current, and similar problems, in the future on their own. An example of what I am talking about is a parent helping a child (adolescent or adult) find ways to work through a tough moral choice on their own, rather than simply providing them an answer. Most of us remember the solutions we work through on our own and can do it again, even though we might have been guided by someone else the first time or two.

The same *National Catholic Register* article referenced earlier, also suggests a range of useful ways to counsel the doubtful:

- Remind those in doubt that Christ is the Way, the Truth and the Light and that whoever follows Him will never stumble in the darkness (1 John 1:7).
- Volunteer at a suicide prevention hotline.
- Be a mentor for a teenager/young adult through Catholic Big Brothers/Big Sisters.
- Keep sacramentals on hand to give to those in spiritual need.
- Watch out for the signs and symptoms of despair in yourself and others and respond with hope.
- Avoid unloading your negative criticisms or perceptions onto people. The world is full enough of those thoughts already.

- At each example of cynicism, skepticism, doubt and despair which you encounter, offer hope.
- Speak openly of your hopes. Optimism is contagious. You might very well inspire someone.
- It may not be easy to be optimistic all the time but it beats the heck out of the alternative.
- Ask those you encounter about their hopes. Support and encourage them in their pursuit of them.
- Seek out those who have important things to teach and learn from them (Prov. 19:20).

A few additional suggestions:

- Accompany a friend who is struggling with believing to join a parish group for service or faith formation.
- Share a book you have found useful related to the person's faith concern.
- Pray for someone you know who is making a big life decision.
- When asked a question, whenever possible, make sure you mention Jesus and His One, True, Holy, Catholic and Apostolic Church. It's good PR.
- Reach out to a friend/family member who's struggling with his faith to join a prayer group or parish-based program like *Welcome* (formerly Christ Renews His Parish).
- Reach out to those in spiritual need and invite them to Mass. You might just be saving a life.
- Never, ever, ever, ever, ever, ever, ever, ever, ever, ever, ever despair. EVER!

Counseling the doubtful is an act of love because it is helping someone be more certain about what they should do to better love and serve God. Many souls could be saved if Catholics would simply make the effort to lovingly speak the truth to their neighbors.

Admonishing the sinner is possibly one of the most difficult, or if not the most difficult, the most delicate of the works of mercy to actually practice. On the surface, this Spiritual Work of Mercy sounds like a call to minding other people's business; or even more disturbing, minding other people's sinfulness. Father Andrew Apostoli, in an article in *Envoy Magazine* (2008) rightly observes: "To admonish the sinner begins by admonishing one's self. After all, we are all sinners. Humility is the virtue by which we recognize our sinfulness and our weakness, thus, realizing we ourselves depend upon God's mercy to forgive us our sins and upon His grace to strengthen us to resist sin in the future. Without humility, we will not admit our sins honestly to ourselves and, when needed, to others also. Since human weakness is always present due to Original Sin and our own past personal sins, we know that we must struggle each day to resist evil and do good."

One of the most memorable passages from the New Testament providing insight into this work of mercy is from Luke 6:41-42 (a nearly identical account appears in Matthew 7:3-5):

"Why do you notice the splinter in your brother's eye, but do not perceive the wooden beam in your own? How can you say to your brother, 'Brother, let me remove that splinter in your eye,' when you do not even notice the wooden beam in your own eye? You hypocrite! Remove the wooden beam from your eye first; then you will see clearly to remove the splinter in your brother's eye."

So, getting our own house straight is the first order of business.

Admonish usually means to rebuke, reproach or reprimand; but it also means to caution, advise or guide. When this second set of meanings is acted upon with unconditional love and humility, we are on the right path to providing real help to someone who needs guidance. Apostoli points out two other things we must keep in mind. The first is "we must practice what we preach!" The second is avoid the error of the Pharisees, "the terrible attitude of self-righteousness with its judgmental view of others", being "quick to condemn sin in others but overlooked it in themselves…to carry out this work of admonishing the sinner, a person must have a sense of compassion for human weakness, and we can only learn that by recognizing our own weaknesses. If we fail to do so, we will be throwing a lot of stones at other people, and this would not be the Gospel attitude." John 8:1 is pretty clear, *"Let the one among you who has no sin cast the first stone."*

Some might argue if we see someone doing something they should not be doing it is none of our business. The counter argument, though, is that if we see someone in distress, it is our obligation to help. For instance, if we saw someone drowning, we certainly would not just stand and watch – we would, at least, try to do something to help. When we see a loved one or friend clearly on the wrong path, their eternal salvation may be at stake. Would it not be just as wrong to stand and watch someone spiritually drowning? In much the same way that we would throw a life preserver to someone in the water, we need to do the same thing spiritually for a person in spiritual peril. There is nothing more important in a person's life than the eternal salvation of their soul.

Pope Pius XII prophetically warned attendees of the 1946 National Catechetical Congress of the United States, via live radio broadcast: "Perhaps the greatest sin in the world today is that men have begun to lose the sense of sin." A decade or so later, Bishop Fulton Sheen echoed similar concerns. He observed that "not long ago, many did not even believe the Blessed Mother was without sin, while today, no one sins!" The point here, hopefully, is obvious. Both as individuals and as a society, we seem to do a pretty good job of denying our sinfulness. The natural reaction by most of us when a sinful action is brought to our attention is to recoil, be defensive, get angry, etc. Our egos are bruised. Having our errors pointed out to us can really hurt, so admonishing the sinner must be approached with a great deal of unconditional love, humility, compassion and delicacy. Self-righteousness has no part whatsoever in administering this beautiful Spiritual Work of Mercy. We must focus on the *actions* that are wrong, not the *person* doing those actions – a foundational attitude that should guide our dealings with everyone. We have no right to judge people, only God does. But helping someone become aware (or more aware) of something they are doing that is sinful or morally dangerous is our obligation as a fellow member of the Body of Christ. What might be an example? Missing mass on Sunday without a valid reason.

There is an old saying, "All that is needed for evil to succeed is for good people to say or do nothing!" Silence in the face of evil allows that evil to continue and even to spread. Bishop Sheen spoke eloquently on this issue: "We don't need a voice that speaks when everybody else is speaking; we need a voice that speaks when everybody else is silent!" I think it critical to keep in mind – no one hated sin more that Jesus, yet no one loved sinners more than He. As brothers and sisters in Christ, we have the moral obligation to insert ourselves into the lives of others when we see them headed astray. However, do we have the courage?

As individuals, and collectively as followers of Christ, we have similar responsibilities to speak out publicly against evils in our society. The most obvious of those evils today is that of elective abortions. While many are actively supporting the legality of abortions up to the point of birth, we must speak out. Nearly seventy-five years ago, Bishop Sheen was spot on when he rightly observed: "The refusal to take sides on great moral issues is itself a decision. It is a silent acquiescence to evil. The [great] tragedy of our time is that those who still believe in honesty lack fire and conviction, while those who believe in dishonesty are full of passionate conviction." Sheen's reference to *honesty* actually goes to the heart of all moral truth. In the context of admonishing the sinner, then, we must speak out in defense of the unborn. We must encourage, support and vote for public officials dedicated to defending life at all stages. Could there be a more merciful thing to do?

Twentieth century theologian, Father Karl Rahner commented, "The number one cause of atheism is Christians. Those who proclaim Him with their mouths and deny Him with their actions is what an unbelieving world finds unbelievable." While this observation should pain our hearts, unfortunately, it is true.

In mercy, we must be willing to act. So . . . are we, by our actions or inactions, validating Rahner's observation, or are we eagerly and courageously willing to step out in faith and love instructing those seeking knowledge, and counseling those looking for ways to navigate difficult decisions? What about humbly admonishing those we see in sinful behavior?

When the going gets tough, the spiritually tough get going.

Reflection

XXI

Forgiveness Is at the Heart of Mercy

Then Peter approaching asked him, "Lord, if my brother sins against me, how often must I forgive him? As many as seven times?"

(Matthew 18:21)

Y OU MAY RECALL, when Peter asked Jesus how many times he must forgive his brother, he set a rather low threshold for himself – seven times? Jesus responded, *"not seven times but seventy-seven times."* Clearly the much larger number was symbolic of *whenever you have been wronged!* The parable that followed is the well-known narrative of the master calling in a large debt from one of his servants. When the servant said he could not pay, the master ordered him, his wife and family and all his belongs to be sold in order to settle the debt. The servant begged for his boss's patience. In response, the master had compassion on him and forgave the entire debt. Then, rather than being grateful for the forgiveness he had been shown and offering similar forgiveness to his fellow servant, he instead beat his colleague and demanded repayment in full for a debt much smaller than the one he himself had been forgiven. Much to his surprise, his fellow servants ratted him out. When the master of the house heard what had happened, his response was swift, decisive and firm. He turned the evil servant over to the torturers until he paid in full. The evil servant had begged for forgiveness – and it was granted to him – but when he was given the opportunity to show forgiveness, his response was quite the opposite. The point of Jesus' parable is crystal clear:

So will my heavenly Father do to you, unless each of you forgives his brother from his heart." (Matthew 18:35)

Because we have already been forgiven, we must unwaveringly forgive others.

A beautiful passage from Sirach (27:30-28:7) further clarifies the importance of forgiveness:

> *Wrath and anger, these also are abominations, yet a sinner holds on to them. The vengeful will face the Lord's vengeance; indeed he remembers their sins in detail. Forgive your neighbor the wrong done to you then when you pray, your own sins will be forgiven. Does anyone nourish anger against another and expect healing from the LORD? Can one refuse mercy to a sinner like oneself, yet seek pardon for one's own sins? If a mere mortal cherishes wrath, who will forgive his sins? Remember your last days and set enmity aside; remember death and decay, and cease from sin! Remember the commandments and do not be angry with your neighbor; remember the covenant of the Most High, and overlook faults.*

The mercy of forgiveness is, frankly, therapeutic. Our day-to-day interactions and relationships are often peppered with misunderstandings, hurtful words and attitudes, unkept or broken promises, unkind behavior, thoughtlessness, deception and a host of other words and actions that hinder loving conversations and relationships. Some of those unkindnesses are intentional, but many are not. Often, offenders are not even aware they have harmed us in some way. When we encounter such bumps in the road, we have the choice of simply brushing them off and forgetting about them (or burying them); or we could react with an eye-for-an-eye type of response; or we could calmly let the other party know we have been hurt and give them the opportunity to clarify or make amends. If we opt for the first choice, what often happens is we begin to subconsciously *compile a list of offenses.* Unfortunately, when that list gets to a certain point, anger erupts and a comment like "you always . . . ," or "you never . . . " results, and little to no reconciliation occurs. If we opt for retaliation, outcomes are seldom if ever fruitful. However, if we choose the third option, we have a really good chance of working positively through the issue and getting a favorable result, which often includes a sincere apology. In my experience, when someone apologizes for hurting me in some way, I can express genuine forgiveness – and the result is often a strengthening of the relationship I have with that person.

A critically important concept about forgiveness, which we learned as children, is framed in the words of the *Our Father*, "Forgive us our trespasses as we forgive those who trespass against us." This passage is pretty straight forward – because we have been forgiven, so should we forgive those who have offended us. As a reminder, when the apostles asked Jesus how they should pray, this is the prayer He taught them.

The connection between an apology and forgiveness is real. When I was just seven years old and preparing to receive the Sacrament of Reconciliation (called the Sacrament of Penance or simply Confession at that time), I learned the Act of Contrition. The version I learned then (and still pray many decades later) is:

> O my God, I am heartily sorry for having offended Thee, and I detest all my sins because I dread the loss of Heaven and the pains of hell, but most of all because they have offended Thee, my God, Who art all good and deserving of all my love. I firmly resolve, with the help of Thy grace, to confess my sins, to do penance, and to amend my life. Amen.

While this prayer (or one of the many variations of it) is an integral part of the Sacrament of Reconciliation, it can be prayed any time. You may want to consider praying it before going to sleep each night! The Act of Contrition, in a real way, is complete in itself. It contains a genuine apology to my Loving Father and an expression of sorrow for the evil things I have done. The primary reason I am asking for forgiveness is because I have offended the ultimate source of love, kindness and mercy who deserves my unconditional love and devotion. In my human weakness, however, fear of punishment is certainly one reason for apologizing, although clearly not the best. The prayer also is my call to action – I will confess my sins in confession (to a priest, acting in *persona Christi*), make a firm resolution not to commit those sins again, make amends by doing what the confessor deems appropriate (most often saying some prayers), and commit to a genuine effort of getting myself back onto the path toward holiness.

Forgiving offenses willingly is a Spiritual Work of Mercy that many of us struggle with, yet we have been given ample examples of Jesus' forgiveness, including His forgiveness of the *good thief*, Dismas, just before He Himself died on the cross. Likewise, recognizing our own need to ask for forgiveness when we have done something wrong is very difficult. Even though Dismas was near death, he courageously admitted his sinfulness and sincerely begged for forgiveness. Recall Jesus' loving words of forgiveness in response, "Amen, I say to you, today you will be with me in Paradise." Matthew Kelly (2019) argues that Dismas was actually the *first saint*!

Closely connected to *forgiving injuries* of any sort, is another Spiritual Work of Mercy, *to bear wrongs patiently*. In reflecting on which of these two comes first, as in the-chicken-or-the-egg argument, I think a valid case could be made for either. But no matter, being patient when wronged takes a lot of kindness and courage. In fact, doing so requires a deliberate act of our will, and that act is fueled by grace, which is supernatural. Bearing wrongs patiently is hard. In her wonderful book, *"Scandalous Mercy,"* Sister Emmanuel Maillard (2017) retells the remarkable story of a Dutch woman, Corrie Ten Boom, who lived in Harlem, Holland with her father and sister, at the outset of World War II. While I have read Corrie's story elsewhere, the account Sister Emmanuel shares is the most compelling I have seen. The Ten Boom's were watchmakers, simple people, devout Christians. They quietly opened their doors to Jews who were trying to escape the attention of the Gestapo. In the midst of the arbitrary arrests and disappearance of many of her neighbors, Corrie prayed, "Lord Jesus, I offer myself to You for Your people, in any circumstance, in any place, at any time." Her prayer guided her actions. For nearly two years, she and her dad and sister worked with dozens of Jewish men and women to protect others from being arrested. Many of them acted as aides to maintain contacts with those who needed help. One such instance revolved around information the aides had obtained that a hundred Jewish babies were to be assassinated. Disguised as German soldiers, several of them managed to move the babies to safety.

Eventually, the kindness of the Ten Boom family to those being hunted down was discovered and the three of them were arrested based on the word of a neighbor, Jan Vogel, who had cast his allegiance with the German secret police. They were put into prison, then eventually sent to a work camp in Germany. By way of a remarkable coincidence, Corrie found out the name of the neighbor who turned them over to the Gestapo. She commented later that had Jan been standing in front of her she would have killed him. Within a week of finding out the traitor's name, the hate and disgust she had for him caused her to become seriously ill both physically and emotionally. By contrast, her sister, Betsie, had made a personal choice to pray for Vogel. Eventually, Corrie got to the point she prayed, "Lord Jesus, I forgive [him], as I ask You to forgive me. I would have done him harm. Bless him and his family as well this very minute." After weeks of little to no sleep, her preoccupations with thoughts of him vanished – but a few weeks later, Corrie suffered the horror of witnessing her sister being inhumanely tortured to death. Ironically, in the midst of her sorrow, because of an administrative error, Corrie was transferred back to Holland from the notorious camp where she had been held prisoner. Just one week later, nearly all of the prisoners at Ravensbruck were summarily executed.

All of these events could have poisoned Corrie for life, but instead she allowed herself to be guided by her faith and inspired by the remarkable conversation she had with her sister just before her sister died. Betsie's last words were, "We have to tell the world what we have learned here… We have to tell them that He (God) will always be able to bring us out of the abyss, no matter how deep it might be. People will listen to us, Corrie, because of what we have experienced here. I pray every day that we will be able to show, even to our persecutors, that love is greater than anything else."

Not long after the war ended, Corrie opened a rehabilitation center to care for survivors of the holocaust. Those who came to her were wounded physically, emotionally and spiritually. She knew there was only one way they would be healed, and that was through the way of forgiveness. Interestingly, for many of her Dutch countrymen, forgiving their German oppressors was not nearly so difficult as forgiving their fellow compatriots.

Someone suggested to Corrie that she repurpose an old concentration camp to continue her reconciliation work, which she did. An addendum to the final conversation Corrie had had with Betsie was her sister's insistence that a concentration camp in Germany be used for this eventual work! Betsie's vision was a converted concentration camp "without barbed wire, where people destroyed by hate and violence could come freely to learn to love again…We would paint the gruesome barracks bright green, and, in front of the windows, we would put boxes of blooming flowers." Corrie soon welcomed 160 German refugees, knowing full well that, "the merciful love of Jesus was always near to the victims as well as the guilty, to the sufferers as well as to the authors of their suffering." (Maillard, 2017).

Learning that her betrayer, Jan Vogel, had been convicted of war crimes and sentenced to death, Corrie wrote to him, detailing the gruesome deaths of her father and sister and disappearance of her nephew. She concluded her letter, "As for me, I lived through the indescribable nightmare, but I have forgiven you. It is Jesus who has given me the strength. He said, 'Love your enemies!'" She also sent him a Bible – with "love your enemies," underlined. Vogel wrote back to her saying, "Your forgiveness is such a great miracle that I have dared to say, 'Jesus, if You have put into the heart of your disciples a love as great as that, then there must be hope for me!' After reading in the Bible you sent me that Jesus died on the cross for the sins of the world, I surrendered into His hands my abominable sins, and I know that He has pardoned me, because your forgiveness has convinced me of the reality of the forgiveness of Jesus." A few days later, Vogel gave his soul back to God.

Corrie wrote to two other Dutch compatriots who had been imprisoned for their war crimes. These two actually beat Corrie and Betsie unconscious one day in the prison camp. She offered her full and complete forgiveness and her own prayers that they would accept the forgiveness of Jesus. Both men answered her. The first said, "I know what harm I've done to your family. The fact that you have been able to pardon me is tangible proof that Jesus can pardon me. I have confessed to Him all my sins." She was thrilled. The second, however, said, "I am not only responsible for the death of your loved ones, but for the extermination of thousands of Jews. I only regret one thing, not having been able to kill more of them as well as people like you." Corrie was shaken to the core, but she was determined not to allow her shock to deter her campaign of mercy through forgiveness and reconciliation.

Just a few years later, Corrie was giving a presentation on forgiveness and reconciliation at a church in Munich. Her message was a testimony to the forgiveness of God for every person, intended to heal the many who had been conquered and were desolate and devastated by the loss of their homes and families. At the end of her presentation, a man approached her with an outstretched hand, complimenting her on her talk. Corrie looked at him and knew instantly that he had been one of the prison guards who had so cruelly beaten Betsie. She knew in her heart she must forgive him, in exactly the same way she had just encouraged others to do, but she could not. The man then said to her, "Marvelous message. How wonderful it is to hear, as you said, that He has washed away all of our sins." She would not allow herself to engage the man, to shake his hand or to look into his eyes. He then commented that she had mentioned in her talk the name of the Ravensbruck concentration camp. He admitted to her he had been a guard there. Then, almost in a stream of consciousness, he said to her, "At Christmas time I became a Christian, and I know that God has pardoned me for the atrocities I committed then. However, I begged Him to give me an opportunity to ask for forgiveness personally from just one of the victims! That's why I'm asking you: 'Can you forgive me?'" Again, he offered his hand. Knowing she had to fight off all the vengeance and anger she was feeling in that moment, she tried to muster a smile, but nothing. Then, she clearly recalled that Jesus said, "If you do not forgive others for their trespasses, your heavenly father will not forgive you in return." So, Corrie gathered all the strength she had, reached out and took the man's hand. Much to her astonishment, she felt a strong current running down her arm, through her hand, into his. Her heart nearly exploded with the warmth of God's love. Completely overwhelmed, she looked deeply into the man's eyes, with her own eyes flooded with tears of joy and she said, "Brother, I forgive you with all my heart."

Stories such as Corrie Ten Boom's are not unique. Immaculee Ilibagiza, a survivor of the 1994 Rwanda genocide, documented her horrifying experience in a wonderful book, *Left to Tell* (2006). When the Hutu took power and began to execute members of the Tutsie tribe and moderate Hutu, Immaculee's dad sent her to stay with a friend, a Hutu pastor, for her protection. For 91 days, she and seven other young women survived in a 12-square-foot bathroom in the pastor's house, fearing constantly they would be found and killed. Immaculee spent much of her time silently praying the rosary, coming to realize part-way through the ordeal, she no longer hated those who were hunting down her and her comrades. In meditating on the Sorrowful Mysteries, she recalled what Jesus said just before He died, "Father, forgive them for they do not know what they do." Those words transformed her heart from hate to love and forgiveness. During the three months Immaculee was in hiding, her entire family was executed by a man who she later found out had been a neighbor, a man she had known for years. She went to visit him in prison after all the horror was over, and forgave him. She, too, experienced a flood of warmth and peace flow through her as she extended mercy to that man, who, she described as broken and "in a bad place."

These two stories of remarkable acts of mercy through forgiveness, are likely well beyond what most of us will ever experience in our lives. Yet, in studying both cases, we can begin to grasp the power we have, and the peace we can achieve, when we choose to shower our love and forgiveness toward those who have wronged us. "Father, forgive them for they know not what they do."

On an entirely different level than the two cases just described, I have personally experienced much peace and comfort, both by asking for forgiveness from those I have offended and by granting forgiveness to those who have hurt me in some way. I have also discovered that when I ask genuinely for forgiveness, even if the other person does not accept my apology, or does so lukewarmly, there is a real peace that settles on my heart.

An entire chapter could be written just on holding grudges, but I will not do so. Having said that, holding grudges does no one any good, not the least of which is the person holding the grudge. There are classic tales of grudges (e.g., the Hatfields and McCoys) that lasted not just generations, but centuries, even millennia (e.g., in many parts of the Middle East). Without having done extensive research to verify this assertion, I think it safe to say that none of those grudges did anyone any good. Grudges, frankly, weigh a lot, emotionally. If we insist on carrying that dead-weight around with us, we should expect the extra (emotional) load to wear us out. No one can force us to carry a grudge – that choice is ours alone – and, only we can choose to leave it behind. Love, patience and forgiveness are strong medicine.

One of the most effective addiction recovery programs ever implemented is the so-called *12-Step Process*. Interestingly, Step 9 of that process is forgiveness. Making amends may seem like a bitter pill to swallow, but for those serious about recovery, it is great medicine for the soul. For addiction recovery, or simply making up for hurting someone, a critical part of the formula for healing is the same – forgiveness. If we have caused someone pain, we must apologize sincerely and graciously ask for forgiveness. If we are the victim of someone's wrath, we must be willing to forgive when they apologize.

We need not look any farther than our extended family to see the pain, frustration, anger, disappointment and grid-lock caused when someone (or *several someones*) says or does something hurtful. Upon the death of a loved one, look no farther than to those who might be beneficiaries (of anything) to see how petty jealousies arise, fights ensue and relationships fracture because of *stuff*. Family squabbles and disagreements between and among friends cause great pain. Participants know they are right and the other person(s) is (are) wrong and are unwilling to budge. Sound familiar. One of the worst consequences of such disagreements is the relational distance that grows between those involved. Let me repeat, holding grudges benefits no one. As children of God, we must put such issues behind us.

Genuine forgiveness and genuine bearing of injuries patiently both require that we look beyond ourselves. Because the gift of mercy we receive from God is His love directed toward us the sinner, our duty of mercy requires that our mercy must be directed, through forgiveness. toward those who have injured us. Forgiveness must start within me, but it is not about me. Mercy is my willingness to lovingly treat others (who have offended me) in the same way God lovingly treats me (who has offended Him). The salve of mercy through forgiveness heals many wounds.

"Father forgive them, for they know not what they do."

Reflection

XXII

Pray for the Living and the Dead

Have no anxiety at all, but in everything, by prayer and petition,
with thanksgiving, make your requests known to God.

(*Philippians 4:6*)

How many times, in a moment of need, have you asked someone to pray for you, or for some outcome or someone near and dear to you? How many times have you been asked to pray for someone in their time of need? For most of us, I suspect the answer to both questions is, *many*. When we are in any kind of need, asking for prayer support is a pretty natural thing to do because in a very real way it is a call for help. I suspect the reason we happily offer prayers for others when they ask us is because we know doing so is important to them and because we simply want to help. Keep in mind, praying for others is an important way of building a relationship with them, too. Truth is, we likely are also willing to help others because we have been the recipients of the grace and warmth that comes from others praying for our intentions, whatever they might be. Each time we pray for someone else's intention, we are committing a merciful act. Whenever we ask someone to pray for us, we are giving them the opportunity to do the same.

So why might we ask a loved one or friend to pray for us? Probably a million different reasons. One might be for our health. Others might include success of a surgical procedure, passing an exam, safe and healthy birth of a child or grandchild, outcome of an election, getting a job, successful completion of a project, safe travel, help in finding or selling a home, successful acceptance of a contract, comfort in time of grief particularly with the loss of someone special in our life, passage of legislation that would protect the sanctity of human life at all stages of life and safety for a loved one in the midst of danger, to name just a few. All these and other reasons likewise motivate others to ask us to pray for their intentions.

More than a half dozen years ago, my wife, Laurel, was diagnosed with cancer. While it was caught early, our decision for her treatment was to have the disease removed surgically, as soon as possible. We shared her situation with our children, family and friends and in each case asked them to please pray for a successful outcome for her, the defeat of the disease. Well, they did. And then, they in turn asked others to do the same for her. Laurel received many notes and cards from individuals and small groups that had been made aware of her situation with the message, "we are praying for you." In a number of those cases, we had no idea how, or by whom, they were asked to lift her up in prayer! We went through all the preliminaries, the surgery and recovery almost as though we were riding a tidal wave of grace and blessings, without fear, without anxiety, with a genuine sense of calm. The only reasonable explanation we had, as people of faith, was God heard our prayers and the prayers of others. He answered those prayers with ridiculous grace and a scandalous outpouring of His mercy.

Several years later, the cancer word returned to our family, this time it was me. We knew how our prayers and the prayers of scores of others carried us through Laurel's situation, so there was absolutely no hesitancy in asking others to pray for me, and they did! Once again, throughout the preliminaries, the surgery and recovery and follow-up, both of us felt genuinely at peace, full of hope that all would be fine. As repetitious as it sounds, the real feeling of moving through the entire ordeal on a tidal wave of prayer support generated a genuine sense of peace and comfort.

By the grace of God, Laurel is eight years out and I am four years out and we are both doing well. Do we have regular checkups? Of course. But we are blessed, hopeful and at peace going forward because we know and have felt the very real power of prayer and the generous mercy of our Loving Father. The reason for sharing these two health-related stories is simply to provide a real and personal experience of having been on the *receiving end* of the prayers by others. We know what it feels like to be supported in prayer by others, so we are always willing to pray for their intentions when they ask.

Praying for others is a wonderful way to focus our attention away from ourselves; and raise up someone else's needs to our Loving Father and lift them up in one of the most caring ways possible. A beautiful and natural consequence of looking outward from ourselves to help others is that it allows us to actively nurture our personal relationship with our Creator at the same time.

Praying for loved ones and friends, or for their intentions, is not too hard to get our arms around. However, praying for those who are unloving, hurtful, conniving, irritating, emotionally distant and even hateful can be very difficult. But Christ did not say we should pray only for those who are close to us. No, He challenged us to pray for the living – period! Near as I can tell, that includes the likeable and unlikeable alike. Let me provide an example or two of how and why to pray for those who cause us angst in some way.

One unpleasant person that immediately comes to mind is the nosey neighbor who stays busier minding our business than his own – interestingly, this *neighbor* could just as easily be a relative! Far too often, our response when we encounter such people is to be irritated, frustrated, even angry with them. In short, their annoying ways cause us to *react*. Reacting, however, is an unfortunate response because when we react, we allow others to take control of our behavior. Stephen Covey's first habit of highly effective people is to, "Be Proactive." Being proactive means choosing our behavior, attitude and words (that are truly Christ-centered), rather than being duped into reacting in ways that are me-centered. When we give up control of our emotions, even the best of us retreats into the background and lets our egos rush forward and leap into action. When that happens, we say things we should not, do thing we know we should not and often hold grudges, or if not grudges, at least harbor hurt feelings. When that equation takes charge, we are not inclined to nurture loving relationships – and yet, we know we must love everyone. So, what to do? Personally, after unsuccessfully trying a variety of different things to counteract my ill feelings, I find the only thing that consistently works for me is to pray for the source of my irritation. If only I could condition myself to begin praying sooner!

Father Larry Richards (2009) provides an insightful perspective for dealing with those who irritate us. As his story goes, at one point in his career Father Richards taught at an all-boys Catholic high school. One year, there was a student who seemed to know exactly where Father kept his last nerve and regularly poked at it. He knew the kid was getting to him, but no matter how hard he tried not to let him get under his skin, the young man continued to drive him nuts. One day, during a holy hour, Father confessed privately to Jesus he could not put his dislike for the guy behind him, even though he knew he must. Finally, after arguing with Him, he finally realized he simply needed to ask Jesus to love the kid for him; after all, if we are really true believers in Christ, we must accept the reality that He lives within us! Father Richards said, "I had to get out of the way and let Jesus live in and through me." Maybe, just maybe, we could learn a valuable lesson from Richards' experience. When we truly surrender our lives to Jesus and allow Him to live in and through us, we will not need to deal with those who get under our skin on our own, He will love them for us – and we will, in turn, learn to do the same.

Many Christians, and other people of faith, believe that when a person who has led a good life dies, they go straight to heaven. But many have a different view, for example, Catholics, Eastern Orthodox and some Jews. Purgatory, or what is generally referred to as after-death purification, is a belief that has been part of the Catholic faith since the time of Christ, arguably even before. With no intention of providing a comprehensive theological defense of the reality of purgatory, I would like to provide a bit of background to support the merciful act of praying for the dead. After all, if there were no purgatory, praying for the dead would not be important. If, however, there is a purgatory – and I firmly believe there is – praying for the dead makes perfect sense. Doing so, in very simple terms, is all about our genuine desire to help our loved ones fully experience the joys of heaven.

While still an Anglican priest, Newman's research into the writings of the early Church fathers, and his in-depth study of Catholic doctrine, led him to conclude purgatory was a reality even though his conclusion broke with Anglican Church doctrine at the time. About two decades after his conversion, Newman wrote, *Dream of Gerontius,* an eloquent explanation of his understanding of purgatory as the final cleansing for our passing from this life to our eternal reward. An abridged version of his poem is presented in Reflection XII of this book.

Wisdom 3:1-9 provides a beautiful explanation of the cleansing process we encounter after we die:

> *The souls of the just are in the hand of God,*
> *and no torment shall touch them.*
> *They seemed, in the view of the foolish, to be dead;*
> *and their passing away was thought an affliction*
> *and their going forth from us, utter destruction.*
> *But they are in peace.*
> *For if before men, indeed, they be punished,*
> *yet is their hope full of immortality;*
> *chastised a little, they shall be greatly blessed,*
> *because God tried them and found them worthy of himself.*
> *As gold in the furnace, he proved them,*
> *and as sacrificial offerings he took them to himself.*
> *In the time of their visitation they shall shine,*
> *and shall dart about as sparks through stubble;*
> *they shall judge nations and rule over peoples,*
> *and the LORD shall be their King forever.*
> *Those who trust in him shall understand truth,*
> *and the faithful shall abide with him in love:*
> *because grace and mercy are with his holy ones,*
> *and his care is with his elect.*

As Christians, each one of us has the hope of heaven because Jesus died for us and rose from the dead. Through His suffering, death and resurrection the doors to eternal life have been opened to us. But sin has taken its toll on us, even though we have remained faithful to God. "Think about times when someone forgave you for an angry outburst of hurtful words, but the pain that you caused that person still lingered. Can any of that coexist with God? Those lingering consequences of sin?

215

The mixed motives? No. Thanks be to God, when we die in friendship with Him, we are saved. But for those persistent effects of sin, God offers us opportunities to be purified and cleansed even more deeply, like gold that is refined to remove impurities (Wisdom 3:6). In his encyclical *Spe Salvi (Saved in Hope)*, Pope Benedict XVI says that when we come face-to-face with Jesus, "all falsehood melts away." As we encounter Him whose love has conquered all evil, "we absorb the overwhelming power of His love" into our hearts. That love is so strong that it burns away whatever evil or sin remain in us. Benedict calls this "the pain of love." It's something that can be painful – but joyful too – because it ultimately brings us salvation. We can look at it as God's way of loving the sin out of us." (*Word Among Us*)

Saint Paul's letter to the Romans 6:3-9 explains it this way:

Are you unaware that we who were baptized into Christ Jesus were baptized into his death? We were indeed buried with him through baptism into death, so that, just as Christ was raised from the dead by the glory of the Father, we too might live in newness of life.

For if we have grown into union with him through a death like his, we shall also be united with him in the resurrection. We know that our old self was crucified with him, so that our sinful body might be done away with, that we might no longer be in slavery to sin. For a dead person has been absolved from sin. If, then, we have died with Christ, we believe that we shall also live with him. We know that Christ, raised from the dead, dies no more; death no longer has power over him.

Knowing what we know about Jesus' suffering and death for us, I believe praying for the dead, is all about our genuine desire to help our loved ones experience all the joys of heaven as quickly as possible. The fourth commandment is *Honor your father and your mother*. Is there a more loving way to honor them in death than to pray for the repose of their immortal soul? The same could be said of praying for anyone who has died. Ask the Holy Spirit to help them pass through the "pain of love" described by Pope Emeritus Benedict XVI, so that they can see

God face-to-face! Know that if the souls you are praying for have already reached their full cleansing, your prayers will simply pass along to those whose souls are most in need. What a wonderful and merciful way to honor them.

P.S. I have never seen a post script added to a chapter (or reflection) before, nor have I ever considered adding one before now. However, I need to do so here. Without question, praying for the living and dead is a powerful way of showering others with mercy. But there is another, deeply personal and related act of mercy I experienced several months ago that I cannot allow to pass without sharing it, specifically, ***praying with the dying***. The day my dear friend, Jim Stone, told me his doctors had just informed him he only had a few months to live, I was devastated. I said, "you know we are praying for you every day, right?" He acknowledged he knew. I then asked what else I could do to help comfort and support him beyond praying for him. His response surprised me, but in a way I could never have imagined. Jim asked that when we got back to town, would I come pray the Liturgy of the Hours – Morning Prayers with him. He dearly loved those prayers. It was this very man who taught Laurel and me to pray this daily devotion. Needless to say, I assured him I would be there every morning he felt well enough for me to be there. So, for the next two weeks or so, about every second day, at nine in the morning, I was blessed beyond measure to pray these beautiful morning prayers with my friend. On one occasion, Laurel went with me – that day, along with Jim's wife Beverly, the four of us prayed Morning Prayers together. As my time to pray with Jim continued, he got progressively weaker to the point that the last few times we were together, he could not even hold his prayer book, so I mostly prayed the prayers aloud in his presence. Every time I thought he might have dozed off, he would, from memory, complete one of the prayers out loud, sometimes with a twinkle in his eye.

My reason for including this addendum is simply to affirm that praying with Jim in his final days on earth, not only gave him a genuine sense of warmth and peace, but it also provided me a true sense of comfort in his death, beyond anything I could have imagined. I can attest to the truth of Jesus' words, recorded in Luke 6:38:

Give and gifts will be given to you; a good measure, packed together, shaken down, and overflowing, will be poured into your lap.

My lap overflowed.

On the morning Jim left this life and began his eternal reward in heaven, he was surrounded by his family, and a dear priest friend, who were praying with him to the end. What glorious peace, what glorious satisfaction, what a magnificent send-off. I know each of those who were there with him experienced the outpouring of God's mercy, knowing full well He was there to welcome His servant home.

I will never forget the blessings I experienced having the opportunity to pray with my friend during his final weeks. If ever given the chance to do the same for another, I hope I will eagerly jump at the chance. *For the sake of His sorrowful passion, have mercy on us and on the whole world.*

EPILOGUE

Lord, Help Me Learn to Be Third

"You shall love the Lord, your God, with all your heart, with all your soul, and with all your mind. This is the greatest and the first commandment. The second is like it: You shall love your neighbor as yourself. The whole law and the prophets depend on these two commandments."

(Matthew 22:37-40)

THE FIRST HALF of this book reflects on the enormity of God's unconditional gifts of grace and mercy. Those gifts define Him as the "true north," the true "number one." The second half, by contrast, reflects on my responsibility, actually my obligation, to be gracious and merciful to everyone I encounter along my life's journey. That being said, God who is the giver of all gifts must rightly be my highest priority – and to obey the *greatest commandments* as defined by Jesus, my neighbor has to be my second. God is first and my neighbor second. By deduction, then, my rightful place is third. In the spirit of full disclosure, I must confess this desire to be number three is not original, I borrowed it from Father Larry Richards. I have heard him encourage parishioners and audiences on multiple occasions to get their priorities straight and keep them straight.

My response to the ridiculous grace and scandalous mercy God showers on me, must be in-kind to those around me, to the best of my ability, as frequently as possible. I receive gifts from Him, so I in turn share them with others. In the very simplest of terms, the giving all starts with God, but flows through me to others, so God the Father, Son and Holy Spirit must be first and foremost in my devotion, guiding all of my thoughts, words and actions. The fruits of my willingness to truly put God first is putting others second. With that in mind, I would like to take a crack at explaining why we should happily strive to put ourselves third, why it is important to do so, and why it is so difficult.

The First Commandment is clear – *I am the Lord your God, you shall not have strange gods before me.* The Second and Third Commandments are also about honoring God as our highest priority – *You shall not take the name of the Lord your God in vain,* and, *Remember to keep holy the Lord's Day.* Actually, if we do not prioritize our thinking and devotion to our Creator, we are not really Christians. Unfortunately, our society is intoxicated with promoting the notion of looking out for ourselves first, no matter what. We often hear, "got to look out for number one." Yet even for those who rightly prioritize their relationship with God as most important, looking out for themselves next is not right-thinking.

Legitimately we could ask, "What about me? Am I not important?" Saint Paul provides a pretty clear and straight forward response to these two nagging questions in his beautiful letter to the Philippians (2:3-6):

> . . . *humbly regard others as more important than yourselves, each looking out not for his own interests, but [also] everyone for those of others. Have among yourselves the same attitude that is also yours in Christ Jesus . . .*

All of this seems pretty simple. Right? So, what's the big deal?

Well, speaking only for myself (although you may find this rings true for you, too), the big deal is I have a real knack of putting myself in first or second place, in spite of my best intentions! Follow me around for a while, watch what I do and listen to what I say – you will clearly see that while I might talk about God being first in my life and others second, my words and actions often demonstrate something quite different. For example, because I like being productive, I often plan my day to get *important* stuff done, even delaying my morning prayers so I can get started early. My stinking-thinking goes like this: I've got something that needs doing now, so I will just postpone morning prayers until later, after all, I have the rest of the day to pray. But when *later* comes, so does the end of the day, and I have fallen asleep – often without even remembering I had promised God I would visit with Him later. While this scenario often plays out with the best of intentions, follow-through on the most important order of the day slips through the cracks. Surely, I will do better tomorrow! Sound familiar? Simply waking up a few minutes earlier than normal on days when I have to be up and out early would solve the problem. If God really is first in my life, my highest priority should be focused on my relationship with Him. After all, He is the author of life; the giver of all gifts; the loving Father that cannot be out-given; the very source of unconditional love; and the one who showers me with ridiculous grace and scandalous mercy in spite of how I treat Him.

Sadly, consciously or unconsciously, we frequently elevate many things above God – image, career, social status, addictive substances, cars, houses, entertainment and all grades of other stuff that we allow to become godlike. If you doubt it or think this is harsh, just look at how you prioritize. Where is your time focused? Where are your resources focused? What activities take priority over everything? If God really is first in our lives, we must give Him top billing and generously share our first fruits (including our time), whatever they may be.

When Jesus was asked which was the greatest commandment, He answered:

> *"You shall love the Lord, your God, with all your heart, with all your soul, and with all your mind. This is the greatest and the first commandment. The second is like it: You shall love your neighbor as yourself. The whole law and the prophets depend on these two commandments." (Matthew 22:37-40)*

That God should be first is clear, Scripture says so. *You should love the Lord, your God.* But then Jesus immediately added, *You shall love your neighbor as yourself.* He could have put different focus on this second commandment, but He did not. Instead, Jesus was clear that our neighbor should be loved next after Him. Of course, we should love ourselves, if for no other reason than we were each created in His image and likeness, and because Christ lives within us. But knowing that, and knowing that our neighbor was also created in God's image, Jesus challenges us to love beyond ourselves because He is the source of all love, and He wants us to love others outside ourselves just as He loves us. Saint Paul, in Galatians 2:19-20 provides an inciteful description of what should motive us to love others:

I have been crucified with Christ; yet I live, no longer I, but Christ lives in me; insofar as I now live in the flesh, I live by faith in the Son of God who has loved me and given himself up for me.

Wow. Christ lives in me! If I really believe that He lives in me, how could I not put others ahead of myself. Jesus not only put each of us ahead of Himself, He gave His life to prove it. John 15:12-13 is very clear:

This is my commandment: love one another as I love you. No one has greater love than this, to lay down one's life for one's friends.

Why then, do we struggle so with putting others ahead of ourselves? Frankly, I suspect many of the reasons are remarkably parallel to the issues with which the Scribes and Pharisees struggled. Interestingly, one day, right after Jesus taught a large crowd,

The greatest among you must be your servant. Whoever exalts himself will be humbled; but whoever humbles himself will be exalted. (Matthew 23:11-12

He admonished the Jewish church leaders with a withering litany of, what I often refer to as, the *woe to you's*. Each of the *woe to's* pointed out a specific behavior or attitude the Scribes and Pharisees chose to live by that lifted themselves up at the expense of others. He called them on the carpet for their pridefulness, arrogance, hypocrisy, and elitism. I have often wondered how I would have behaved if I had held one of those positions.

While it is pretty easy to sit in our easy chairs two millennia later and criticize those early church leaders, we also suffer from parallel attitudes, motivations and self-righteousness today. Our interactions might take on different details, but the result of living self-centered lives play out in remarkably similar ways. Our society today has developed a well-honed propensity for encouraging us to hold ourselves in high esteem while looking down on others. We have come close to developing such behavior into an artform. We need look no further than the way we talk with one another to demonstrate my point.

Bearing with one another through love in today's society is not one of our strong suits. Let's be honest, our lack of kindness, patience and lack of deference to the opinions of others has created a hostile social environment. For example, many of us disagree with each other in very disagreeable ways, even within our families. But disagreeing disagreeably reaches much deeper – even beyond the discourse between liberals and conservatives, or Catholics versus non-Catholics, etc. In fact, we need to look no further than exchanges of ideas within our own faith tradition. Among those who identify themselves as Catholics, nearly half believe abortion should be legalized, yet the Church very clearly teaches (and has always taught) that all life is sacred from conception to natural death. Arguments related to this topic and many others often get very heated. Pretty hypocritical to cast stones at others for vitriolic conversations when we cannot even focus on civil discourse within our own faith community.

Many accuse social media platforms and the around-the-clock news mania as being the cause, and while that might be partly true, I believe each of us need look no further to find the cause than the nearest mirror. A remarkable part of uncivil conversation is founded on what St. Paul called vainglory pride. Another way of saying the same thing is that most of us are quick to justify ourselves and our *rightness*, rather than second guessing ourselves for the good of others. My opinion makes more sense than yours. My ideas are more creative than yours. My analysis is more insightful than yours. My data are more robust than yours. And on and on. When our egos get deeply involved in a conversation, we likely do not even hear what the other person is saying to us because we are far too busy writing the script for what we will say when the other person has the decency to shut-up. Frequently, we don't even let the other person finish their thought before we insist on blurting out the script we have just written. They, in turn, not liking how the conversation is going, interrupt us before we finish our thought, so round two begins. In truth, this kind of exchange is a verbal battle with a clear intent of winning, not an exchange of ideas for the purpose of learning or better understanding a point of view different from our own. To be sure, if my primary purpose in any conversation or debate is to win, then clearly, I am elevating myself to a higher place than you. If I only care about winning an argument, my intent is for you to lose. Impossible to prioritize you as second and me third with such motivation.

But Saint Paul in Ephesians 4:1-3 teaches us an important lesson:

> *I, then, a prisoner for the Lord, urge you to live in a manner worthy of the call you have received, with all humility and gentleness, with patience, bearing with one another through love, striving to preserve the unity of the spirit through the bond of peace."*

As intimidated and helpless as we might feel at any moment during our quest to lift others up, we have a remarkable history and legacy from which to learn. The saints are wonderful examples of people, just like us, who rose above the temptation to focus on themselves and their personal needs in order to serve the needs of others. Countless examples could be presented here, but I will mention just a few. Saint Maximillian Kolbe, one of our modern-day saints, volunteered to take the place of a fellow Auschwitz prisoner, a husband and father, who had been picked to be starved to death in a vicious experiment. Saint Teresa cared for the poorest of the poor in the streets of Calcutta, not doing big things but doing many small things with great love. St. Theresa of Lisieux similarly lived her life dedicated to doing small kindnesses with great love. Saint John Vianney, who nearly flunked out of the seminary, spent countless hours hearing confessions, listening to penitents, providing loving council and absolving them of their sins. His loving spirit touched the lives of hundreds of thousands, all done quietly from a tiny outpost in rural France. These four saints lived their lives, one moment at a time, focused on God but caring for those around them. Matthew Kelly (2019) suggests that the saints did not actually live holy lives; instead, they lived lives filled with holy moments. He defines a holy moment as, "a moment when you make yourself completely available to God. You set self-interest aside, you set aside what you want to do or feel like doing, and for that moment you do exactly what you sense God is calling you to do." He goes on to say, "the brilliant and beautiful truth is you (we) are just as capable of collaborating with God to create holy moments as the saints were."

So, how does all of that relate to my desire to be third? First, I must take to heart the glorious realities of God's unconditional love for me poured out in the form of His ridiculous grace and scandalous mercy, as reflected upon in the first half of this book. Second, I must be willing to live the duties outlined in the second half of this work and create as continuous a stream of holy moments as possible. And finally, in addition to practicing the Spiritual and Corporal Works of Mercy, I must do much more. What might *more* include?

- Be kind, to everyone – being kind costs nothing, except possibly a bit of time. What possible justification could be made for not being kind? The only reason I can think of for not, is that I consider my thoughts, needs, desires and welfare to be more important than yours.

- Listen, attentively – many wise people maintain that one of the greatest honors we can show another is to actually hear what they have to say. Listening requires patience, kindness and a genuine desire for a positive relationship with the person speaking.

- Avoid the temptation to interrupt.

- When you offend someone, apologize sincerely and quickly – not doing so is laying the foundation for a seriously damaged relationship.

- Pray the rosary often (daily) – praying the rosary is a beautiful way to honor the Blessed Mother who is the perfect model of someone totally dedicated to serving others. Nourishing our relationship with her will result in her helping us lift others up.

- Look for the best in everyone – when we do, we will see Christ's face in each of them.

- Think the best of everyone – when we do, we will remove artificial barriers to loving them. Thinking the best of everyone requires that we not assume or prejudge what another is thinking, meaning or intending.

- Be genuinely happy for others when they excel, are honored, or succeed in any way – if we view the world with what Stephen Covey (1989) calls an *abundance mentality,* we will be imitating the example Christ modeled. The success of others is theirs, and we should not in any way be threatened by it, so celebrate them enthusiastically.

- Don't hold grudges – there is no gain whatever in harboring ill will against another.

- Emotionally, grudges and anger weigh a lot and they rob us of the energy we need to treat others with love, dignity and respect.

- Share your time, talent and treasure generously – stewardship is how we live out our spirituality. Give unconditionally, looking for nothing in return.

- Be open to the ideas and feelings of others – when we listen to others, we allow them to teach us something we do not know. Learning from someone is a wonderful way of showing them respect.

- Do not judge others – remember, God will judge us the way we judge others.

- Do not prejudge others – because we really don't know what is in another person's mind and heart, we should not pretend we do. A corollary to prejudging is, *do not assume,* instead, seek information and clarity.

- Be fully present – there are few greater honors you can convey on someone than to be fully present when you are with them. What does that mean? When you are with someone, ensure your attention is fully focused on them. That means eye contact and a genuine sense of empathy and caring. It's not about you, it's about them, whether family member, friend or perfect stranger.

- Concentrate on the *small stuff* – in the manner of St. Theresa of Lisieux, when we concentrate on the *small stuff* and do it with love, we create a "steady stream of opportunities to collaborate with God and create holy moments. Each is a chance to let somebody know someone cares, sometimes with a small gesture and sometimes in more significant ways." (Kelly, 2019)

- Give away every ounce of knowledge and wisdom you have – what better way to subordinate yourself into third place than sharing completely the gifts of knowledge and wisdom you have acquired over your lifetime. All you have has been given to you, so selflessly give it away so others can benefit.

Being third is hard work, really hard work. So, in light of this challenge, I would like to close by paraphrasing some beautiful thoughts on just why I must be third in order to live out what Jesus said in John 15:9:

"As the Father loves me, so I also love you."

The love of God the Father for the Son is perfect in every way. It is unconditional, all-consuming and totally selfless. Jesus receives all He needs, but that love cannot be contained, it cannot be kept to Himself. So, the love of the Father overflows from Jesus' heart to us. In much the same way the Father's love overflows from Jesus, Jesus's love for us cannot be contained either, so it must pour forth from our hearts onto others in the same unlimited and unconditional way. Loving unconditionally can be a real challenge, but that is what we are asked to do. The first and most important step in learning to overcome the challenge to love with the Father's Heart is to let God love you. To be sure, for many of us accepting the reality that God loves us is hard to do. Yet if we can accept that God loves us unconditionally, we will start to see His love automatically flowing from us as a river of ridiculous grace and scandalous mercy, allowing us to focus on others. (Catholic Daily Reflections.com, 2019). In turn, as we focus on others, we will begin living our lives with aggressive humility, being passionately dedicated to the loving service of others (Armbruster, 2010).

One of our faith's greatest intellectuals and Doctor of the Church, Saint Thomas Aquinas, taught us a profound lesson, but in very simple terms: "The love of our neighbor requires that not only should we be our neighbor's well-wishers, but also his well-doers." I believe being *third* requires me to not only be a well-wisher of each of those I encounter; I must also be a well-doer for them. St. Paul's instruction to the Philippians (2:3) provides a simple and practical foundation for what it means to be third:

> *Do nothing out of selfishness or out of vainglory; rather, humbly regard others as more important than yourselves.*

In my experience, loving God above all things is much simpler than loving my neighbor. But the inspired word of God is clear, I must regard others as more important than myself. Dorothy Day provided a wonderful litmus test: "I really only love God as much as I love the person I love the least."

Not sure about you, but I have some serious work to do in learning to be third!

WORK CITED

Armbruster, Jeffrey T., *Some Practical Lessons in Leadership – Observations from Daily Life*, CreateSpace, 2010.

Armbruster, Jeffrey T., *Live Humbly, Serve Graciously – Reflections on Baptism, Mission and Service*, CreateSpace, 2016.

Barron, Robert, *Pope Francis and True Mercy*, Word on Fire, October 13, 2016.

Bickerstaff, Michael, *Jesus Offers You Living Water*, Integrated Catholic Life, 2019.

Cantalamessa, Raniero, *The Gaze of Mercy*, The Word Among Us Press, 2015.

Catechism of the Catholic Church, Doubleday, 1995.

Catholic-Daily-Reflections.com, *Unlimited and Unconditional Love*, May 23, 2019.

Catholic Encyclopedia, catholic.com/encyclopedia.

Chaput, Charles, *Render Unto Caesar*, Image Books, Doubleday, 2012.

Christian Prayer: Liturgy of the Hours, Catholic Book Publishing Corp., 1976.

Coren, Michael, *Why Do Bad Things Happen to Good People*, Christianity Today, 2012.

Covey, Stephen, *7 Habits of Highly Effective People*, Simon and Shuster, 1989.

Douay-Rheims Bible, 1899.

Eden, Dawn, *Saint Ignatius and Memory*, IgnatianSpirituality.com, 2012.

Francis I, *Evangelii Gaudium (The Joy of the Gospel)*, Vatican Press, 2013.

Francis I, *Misericordiae Vultus (The Face of Mercy) – Bull of Indiction of the Extraordinary Jubilee Year of Mercy*, Vatican Press, 2015.

Francis I, *Laudato Si (On Care for Our Common Home)*, Word Among Us Press, 2015.

Francis I, *The Name of God is Mercy*, Random House, 2016.

Francois-Angel, Jackie, *Empowering Mercy* in *Beautiful Mercy* (Matthew Kelly, editor), 2015.

Groeschel, Benedict, *Heaven in Our Hands – Living the Beatitudes*, St. Anthony Messenger Press, 1994.

Hunt, Allen, *Life's Greatest Lesson: What I've Learned from the Happiest People I Know*, DynamicCatholic.com, 2013.

Ilibagiza, Immaculee, *Left to Tell – Discovering God Amidst the Rwandan Holocaust*, Penguin Random House Publishers, 2006.

Kelly, Matthew, *Perfectly Yourself – Discovering God's Dream for You*, Random House Publishing Group, 2006.

Kelly, Matthew, *Beautiful Mercy*, Beacon Publishing, 2015.

Kelly, Matthew, *Perfectly Yourself*, Beacon Publishing, 2017.

Kowalska, Maria Faustina, *Divine Mercy in My Soul – Diary of Saint Maria Faustina Kowalska,* Marian Press, 1981.

Kreeft, Peter, *Making Sense Out of Suffering*, Servant Books, 1986.

Kreeft, Peter, *Making Choices – Practical Wisdom for Everyday Moral Decisions*, Beacon Publishing, 1990.

Kreeft, Peter, *How to Win the Culture War*, InterVarsity Press, 2002.

Kreeft, Peter, *The God Who Loves You*, Ignatius Press, 2004.

Kreeft, Peter, *How to Be Holy – First Steps in Becoming a Saint*, Ignatius Press 2016.

Kushner, Harold, *When Bad Things Happen to Good People*, Random House, 1981.

Langford, Joseph, *I Thirst – 40 days with Mother Teresa*, Augustine Institute, 2018.

Lewis, C. S., *Mere Christianity*, Harper Collins Publishers, 2001 (originally published, 1952).

Maillard, Sister Emmanuel, *Scandalous Mercy – When God Goes Beyond Boundaries*, Children of Medjugorje, 2017.

Newman, John Henry, *The Mission of My Life*, in *Meditations on Christian Doctrine, Hope in God – Creator, March 7, 1848*.

Newman, John Henry, *God's Will the End of Life*, from *Discourses Addressed to Mixed Congregations*, 1849, in *Favorite Newman Sermons* (Daniel M. O'Connell, editor), The American Press, 2nd ed., 1940.

Newman, John Henry, *Discourses for Mixed Congregations, Discourse 18*, 1849, in *A Newman Reader* (Matthew Muller, editor), *Our Sunday Visitor* (modernized in 2019).

Newman, John Henry, *Dream of Gerontius*, Newman Reader – Writings of John Henry Newman, The National Institute of Newman Studies, 2007.

Newman, John Henry, (Edited by Christopher O. Blum), *Waiting for Christ*, Augustine Institute, 2018.

Nouwen, Henri J. M., *Can You Drink the Cup?*, Ave Maria Press, 1996.

Rickert, Scott, *What are Patron Saints? A Brief History and How They are Chosen*, LearnReligions.com

Rohr, Richard, *The Naked Now – Learning to see as the Mystics See*, The Crossroad Publishing Company, 2009.

Sayers, Dorothy L., *Creed or Chaos?*, Sophia Institute Press, 1949.

Stangaro, Angelo, *89 Practical Recommendations for the Spiritual Works of Mercy*, National Catholic Register, 2017.

The Word Among Us, a Catholic devotional magazine based on the daily Mass readings.

Thierfelder, *Less Than a Minute to Go*, Saint Benedict Press, 2013

U.S. Conference of Catholic Bishops, *To Be a Christian Steward – A Pastoral Letter on Stewardship*, 2013.

Williams, Thomas D., *Spiritual Progress*, Hachette Book Group, 2007.

ABOUT THE AUTHOR

PHOTO BY PETER MOLLOY

JEFF ARMBRUSTER WAS born into a Roman Catholic family and has been active in church activities his entire life, including serving as a lector and an Extraordinary Minister of the Eucharist. He has been involved in pastoral planning, Christ Renews His Parish, and teaching adult education courses. Jeff, and his wife Laurel, together taught high school CCD and as a sponsor couple, prepared 25 couples for marriage. Over the years he has trained parish ministry leaders on teamwork concepts, and has facilitated in-depth internal assessment processes for two religious orders. Jeff has given spiritual talks at many Catholic and non-Catholic churches across Georgia and South Carolina. He is a founding member of the Steering Committee for Catholic Charities Atlanta's Leadership Class and has mentored a member of each class in the program's 10-year existence.

Jeff has been fully retired for about five years. For about 14 years, he was Senior Consultant, Armbruster & Associates, LLC, and provided customized training, coaching, and consulting services to a wide range of clients, particularly in the areas of principle-centered leadership, emotional intelligence, teamwork effectiveness and one-on-one executive coaching.

Jeff retired from the U.S. Geological Survey in 2001, after more than 37 years of public service. During his career with USGS, he spent 15 years working in the field of hydrology (he has both a BS and MS in Civil Engineering) and 20 years managing scientific research programs. During his final two years, he was a member of the USGS's Executive Leadership Team and served as one of the agency Director's senior policy advisors.

He is the author of two other books: *Some Practical Lessons in Leadership – Observations from Daily Life* (2010), and *Live Humbly, Serve Graciously – Reflections on Baptism, Mission and Service* (2015)

Jeff lives in Peachtree Corners, Georgia, with his wife and best friend, Laurel. They have two children, both married, and four grandchildren, so far! In his leisure time, he enjoys reading, traveling, woodworking, writing and playing golf.

NOTES

NOTES

NOTES

NOTES

Made in the USA
Columbia, SC
30 December 2021